ABOUT THE AUTHORS

George Franki and Clyde Slatyer, who met when serving as seamen in the RAN in World War II, have shared a lifelong interest in Australian military history, especially of the First AIF. After World War II, Franki graduated in dentistry from the University of Sydney, then joined the Royal Australian Army Dental Corps and served in Australia, Japan and Korea. Later, he gained qualifications in librarianship and became Biomedical Librarian of the University of New South Wales.

Clyde Slatyer, BA, DipEd, taught for twenty years at Sydney Grammar School and is an experienced teacher in adult education. He was commissioned as a lieutenant in the Royal Australian Naval Volunteer Reserve in 1968. His interest in two world wars has been motivated by his father's service in the 1st Australian Light Horse Regiment on Gallipoli and in Palestine and the service of his three brothers in the Second AIF.

MAD HARRY

HARRY MURRAY

VC CMG DSO and Bar DCM C de G

AUSTRALIA'S MOST DECORATED SOLDIER

GEORGE FRANKI

and

CLYDE SLATYER

First published in Australia in 2003 by Kangaroo Press,
an imprint of Simon & Schuster (Australia) Pty Limited
20 Barcoo Street, East Roseville NSW 2069

A Viacom Company
Sydney New York London

Visit our website at www.simonsaysaustralia.com.

National Library of Australia
Cataloguing-in-Publication data

Franki, George.
    Mad Harry: Harry Murray, Australia's most decorated soldier.

    Bibliography.
    Includes index.
    ISBN 0 7318 1188 7.

    1. Murray, Harry, 1880–1966. 2. Australia. Army.
    Australian Imperial Force (1914–1921) – Biography.
    3. Soldiers – Australia – Biography. 4. World War, 1914–1918 –
    Biography. I. Slatyer, Clyde. II. Title.

940.394

Front cover portrait of Harry Murray by George Bell. Held by the Murray family.
Cover design: Anna Soo Design
Internal design: Asset Typesetting Pty Ltd
Typeset in Adobe Garamond 12pt on 16pt by Asset Typesetting Pty Ltd
Printed in Australia by Griffin Press

10 9 8 7 6 5 4 3 2 1

Dedicated to the memory of my cousin, Sergeant Brian John Troy Johnson, 25 Squadron RAAF, who lost his life on air operations, 14 February 1945, aged nineteen years. G.F.

Dedicated to the memory of the millions of people of all races who lost their lives in two hideous world wars, in the hope that one day war of any kind will cease to be a human option. C.S.

IMPERIAL AND METRIC MEASUREMENTS

Length
1 inch = 25.4 millimetres
1 foot = 0.305 metres
1 yard = 0.91 metres
1 mile = 1.61 kilometres

Weight
1 pound (lb) = 0.45 kilograms

Money
12 pence = 1 shilling
20 shillings = £1

CONTENTS

John Monash, William Birdwood and Harry Murray, VC,
Perth, December 1919

PREFACE

In the photograph opposite appear three of the most famous figures of the Australian Imperial Force (AIF) of World War I. The photograph was taken in Perth in December 1919. On the left is Lieutenant General Sir John Monash, who commanded the Australian Corps of five divisions from May 1918. Next to him is General Sir William Birdwood (later Field Marshal, 1st Baron Birdwood of ANZAC and Totnes) who led the Corps from 1914 to May 1918.

The third figure in the photograph is a younger man, a well turned out officer holding the rank of lieutenant-colonel, who has two rows of medal ribbons — these include a VC, a CMG, a DSO and Bar, a DCM and a Croix de Guerre. In September 1914, this man, Harry Murray, a timber cutter, had enlisted in the 16th Battalion of the AIF as a private soldier. In the history of the 16th Battalion, Cyril Longmore states: 'To Murray belongs the honour of rising within three and a half years from a machine-gun private to the command of an M.G. [machine-gun] battalion of 64 guns and of receiving in the process more fighting decorations than any other infantry soldier in the British Army in the Great War — rewards and decorations every one of them richly deserved.'[1]

On Gallipoli, Murray transferred to the 13th Battalion, with which he served until March 1918. In his Foreword to the history of the 13th, J.M.A. Durrant observes:

The outstanding character in our history is Lieut.-Colonel H.W. Murray V.C., C.M.G., D.S.O. (and bar), D.C.M. He also received the French Croix de Guerre. He was known to the men as 'Mad Harry,' but there was considerable method in his madness. No officer took more care to avoid losing men, and he took astonishing risks while personally reconnoitring, with the sole object of saving his men. A quick thinker in times of danger, he displayed extraordinary energy, resolution and courage.[2]

After World War I, Murray lived a secluded life on sheep stations in the Queensland bush. He avoided publicity and the story of his life has not been written. This work attempts to do justice to the memory of Australia's most decorated soldier.

ACKNOWLEDGMENTS

We wish to thank Douglas Murray and Clem Sutherland, son and daughter of Harry Murray, for the assistance they gave and the hospitality they showed when this book was being written. Joseph Cocker, nephew of Harry Murray and the family historian, provided much information and was also most hospitable. Major General Gordon Maitland was very supportive of the project and introduced us to the publishers, Simon and Schuster. Joseph Crumlin, a noted authority on the Gallipoli campaign, provided many insights. The staffs of the Mitchell Library, Sydney, the Society of Australian Genealogists and the Australian War Memorial were of assistance when research was being carried out. Ron Drummond gave advice on computer tasks and Cameron Slatyer painstakingly produced the maps. Julia Collingwood and Clare Wallis of Simon and Schuster were helpful and pleasant. Carl Harrison-Ford skilfully edited the manuscript.

We also wish to thank the following persons who, in various ways, were of assistance: Paquita Crouch, Brian Foote, Ruth Littler, Tom Marshall (Sydney), Tom C Marshall (Canberra), Pauline Nolan, Lilia Galace Rathbone, Don Reid and Dick Thompson.

Finally, we wish to record our gratitude to our wives, Therese Franki and Judith Slatyer, for the encouragement they showed to us at all times during the years when the book was being written.

George Franki and Clyde Slatyer — January 2003

1

TRADE OR CALLING — BUSHMAN

These men I know have rough tongues and hard bitter faces,
Their laughter comes readily, but there's harshness in its ring.
They've spent their days with bent backs in bleak, unlovely places
In mill, and trench, and coal pit, at work of soldiering.

— Vance Palmer, 'These Are My People'

Henry William Murray was born on 1 December 1880 at Evandale, a hamlet 19 kilometres south of Launceston in northern Tasmania. He was the eighth of nine children of Edward Kennedy Murray and Clarissa Murray, née Littler. Two brothers and five sisters were older than he, and one sister was younger. Writing in 1920 to Charles Bean, leading historian of Australia's part in World War I, Murray stated: 'Re the information you ask. Born near Launceston 1 December 1884. [Murray's birth certificate states he was born in 1880.] The nearest township to my home was Evandale but Launceston was almost as close and I usually give my native town as Launceston. You can, however, please yourself — for I do not truly belong to any village or town but am a true child of the soil and jolly glad to be back on it.'

On his father's side of the family, he came of convict stock. A great-grandfather was a Scot, Kennedy Murray, convicted in Glasgow in 1786 of stealing from the house of a widow, Agnes Dunlop, a box containing six small knives, a pair of striped garters and some 'knittings' with plated buckles. At his trial, Kennedy Murray was described as 'a person of bad fame and character and repute, a thief'. Before his trial, he petitioned the trial judge, stating that 'as his character is broken and he can have no prospect [of] living comfortably in this country he is willing rather than risk the issue of a trial to submit to banishment to any of His Majesty's Colonies or Plantations which His Majesty shall please to appoint for such a period of time and under such terms as to your Lordship shall see fit.' He was sentenced to 14 years penal servitude and arrived in Sydney on 14 February 1792 in the transport *Pitt*. Few of the early convicts transported to New South Wales were Scots, most were English or Irish. Indeed, only 80 Scottish convicts had been sent to New South Wales by 1800. In later life, Kennedy Murray claimed to be a son of a Bishop of Edinburgh and a nephew of John Murray, 3rd Duke of Athol. Genealogists reject this, noting that Kennedy Murray was recorded at his trial as being a labourer and illiterate. It does seem unlikely that he was a bishop's son.

Kennedy Murray was sent to Norfolk Island on 1 October 1796. The island had been first settled by a party of 23 in 1788, sent there to farm to provide food for the settlement at Sydney Cove. On Norfolk, Kennedy Murray formed an association with a convict woman, Ann White, and had two children by her — Kennedy Murray junior, in August 1799, and Elizabeth Murray, in March 1802. Ann White was from Cheapside, London; a true Cockney. When aged fifteen, she and Sarah Woolley were convicted of the theft of a roll of cloth at London's Old Bailey. On 28 October 1789 both were sentenced to five years' penal servitude. According to family tradition, the shopkeeper concerned might have made the accusation out of spite. Ann White was transported to New South Wales in 1790 in the transport *Neptune*, one of four ships of the hellish Second Fleet. Of the

1006 convicts who left Portsmouth in January 1790 in the *Lady Juliana, Scarborough, Neptune* and *Surprize*, 267 died at sea and 150 more of illness soon after landing at Sydney Cove.

The conditions endured by Second Fleet convicts rivalled those of African slaves shipped to the Americas. On *Neptune*, 147 of 424 men died and 11 of 78 women. John White, surgeon of the colony, visited the ship on arrival and reported: 'A great number of the convicts were lying, some half and others nearly quite naked, without bed or bedding, unable to turn or help themselves. The smell was so offensive that I could scarcely bear it. Some of these unhappy people died after the ship came into the harbour before they could be taken ashore. The misery among them is inexpressible. On coming into contact with the fresh air, men fainted and died.'

For a convict girl of sixteen, as Ann White was when transported, there was little choice but to seek the protection of a male if rape was to be avoided and, over the years, she had a number of consorts. Before her association with Kennedy Murray, in Sydney Cove she married John Scott, a sailor from HMS *Sirius*, and on 24 July 1791 had a child, Elizabeth Ann, by him. The child died four months later. With Scott, in October 1791, she went to Norfolk Island where they settled. After some years, however, Scott left her on Norfolk and, it is said, accepted a passage to Asia.

A close neighbour of Ann White's on Norfolk was her partner in crime, Sarah Woolley. Like so many convict women, Sarah Woolley prospered in Australia. She had six children by two husbands and became a prominent resident in the Hawkesbury area. On her death in 1809, the *Sydney Gazette* reported: 'The funeral was numerously and respectably attended, many persons travelled ten to twenty miles to pay this last tribute of respect to a departed much lamented friend whose kindness of disposition and obliging manners have ever been the admiration of all who were acquainted with her; as a mother and a wife her conduct was exemplary; and her loss will for ever be sincerely regretted by a disconsolate husband and family of six children.'[1]

In 1802, Kennedy Murray was granted a ticket-of-leave from Norfolk Island and returned to Sydney Cove, without Ann White. According to one record, he sailed for Van Diemen's Land (Tasmania) in the schooner *Governor Hunter* on 22 April 1805. He spent some time in Penrith, NSW, before going to Van Diemen's Land, marrying Ann Parker, a convict, who had arrived in Sydney on 17 March 1803 in the *Glatton*. Three sons were born of this marriage: William, Henry and James. Ann White formed an association with another convict, Richard Sydes, on Norfolk Island and had a further four children by him. On 20 January 1813, she and Sydes left Norfolk Island in the *Lady Nelson* and came to Tasmania, where at Launceston, on 14 March 1814, they were married. Kennedy Murray's two children had accompanied them to Tasmania. All the inhabitants of Norfolk Island were evacuated, most to Tasmania, by 1814; the island was resettled in 1825. Ann Sydes (White) died at Launceston in 1820, aged 46 and having lived 29 years of her life on islands far from the crowded slums of Cheapside. She is believed to have had 44 grandchildren.

Kennedy Murray lived to the great age, especially for those days, of 89, dying in 1853. His son, Kennedy Murray junior, prospered, receiving large land grants. On 20 April 1831, he wrote to George Arthur, Lieutenant-Governor of Van Diemen's Land, requesting more land, stating in his letter that he had 'built a dwelling house, (known as Prosperous House), a school house, stable, granary and store house, outhouses for Crown servants all of which are completed in the best workmanlike manner — value £500'. Also, he noted that he had five convict servants and two and a half miles of post and rail fencing enclosing his paddocks. His petition was successful: a month later he received a notification that he had been granted a further 320 acres. Kennedy Murray junior died in 1860, leaving sixteen children by two marriages.

Harry Murray's mother, Clarissa Littler, had married Edward Kennedy Murray, grandson of the convict, on 27 June 1867 in Launceston. Her father, Charles Littler, migrated to Tasmania from Essex in 1837 as the family silk mills were suffering financial problems. The Littlers were a prominent 'county' family which produced many naval and military officers. The Tasmanian Littlers can trace their family tree back to 1218.

Harry Murray became aware of his ancestry only in his latter years, when family research carried out by younger members of the family disclosed the convict ancestors. Murray was noncommittal about the revelation and did not appear to be disturbed by it.[2] Certainly, his mother did not know and was proud to have married into the Murray family. Her generation believed that the original Murray of the family in Australia was a free settler, John Murray, who had settled first in Victoria before moving to northern Tasmania[3]. In nineteenth-century Australia, children of convicts almost certainly knew of their parents' backgrounds but, considering it shameful, did not disclose the fact to their own children. Until recent years, when it has became a matter of pride for many to claim such an ancestor, the 'convict stain' in the family was well hidden.

Harry Murray attended Evandale State School until he was fourteen, when he was withdrawn by his father who required him to work on the family farm which was not doing well. This embittered him, as his elder brothers, Albert Edward and Charles Stewart, had received a good secondary education at the prestigious Launceston Church Grammar School. His rancour towards his father lasted all his life. On a post-World War II visit to Launceston, his nephew, Joseph Murray Cocker, son of his favourite sister, Annie (Dot) Cocker, suggested to Harry Murray that he pay a visit to the grave of his father in Evandale. Murray refused, saying: 'No. I haven't got any time for him. I have nothing to thank him for.' Cocker was surprised at his uncle's vehemence. A few days later, however, Murray proposed to his nephew that they make a visit to the Launceston airport, and on arrival he instructed Cocker to go further, to the Scots Kirk in nearby Evandale. He then left the car and walked straight over to his father's grave which was overgrown with blackberries. Soon thereafter, Harry Murray approached the authorities and paid to have the grave permanently maintained.

Harry Murray rarely discussed his father with his own son, Douglas, although he did relate one story to him that indicates his father's sternness and Harry's unpleasant memories of him. When he was a small boy, he cut up some sticks to fashion little spears and threw them at a family cow — a typical childhood prank. Murray senior saw him doing this and thrashed him with the sticks with such fury that the sticks were broken.

Despite the shortness of his formal education, in later life Murray showed that he was a literate and well-read man. His letters are well composed and lack mistakes in spelling. During the 1920s and 1930s he wrote a number of articles for *Reveille*, the magazine of the NSW Branch of the Returned Sailors' and Soldiers' Imperial League of Australia (RSSILA), later the Returned Services League of Australia. In these articles he showed a capacity for vivid description and made numerous classical allusions. On leaving school, his mother continued his education, especially in English. Clarissa Murray died in 1932, aged 93. Joseph Cocker, her grandson, was taught by her until he attended Scots College, Launceston, and recalls her as a well-educated old lady, authoritarian in the Victorian way; she kept a walking stick by her when instructing him, and if he made a mistake in spelling or in reciting his tables he was punished.[4]

From the age of ten, Murray was accustomed to firearms, shooting possums on the family farm. He showed an early interest in military matters: he had six years part-time soldiering, 1902–1908, in the Launceston Volunteer Artillery Corps, which had been founded in 1860. Murray became a crack rifle shot; 'I knew the man I got a fair shot at was not likely to trouble me further,' he later wrote.[5]

In 1908 he migrated to Western Australia where his two brothers had settled in the late 1880s. The family fortunes had deteriorated; the property in Tasmania was on 'starvation country,' subject to droughts and with poor soil, and there was not a living on it for the three brothers. It was not uncommon, in those days, for young men from the eastern States to migrate to New Zealand or Western Australia in search of work. Henry Lawson, in his short story, *For Auld Lang Syne,* describes wharfside farewells to 'old mates' leaving for the west or New Zealand. Murray was first employed on the wheat farm owned by his brother Charles who provided food and lodging but was not prepared to pay wages to his younger brother. Harry Murray then found work as a courier for a mining company at Kookynie, north of Kalgoorlie, travelling along 'camel pads' by bicycle or on horseback, carrying gold and mail. 'Blacks were hostile and some bad lads with white hides were about. I travelled the track fortnightly and everyone knew what I carried. Occasionally I would let the loungers see what I could do with a .32 carbine,' he later wrote.[6]

When he enlisted in 1914, he was working near Manjimup, a timber town in the karri forests of the south-west, employing a gang of sleeper cutters. All his life, Murray was a fine axeman, having developed skills through practising with his workers when they were preparing for wood-chopping competitions.[7] In later years, when Joseph Cocker sought to draw him out on his time in the west, he was told: 'I don't want to talk about those days. They weren't happy days.' His occupations were extremely dangerous and arduous, mixing with rough bushmen, and he built up a strong physique and durability plus self-reliance, which were to fit him for his experiences in the Great War.

On 4 August 1914, Great Britain declared war on the Central Powers, Germany and Austria. Australia, as part of the British Empire, followed the mother country into war. Andrew Fisher, later to be Prime Minister, during an election campaign on 31 July made the portentous promise that Australia supported the Mother Country 'to the last man and the last shilling'. An expeditionary force of 20,000 men was promised and soon raised as the 1st Division, made up of the 1st, 2nd and 3rd Brigades. Major-General William Throsby Bridges was appointed to command the contingent, which he named the Australian Imperial Force.

Harry Murray enlisted in the AIF on 30 September 1914 in Perth. He would have joined up earlier, but it took some weeks to dispose of his business. His enlistment records state that he was born in Launceston; his next of kin was his mother, Clarissa Murray, of 33 Erina Street, Launceston; his age was 30 years and his 'trade or calling' was 'Bushman'. His age was in fact 33 years and 10 months. His medical examination described him as 5 feet 8½ inches tall; 10 stone 12 pounds in weight and having a chest measurement of 36 inches. He was about average height for Australian males of his day and was muscular and solidly built. His eyes were dark green and his hair dark brown. He gave his religion as Congregational. When he enlisted for service in World War II, however, he gave it as Church of England, and he was buried from a Presbyterian church in Brisbane. Harry Murray was casual in his religious affiliations and rarely attended church.

In his later years, when he was over 70, Murray wrote what he called 'Some Reminiscences' for his son, Douglas. The document is of eleven typed pages. In it he stated that his first preferences in the army on enlistment were the artillery or light horse but there were no vacancies. He was posted to the 16th (infantry) Battalion and refused a commission when offered to him as he wished 'to find out what it was like as a private. I learned a lot that was useful later on Gallipoli.' Although Harry Murray's enlistment date was 30 September, only eight weeks after the formation of the original Expeditionary Force was announced, by that date its full complement had been raised. Those who enlisted in late September and October were sufficient to raise another brigade, the 4th, which was unique, as it was the only brigade whose battalions were raised in every state in Australia. The 13th Battalion was recruited in New South Wales, the 14th in Victoria, the 15th in Tasmania and Queensland, and the 16th in Western Australia and South Australia.

The Brigade, comprised mainly of men from country areas, developed a reputation for toughness and independence and it took part in most of the fiercest engagements in which the AIF was involved. Its battalions are amongst the most famous in Australian military history. The humorous song of the Brigade was:

The Fourth Brigade are happy,
The Fourth Brigade are free,
The Fourth Brigade are happy
When they are on the spree.
They never, never quarrel,
They never disagree,
And the pass word of the Fourth Brigade is
'Come and have a drink with me.'

Murray was originally allotted to A Company of the 16th, his regimental number being 315. He applied to join the machine-gun section, which consisted of two Maxim guns manned by one officer and seventeen other ranks, and was delighted when accepted. He attracted the attention of the second in command of the Battalion, Major L.E. Tilney, who was to say of Murray in 1920: 'I first noticed Murray in Blackboy Hill Camp, where he was a member of the machine-gun section. Something in his bearing individualised him from his comrades and before the training was completed it was not hard to recognise a first-class soldier. His interest in his work was so profound that he was not long in perfecting his knowledge and gained his due recognition.'[8]

Another recruit in the machine-gun section was Percy Black, who was to become Harry Murray's close comrade. Described by Bean as 'the old prospector, known from Yilgarn to the Murchison',[9] Black was a powerfully built man with a heavy moustache which was said to give him a resemblance to Lord Kitchener. He was born in Bacchus Marsh, Victoria, on 12 December 1877, eleventh child of Ulster-born parents, William John and Ann Black. Percy Black was accepted for the AIF on 8 September 1914, 'subject to extraction of stumps', the record of his medical examination states. Like so many volunteers for the AIF, he had poor teeth.

On being posted to the 16th Battalion, Black, with an absence of military niceties but with natural courtesy, questioned Major William Mainsbridge, CO of A Company: 'Look here, Mister, I don't know anything about this soldiering game. What crowd would you recommend me to join up with?' The major queried Black's background and, when told he had worked in mines and had some knowledge of machinery, placed him in the machine-gun section. Longmore wrote of Black and Murray:

> *Percy was chosen for his strength, steadiness and reliability; Harry because he had a wonderful eye for ground, was quick in mind and body, and was as keen as mustard. It was one of the wonders of the War that such a tiny unit as that original gun section should include two men who were to do so much to create the traditions of the AIF. I was a staff instructor for several years and handled many machine-gun squads ... but from no other could I get the snap and precision that I got from that little section. At gun work they were on their own, and before the teams were six weeks old they had broken records. 'Action' with a Maxim in 12 seconds is slick work. The best trio in the section could do it in that time — twice out of every three attempts, and any three men picked haphazardly from the section could do it in 16. These figures are not approximate; they are correct. Standard time in the manual was 45 seconds.*[10]

Bean states that Percy Black, on 12 December 1914, set up his machine-gun ready for action in $13^2/_5$ seconds, 'the fastest time known for this operation'.[11]

The Maxim machine-gun was water-cooled, belt-fed and had a rate of fire of 600 rounds of .303 bullets per minute. Black was No. 1 on one of the Battalion's two machine-guns with Murray, his No. 2, feeding the ammunition through. Other members of the section were concerned with provision of ammunition and supplying water for the cooling system. Late in 1915, the Maxims were replaced by Vickers machine-guns.

Another recruit with Harry Murray in the 16th at Blackboy was an English artist, Ellis Silas, who had been in Australia for seven years. A sensitive, aesthetic man, Silas had hoped to be posted to the Medical Corps. From August 1914 to 1916 he kept a diary whose entries show a man totally unsuited to life in the infantry — in training camp or on Gallipoli. Silas wrote (August 1914): 'After the quiet of my studio I find this terrible, life in camp and the uncongenial society of rough bushmen. They are good fellows and seem to think a lot of me.' Whilst at sea (3 January 1915) he wrote: 'At mess today a youth is rather rude to me — my vis-à-vis, a rough Bushman, turns to the youth and says " 'Aven't you got an 'eart; can't you see 'e ain't used to this kind of life like we are?"' Silas's graphic diary entries of his experiences in the early days on Gallipoli are a most valuable record.

At Blackboy Hill, the 16th trained hard. Physical jerks or a route march before breakfast; squad drill, rifle exercises, signalling, gun drill, trench digging for the rest of the day; all sustained by a diet of stew plus bread and jam, according to the battalion history. There were no trained cooks assigned to the kitchens of the training camps of 1914. Volunteers were sought from the ranks or assigned. It was said: 'Armies being armies and officers and NCOs being officers and NCOs, when the call came out for men for the cook house, invariably the dirtiest, slowest, clumsiest and laziest were picked for the job.'[12] By 1918, however, catering in the AIF had improved greatly and unit cooks strived to their utmost to provide hot food for units coming out of the line. Sadly, with heavy casualties there was often more food prepared than could be eaten by the survivors.[13]

On 21 November 1914, the Battalion entrained for Fremantle, boarded the troopships *Andorra* and *Dimboola* and sailed for Melbourne. At Broadmeadows, outside Melbourne, all four battalions of the 4th Brigade combined under the leadership of John Monash, a civilian soldier without active service experience who was to lead the Brigade until 1916. Silas wrote on 7 December: 'Deep mud everywhere. Mile to shower bath and I return from bath dirtier than before I went.' On 17 December, the Brigade marched through the streets of Melbourne, the salute being taken by the Governor General, Sir Ronald Craufurd Munro Ferguson, on the steps of Parliament House in Spring Street, then the seat of the Federal Government. Huge crowds cheered the new soldiers all along the route. Of the 4000 men so heartily cheered, one-third were never to return to Australia. Of the remainder, two-thirds were wounded.

The Brigade embarked from Port Melbourne on 22 December, destination unknown to most of the troops. Seventy-two officers and 2632 other ranks of the 15th and 16th Battalions plus support troops were crowded into Troopship A40, Ceramic, of 18,500 tons burthen. At Albany, Western Australia, the Ceramic was joined by another sixteen transports making up the second convoy of the AIF, destination Egypt. The only naval protection for the convoy was provided by the Australian submarine AE2, which was later sunk in the Sea of Marmora. The troops did not go ashore until they arrived in Alexandria on 1 February 1915. They slept in hammocks, a new experience for them, although Ellis Silas noted in his diary that 'for a joke' some of the hammock ropes were cut halfway through — a very dangerous practice. A ship's newspaper was produced by a transport company and named The Honk: The Voice of the Benzine Lancers. In it, Lieutenant A.P. Imlay wrote of the 16th: 'In the ranks of the 16th — not veterans in age, let it be understood, but men who have seen active service in different parts of the Empire; in Africa, India, China, Ashanti, Egypt, Burma, South America, Mexico and wherever the flag has been under fire.' Murray wrote of the voyage: 'We trained hard on the voyage to Egypt and, amongst other things, I became quite useful at bayonet fighting and reckoned I could hold my own with any German or Turk. We were very crowded on the boat.'[14]

As always, the AIF showed humour. The following appeared in
The Honk:

THE PLAN OF CAMPAIGN
(as suggested by various conversations on board)

To visit Leicester Lounge
"climb the pyramids
"drink beer
"shoot the Kaiser
"drink more beer
"capture Constantinople
"raid the Sultan's harem
"drink more beer
"shave our moustaches (some of us)
"drink more beer
"flirt with French girls
"return home covered with medals and
"drink more beer

From Alexandria, the Brigade entrained for Zeitoun near Cairo, a
7-hour trip; then, still finding land legs after six weeks at sea, marched
to its camp at Heliopolis. The 1st Australian Division was already
encamped at Mena. At Heliopolis, the 4th Brigade joined the
New Zealand Infantry Brigade, the New Zealand Mounted Rifles
Brigade and the 1st Australian Light Horse Brigade. These units
formed the New Zealand and Australian Division under the command
of Major General (later General Sir) Alexander Godley, a British
officer who had been appointed to command the embryonic New
Zealand Military Forces in 1910. The 1st Division and the NZ&A
Division made up the Australian and New Zealand Army Corps
(ANZAC) under the command of Sir William Birdwood, an Indian
Army officer.

'Birdie' led the AIF until 1918 and was, generally, a much loved figure amongst the Diggers. Fearless under fire, known as the 'Spirit of Anzac', he was not a noted tactician or planner and is reported as spending much of his time visiting troops, addressing groups as 'my men', encouraging them and delivering little homilies known as 'Birdie's Bullshit'. Godley commanded the New Zealanders until the end of the war. Much disliked, he had a reputation for ruthlessness in committing the gallant New Zealanders to hopeless assaults. In a letter to his wife, Vic (Hannah Victoria), dated 15 January 1916, Monash stated that Godley 'was cordially hated by all New Zealanders'. The entire force, the Mediterranean Expeditionary Force, was made up of British, Australian, New Zealand and French troops. Commanding the Force was a 62-year-old officer of vast experience in Britain's 'small wars', General Sir Ian Hamilton, who in his capacity as Inspector of Overseas Forces had inspected Australia's newly expanded Citizen Forces from February to April 1914.

The training of the 4th Brigade in Egypt was monotonous, largely consisting of lengthy route marches across the desert with a final simulated assault, with much cheering and flourishing of bayonets, to conclude the exercise. Ellis Silas described these marches as 'trouncing across the desert'.[15] Monash was gratified when Generals Birdwood and Godley informed him that the 4th was the best Brigade in Egypt. On leave, the Australians visited Heliopolis and Cairo and there were disciplinary problems; the men refused to salute British officers and there was much unruly behaviour in the filthy slums. On 2 April 1915, there was a major disturbance in Cairo, the so-called Battle of the Wazir, when 3000 Australian and New Zealand troops rioted and burnt down several buildings used as brothels. Ellis Silas noted in his diary that in Cairo he had 'seen many interesting things' and 'des choses méchants, très méchants' (bad things, very bad).

The Australians were, by April 1915, becoming bored in Egypt, depressed by heat, flies and everlasting sandstorms and, longing for service in France, hoping for a stop in the British Isles first — 'Home' or 'the Old Country' to that generation. In France, the French and British forces had repulsed the initial German push at Mons or on the Marne. The British soldiers were 'The Old Contemptibles', mostly regular soldiers who, in Kipling's words:

... heard the Revelly
From Birr to Bareilly, from Leeds to Lahore;
Hong-Kong and Peshawur
Lucknow and Etawah,
And fifty-five more all endin' in 'pore.'

A year was to pass, however, before the Australians saw France. To assist Russia, a decision was taken to force the Dardanelles, capture Constantinople and defeat Turkey, which had come into the war on the side of the Central Powers in October 1914. In March 1915, a naval attempt to bombard and destroy Turkish batteries on either side of the Narrows failed as two British battleships, *Irresistible* and *Ocean*, and the French battleship *Bouvet* were sunk by mines and other capital ships damaged. A land invasion was then planned for April; British forces to land at Cape Helles, Australians and New Zealanders at Gaba Tepe with diversionary attacks at Kum Kale by the French. For reasons which are still disputed — a theory is that currents threw the landing boats off course — the Anzacs landed at Ari Burnu over 1650 yards north of their objective.

The 1st Division AIF left Egypt early in April 1915 for the island of Lemnos, off Gallipoli, where a large invasion fleet assembled in Mudros harbour. The NZ&A Division followed on 12 April, embarking in the transport *Haida Pascha*, a German prize ship teeming with vermin. On arrival, the invading force practised landings, struggling down ships' ladders encumbered with heavy boots, carrying rifles and equipment and disembarking into large lifeboats. Pay for the men of the 16th was distributed on 14 April, the Battalion history noting that: 'For some it was the last pay they ever received.'[16] Harry Murray wrote: 'We were ready for whatever the Gods had in store. We had no idea what it might be like and wasted no time in speculation. We had youth, health and strength; high adventure awaited us. What more could heart of man desire?'[17]

At noon on April 25 the *Haida Pascha* weighed anchor at Mudros and by 4 pm was off Ari Burnu. The men of the 16th then disembarked, most into the destroyer HMS *Ribble*, then into open boats, and headed for the shore.

2

ON GALLIPOLI

These by the Dardanelles laid down their shining youth
In battle and won fair renown for their native land,
So that their enemy groaned carrying war's harvest from the field
—
But for themselves they founded a deathless monument of valour.

— From an Athenian war monument, c. 440 BC

THE LANDING

The 16th Battalion, 959 strong, landed at Ari Burnu, Gallipoli, at 5.30 pm on 25 April 1915. The first Australians ashore, at 4.30 am on that April day, were from the 9th Battalion, raised in Queensland, and the 11th, in Western Australia; both from the 3rd Brigade, 1st Division. By nightfall, approximately 16,000 Australians and New Zealanders had landed on a strip of beach about 650 yards wide, 30 yards deep, and were fighting their way inland up steep slopes through waist-high, rough undergrowth under machine-gun, rifle and shell fire.

The following is part of the entry for 25 April 1915 from the diary of Private Silas of the 16th Battalion:

5.30 pm We are on the battlefield, well under the fire of the enemy — it is difficult to realise that every burst of flame, every spout of water, means death or worse. For days before we reached the final scene in the 'Great Adventure' we could hear the ceaseless thunder of the bombardment, we have been told of the impossible task before us, of probable annihilation; yet we are eager to get to it; we joke with each other about getting cold feet, but deep down in our hearts we know when we get to it we will not be found wanting. The Assembly is sounded — I have never seen it answered with such alacrity — there is a loud cheer as we gather together in the hold. Here for the last time in this world many of us stood shoulder to shoulder. As I look down the ranks of my comrades I wonder which of us are marked for the land beyond. Perhaps a shell will fly through the side of the ship to answer my question. I don't think I can carry the kit — I can scarcely stand the weight of it. We are descending on to the destroyer Ribble *which is alongside us. Noise of the guns is simply frightful. Colour of the sea beautiful. We are paraded very tightly on the destroyer.*

The men, who were packed together tightly in the boats and heavily laden, feared that they would have no chance of saving themselves if a boat was hit and sunk. Silas fell in the shallows as he landed and had to seek help to regain his feet. He found it 'a magnificent spectacle to see thousands of men rushing through the hail of death as though it was some big game. In Cairo I was ashamed of them — now I am proud to be one of them though I feel a pigmy beside them.' The beach was 'littered with wounded, some of them frightful spectacles'.

On the northern end of the beach, Colonel Pope of the 16th was met by General Godley and ordered to secure Russell's Top, an unoccupied plateau of key strategic importance at the head of Monash Valley in the shadow of that distinctive feature of the Gallipoli skyline, the Sphinx. Russell's Top, on the 25th, lay between the 3rd Brigade, on Pope's Hill, and the New Zealand Brigade, on Walker's Ridge. If captured by the Turks it would have given them a dominating position and allowed them to split the Anzac force. Monash Valley has been described as 'a narrow cleft, which ran for about half a mile to the northeast. Its rocky sides rose, sometimes almost vertically, from the valley floor, creating a claustrophobic oppression not felt elsewhere at Anzac.'[1]

At dusk, the 16th moved into Shrapnel Valley (sometimes referred to as Shrapnel Gully) and then into Monash Valley. After night fell, the Turks played 'funny bugle calls' all night long — they reminded Silas of a 'Cairene bazaar'. The Battalion was to be in continuous action until 30 April. (Walker's Ridge was named after Harold Bridgwood 'Hooky' Walker, Chief of Staff of the Anzac Corps at the landing and later GOC of the 1st Infantry Brigade and the 1st Division; Russell's Top after Brigadier (later Major General) A.H. Russell of the New Zealand Expeditionary Force.)

The following descriptions are based on Harry Murray's 1935 *Reveille* article, 'The First Three Weeks on Gallipoli',[2] and on his Reminiscences. The machine-gun section was amongst the first of the 16th to land at Ari Burnu, and in Murray's boat, in which ten men were hit, he heard what he thought was the whistle of little birds but was in fact machine-gun bullets passing. Murray jumped from his whaleboat before ordered to and landed on rocks with water over his head. He struggled ashore to the beach, soaked, and it was days before he could dry his uniform. Colonel Pope led the 16th up Shrapnel Valley to Monash Valley where packs, weighing 70 pounds apiece, were dumped. The machine-gun section moved to a plateau on Pope's Hill and set up their guns with Percy Black as No. 1 on a machine-gun and Murray as No. 2, passing him ammunition boxes as he emptied them. Night had fallen, but the machine-guns, in Murray's words, 'poured out a tremendous fire into the blackness ahead'.

At dawn on the 26th, the section used their rifles to pick off Turkish snipers. Percy Black 'dropped a Turkish sniper who had been crawling along the side of a cliff about ninety yards away. The poor wretch fell down the steep side, caught his legs in a low fork of a tree, and hung there for days. We all hoped that the shot had killed him and that he did not have to linger in that position.'[3]

In his Reminiscences, Murray described bluntly a bayonet fight that he had soon after the landing:

A few days later, it was decided to move our machine-gun to a better and more forward position. As I was scout, I was sent out to select a suitable position. It was pretty scrubby and, as I very cautiously made my way along looking for a clear high spot, a big Turk bundled out from behind an olive bush and charged me with his bayonet. He thrust at me, I parried him, he parried and we danced around a bit looking for a chance to impale each other. I started to take stock of him and saw his rifle and bayonet were about a foot longer than mine, and he was a very big chap well over six feet. I could easily imagine his skewering me so I squeezed the trigger and ended the fight. I did not feel very brave for what I had done but he is still there and I am here; so even if not sporty at least the result justified it.[4]

During the 26th and 27th, the Turks counterattacked and the machine-gunners were constantly in action. Murray wrote of his friend, Percy Black, that 'he was a deadly shot ... Only for his deadly gunning and determination, I am convinced that the Turks would have succeeded in turning our flank and so forced us off Gallipoli.'[5] Black was wounded in the ear and hand, but kept his gun in action. He is reputed to have said to Colonel Pope: 'That's the beauty of these guns. You can work them with one hand.'

Murray wrote:

There was a heavy demand on the machine-guns, and Black's weapon was so often hit that it became unworkable. He just put it on his shoulder and walked back to the beach to see if it could be repaired by a ship's armourer, but had the great good luck to exchange it for another one instead. The new gun was all brass and shiny — and what a picture of a returning warrior Percy made as he came up the Hill! He might have been Diomed striding back over the plains after interviewing Paris, a splendid physical specimen, afraid of nothing on earth, and glorying in his strength and power. Although his arm was in a sling and his head swathed in bandages, his eyes were beaming with joy at the success of his quest; now he could carry on with the good work and we needed him badly.[6]

For an Australian bushman of the pre-World War I era, Murray was a rarity in one respect — he did not drink any alcohol. He became a moderate drinker during the war. On the third day after the landing, all that time without sleep, Murray was 'a bit sleepy and tired'. Percy Black brought him a drink in a pint pot that he refused as he could smell rum. However, 'as my sergeant he ordered me to, and perhaps I did not need much urging, ... I drank it and in a few minutes felt fine'. In a euphoric state, he sat on the parapet to gain a clear view of a Turk 'who was annoying us'. Black grabbed him by the collar and dragged him back into the trench saying: 'Get out of that, you bloody fool.' Having learned a lesson that strong drink made him too optimistic, Murray never again drank spirits in the front line, as 'One with men under him always needed a clear sober head.'[7]

Silas's diary records the events of those days:

26 April Pope's Hill — daybreak — down in the Valley, in the midst of this frightful hell of screaming shrapnel and heavy ordnance, the birds are chirping in the clear morning air and buzzing about from leaf to leaf; placidly going about its work is a large bee — to think of what might be makes me weep, for fighting is continuing with all its fury.

27 April Still fighting furiously — now all signallers have been wiped out of A and B Companies except myself. Our ships have missed the range and sent eleven shells into us in a minute; I do not think anyone has been hit. For three days and nights I have been going without a stop ... the continual cry of 'Signallers' never seems to cease ... to keep dodging down in dug-outs gets on my nerves — I can't stand being cramped into small places. The Turks have got hold of the names of our officers and keep giving messages purporting to emanate from said officers.

28 April Fighting still continuing with unabated vigour — will this frightful noise never cease? I wonder what this valley will be like when there is no longer noise of firing, no longer the hurried tread of combating forces — when the raw earth of the trenches is overspread with verdant grass. Perhaps here and there equipment of War will be lying with fresh spring sprouts of grass threading through interstices — underneath the little mounds rest sons of a great nation ...

30 April Cannot write — it is all too terrible, too sad — later if I am not killed — I shall write of these experiences ... Fighting still continuing with unabating fury — the men are commencing to look very weary, they do not look as if they can last much longer — how long will this Hell continue?

Guiding a donkey carrying wounded from Pope's Hill and Russell's Top down Monash and Shrapnel Valleys to the beach in those early days on Gallipoli was Private John Simpson (correct name John Simpson Kirkpatrick) of the 3rd Field Ambulance, a stocky 22-year-old ship's fireman from Shields, County Durham, who had been in Australia for four years. Simpson had enlisted in August 1914 in Perth and trained at Blackboy Hill at the same time as Harry Murray. The day after the landing, Simpson had seen the enormous effort required to manhandle stretchers with wounded from the front line down the steep tracks to the dressing stations. Without seeking permission — it was soon granted — he detached himself from his Field Ambulance, acquired several of the donkeys used as water carriers and each day, from dawn into the night, made trip after trip carrying wounded men to safety and treatment. Imperturbable, sturdy and humorous, he soon became famous throughout the hard-pressed Australian units. His Geordie accent confused many, who took him to be an Irishman or a Scot — he was known as Murph or Scotty, but most often as 'The Man With the Donkey'. 'How's the bloke with the donk going?' became a familiar cry. At the top of Monash Valley he camped with an Indian Army artillery unit, the 21st (Kohat) Mountain Battery, commanded by Major Arthur Ferguson, RA, delightfully nicknamed Percussion Sahib by his troops. To the Punjabis and Sikhs of the artillery unit Simpson was known as 'Bahadur — bravest of the brave'. He could not have expected to live long through the shrapnel and sniper fire he faced, and only 23 days passed before he was fatally shot, early on the morning of 19 May. Of all graves at Anzac, his at Beach Cemetery is the most visited by the increasing number of people who visit the Peninsula. His entry in the *Australian Dictionary of Biography* states: 'Simpson and his donkey became a legend — the symbol of all that was pure, selfless and heroic on Gallipoli.'[8]

BLOODY ANGLE

It was a sad and terrible business …
— Harry Murray

By 30 April the Turks, also exhausted and suffering enormous casualties, ceased their attack. The 16th Battalion was relieved by the Queenslanders of the 15th and had a few days' rest in a gully in Monash Valley referred to as Rest Camp or Rest Gully. On that day, Colonel Pope reported to his brigadier, John Monash: 'The limit of physical and mental endurance has very nearly been reached. No matter how willing the men are to endure, the strain will shortly be too great to risk holding such an important section of the line with men at the limit of their powers.' The Battalion, however, had little rest. On 2 May, the 16th was thrown into an attack on the left flank of the Anzac positions, which it was hoped would gain ascendancy on the heights in an area to the south of Russell's Top known as Bloody Angle. The attack failed; the 16th suffered heavy losses. Writing in *Reveille* in April 1939, Murray stated:

> *It was a blunder, and, excepting Bullecourt in April, 1917, the worst stunt I was ever in ... It was a sad and terrible business, and I feel like hurrying over it. The machine-gunners advanced with the infantry, and as we topped the ridge, our men fell like grass before the sweep of an expert mower; but most tragic of all, one of our machine-guns was firing too low, and added to the massacre until we got a message back and stopped it.*[9]

In a letter to his wife, dated 16 May 1915, John Monash wrote: 'The 16th Battalion on 1 May, at dusk, charged the "Razor Ridge" [his term] singing "Tipperary" and "Australia will be there."' How Monash loved the original Anzacs of his 4th Brigade. In the same letter he said:

> *Throughout the whole of the fighting there has never been a murmur of complaint, in spite of the hardships and privations and continuous hours of toil and deafening clamour. The men are as docile and patient and obedient and manageable as children, yet they are full of the finest spirit of selfless devotion. For the most perilous enterprises, whenever volunteers are called for, every man in sight offers instantly, although often it means certain death to many of them. They are always cheerful, always cracking jokes, always laughing and singing, and as I move amongst them and ask 'Well lads how are you getting on?' the inevitable answer is 'First rate Sir' or 'Ryebuck' or 'We're ready for another go.'*

Of Bloody Angle and its aftermath, Silas wrote in his diary:

2nd May ... At 6 pm we march off ... just as the sun was setting, throwing its rich colour o'er all the landscape, we formed up for the final march for the attack — it was difficult going, crawling through the gully which skirted the foot of the hill we were to attack. We were to attack at 7 sharp prior to which our artillery was to support us ... Lt. Geddes looked at his watch — 'It is 7 o'clock, lads' he said, 'come on lads, at 'em.' Up we rushed — God it was frightful — the screams of the wounded, bursting of shells and the ear splitting crackling of the rifles. In a very few minutes the gully at the foot of the hill was filled with dead and wounded — these poor lumps of clay had once been my comrades, men I had worked, and laughed and joked with. Oh God the pity of it.

3rd May Dawn, Oh God, only 250 left of our Battalion — there has been a ceaseless stream of wounded, many cases have died on the way down, until in most places the narrow pass is so cumbered with dead and badly wounded waiting for the stretchers that it is becoming impassable — along the edge bodies are hanging in all sorts of grotesque and apparently impossible attitudes ... One poor fellow, a New Zealander, came tearing past smothered with blood and quite delirious, kissing everyone he passed, upon whom he left splashes of blood ... I think I am about done — thank God men of my temperament are few and far between. I am quite satisfied that I'll never make a soldier, a thousand pities to have been born an artist at a time like this — I do wish I could take War in the same spirit with which my comrades face its horrors.

5th May Have been delirious all night, my nerves have quite gone to pieces ...

10th May Delirious again last night.

11th May Dawn. The Roll is called — how heart-

breaking it is — name after name is called; the reply is a deep silence which can be felt, despite the noise of the incessant crackling of rifles and screaming of shrapnel — there are few of us left to answer to our names — just a thin line of weary, ashen-faced men; behind us a mass of silent forms, once our comrades — there they have been for some days; we have not had the time to bury them.

By 17 May, Silas could take no more. He was ordered to see the Medical Officer of the 16th, who arranged his evacuation. He was treated with sympathy, for in his diary entry for that day he wrote: 'I tell [Captain] Margolin that I am going — he exclaims "Yes, Silas old chap, it's about time too, you're not cut out for this kind of thing; I hope you will get into the AMC [Army Medical Corps] as you have always wanted."' If Silas had been under the iron discipline of the British Army he may well have been shot for cowardice if he failed to function as an infantryman although not physically wounded. On 6 July 1915, at Cape Helles, Private Thomas Davis of the Munster Fusiliers was shot at dawn for cowardice and leaving his post.[10] Silas had prepared sketches on Anzac and after the war produced a number of paintings based on his experiences. Three of them, *Digging in at Pope's Hill, Attack by the 4th Australian Infantry Brigade at Bloody Angle* and *The Roll-Call* — the latter a most moving work — are held in the Australian War Memorial. Ellis Silas lived for most of the remainder of his life in England, working as an artist. He died in London in 1972.

THE TRUCE — BURYING THE DEAD

At 3 am on 19 May, preceded by a heavy bombardment, the Turks launched massive attacks against the Anzac positions on the entire front. For two and a half hours, an estimated force of 42,000 men charged in wave after wave against the Australian positions. The attacks were repulsed with horrific losses to the Turks, 10,000 of whom became casualties. Never again did the Turks attempt a major frontal assault on Gallipoli. They learned their lesson. This was not the case for the Allied command, as in June and August 1915 futile mass frontal attacks were to be made.

The only major penetration of Australian trenches in the Turkish attack was made at Courtney's Post (named after Colonel R.E. Courtney, the original commanding officer of the 14th Battalion). The attack was repulsed by a furious charge led by Lance Corporal Albert Jacka of the 14th, who bayoneted or shot seven Turks. Jacka was awarded a Victoria Cross, the first to an Australian in World War I. Jacka, and Harry Murray, awarded a VC in 1917, were two of the most famous soldiers of the 4th Brigade and of the AIF. They were different in personality. Jacka was outspoken and rebellious; Murray, although firm, was agreeable and diplomatic. Both gained great distinction in France and Belgium, where they won multiple decorations. Murray reached the rank of lieutenant colonel. But for clashes with authority, Jacka would surely have been promoted beyond captain. Murray lived to a great age. Jacka died in 1931, aged 37, of chronic nephritis caused by severe wounds, especially gas poisoning, and tormented by business problems and the failure of his marriage.

After the attack of 19 May, Turkish bodies lay piled up between the opposing trenches. These bodies added to many others, Australian and Turkish, which had not been buried since the landing. The stench from the swollen, decaying corpses was overpowering; unbearable for both sides. A truce was arranged, and on 24 May the guns fell silent as burying parties, Anzacs and Turks, carried out their grim task. Albert Facey of the 11th Battalion, in his classic work, *A Fortunate Life*, describes the scene:

> *I will never forget the Armistice — it was a day of hard, smelly, nauseating work. Those of us assigned to pick up the bodies had to pair up and bring the bodies in on stretchers to where the graves were being dug. First we had to cut the cords of the*

*identification discs and record the details on a sheet of paper we
were provided with. Some of the bodies were rotted so much that
there were only bones and part of the uniform left. The bodies
of the men killed on the nineteenth (it had now been five days)
were awful. Most of us had to work in short spells as we felt very
ill. We found a few men who had been killed in the first days of
the Landing.*[11]

Harry Murray suffered a gunshot wound to his right knee on 30 May
and was evacuated from the Peninsula. In a *Reveille* article, he wrote:

*And now my turn came when a shrapnel bullet pierced my knee.
Mates carried me to the beach. I got sea-sick in the rowing boat
that took me to the carrier. At Mudros I was put on the
Franconia, along with 1850 others, most of them more badly
wounded than I was. We had only seven doctors on board going
night and day, trying to save life, on the operating table. Slight
wounds had perforce to go unattended. I lost all count of days
on the voyage, but will never forget the 'chats' in millions on my
blanket. All I could do was to turn it every hour and try and
keep them on top. Finally Egypt and hospital; clean at last.*[12]

Murray's wound was treated at the Abbassia Hospital, Alexandria. His
military career nearly ended at this time as, although his wound
healed, his knee appeared to be permanently stiff. He was classified
'permanently unfit for further military service' and posted to a hospital
ship for return to Australia. However, on the day he was to join the
hospital ship, 3 July 1915, he persuaded an ambulance driver to take
him to the wharf in Alexandria, where he joined the transport *Scotian*
for return to Gallipoli. His colonel accepted him on return and his
front line service continued. His knee regained some flexibility, but
the wound was to trouble him for the rest of his life. Whilst he was
in Egypt, on 20 June, his name appeared in List No. 3 Awards,

General Head Quarters, announcing that he had been awarded a Distinguished Conduct Medal (DCM), as had Percy Black. The citation for Murray's DCM read: 'For distinguished service on several occasions from 9th to 31st May 1915 during operations near Gaba Tepe (Dardenelles) [sic] when attached to the machine-gun section. During this period he exhibited exceptional courage, energy and skill, and inflicted severe losses on the enemy, he being himself twice wounded.'

Harry Murray's family holds a faded letter dated 22 May 1915 addressed to 'The Co. 4th Infy Brigade, Monarch [sic] Valley, Gallipoli'. The letter, written by Captain J.M. Rose, 'B.M. Off. N.Z. Staff Officer', states:

I have the honour to bring to your notice the excellent work done by Lance Corporal Murray H. of the machine-gun section, 16th battalion. This N.C.O. was wounded on the 27/4/15 but he remained with his section and worked his gun very often under difficult circumstances on Pope's Hill.

He has been very successful in watching the enemie's [sic] movements and in placing his gun in concealed positions and his initiative and energy have been of great assistance to me. Murray is an ideal machine-gunner and the class of man that is required to take charge of machine-gun work.

I forward this recommendation for your favourable consideration.

Rose's recommendation may well have been influential in gaining the award of a DCM to Murray.

The 16th's casualties in the first month on Gallipoli were amongst the heaviest of all the Australian battalions. Nearly 1000 men had landed; by 3 May, 700 were casualties. The Battalion spent June and July 1915 in Reserve Gully employed as working parties, digging trenches and carrying stores and ammunition. The reserve area lay beneath the shadow of the Sphinx, that dramatic landmark on the Sari Bair skyline.

Reinforcements were now arriving, and men such as Murray were returning from hospital. The 16th Battalion history noted that: 'During this period [June–July 1915] reinforcements joined up, and men wounded in the early fighting returned from hospital. It was noticeable the effect that wounds had on men's nerves and daring. Usually men recovered from wounds were cautious. There were exceptions, of course, but they were so noticeable as to prove the rule.'[13] A 'noticeable exception' was Harry Murray, who was wounded four times during the war and was to see over three years more of hard campaigning, never sparing himself and leading attacks time and time again.

Whilst Murray was in Egypt, British forces at Cape Helles had launched a major attack at Krithia. Despite great gallantry, the attack failed and such units as the Royal Naval Division suffered horrific losses. The Collingwood Battalion of the Division suffered so many casualties that it was temporarily disbanded; only one officer survived the attack. Since 1919, there has been a well-attended service every June at the Collingwood Memorial on the Dorset Downs to commemorate the men of the Royal Naval Division who lost their lives in what was called 'the battle of the 4th of June'.

Back on Gallipoli, Murray had a meeting on 11 July with two of his relatives, Charles Littler and Burford Sampson. All three had distinguished service in World War I. In the nineteenth century there had been much intermarriage between the Murray, Littler and Cocker families in northern Tasmania. Charles Littler and Harry Murray were double first cousins. Burford Sampson had married Jane Cocker, whose brother, David, had married Harry Murray's sister, Annie.[14] Charles Littler had an adventurous life. He served with the United States Army in the Philippines c. 1905, enlisted in the AIF in 1914, aged 46, was commissioned on Gallipoli and became Beachmaster responsible for the unloading of all stores and equipment. Affectionately known as 'The Duke of Anzac', he is reputed to have been the last Australian to have been evacuated from the peninsula in December 1915. He transferred to the 52nd Battalion, 5th Division, and lost his life leading his Company at Mouquet Farm in September 1916. Burford Sampson was commissioned as second lieutenant in the 15th Battalion in 1914. In 1918 he led the battalion in the last attacks of the war. Both Littler and Sampson were awarded DSOs.

THE AUGUST OFFENSIVE

An' Sari Bair, O Sari Bair, you seen how it was done,
The transports dancin' in the bay beneath the bonzer sun.

But Sari Bair, me Sari Bair, the secrets that you 'old,
Will shake the 'earts uv southern men when all the tale is told.

—From C. J. Dennis, *Ginger Mick*

During June and July 1915, plans were being prepared for an assault on the heights of Sari Bair and the capture of major features, Hill 971 and Chunuk Bair, and a landing at Suvla, north of Anzac Cove. Control of the heights would mean control of the peninsula. These attacks were to be supported by diversionary assaults at Cape Helles, Quinn's Post, Lone Pine and the Nek. Every one of these actions ended in failure, except for that at Lone Pine, which was attacked by Australians of the 1st Brigade at dusk on 6 August and captured after ferocious hand-to-hand fighting. The attack at the Nek was one of the most poignant of many Australian tragedies of World War I. Two Light Horse regiments, the 8th and the 10th, were almost wiped out as in four waves, without hesitation, they charged directly into Turkish machine-guns; these machine-guns had remained undamaged in a preliminary bombardment which concluded seven minutes early and gave the Turks ample warning of the attack. John Antill, the brigade major of the 3rd Light Horse Brigade, refused to countermand orders to attack despite seeing the fate of the first assaulting wave. The 8th and 10th Regiments were raised in Victoria and Western Australia. In Bean's memorable words: 'The flower of the youth of Victoria and Western Australia fell in that attempt. The cost to the smaller population of the West was particularly severe — hardly a pioneer family but mourned its one or more dead.'[15] In 1919, a War Graves unit sent to bury the dead and organise cemeteries in the Anzac area found the bones of 350 light horsemen at the Nek, unburied in the open in a space barely the size of three tennis courts.

New Zealanders of the Wellington Regiment, with some support from the 7th Gloucesters, in one of the great feats of arms of World War I, fought their way up Rhododendron Ridge, gained the heights of Chunuk Bair and held it against continuous counterattacks. The New Zealand Memorial on Gallipoli is at Chunuk. Visitors look down the steep incline leading to the summit and wonder how any body of men could have won that crest. The exhausted Wellingtons were relieved at nightfall on 8 August, with only 70 men of the 760 who had taken part in the initial assault still standing. Their valiant colonel, William George Malone, was dead. The next morning, raw British troops taking their place were overwhelmed by a further attack and Chunuk was back in Turkish hands, never to be surrendered by them again. Bean, writing of the survivors of the Wellingtons, stated: 'Throughout that day not one had dreamed of leaving his post. Their uniforms were torn, their knees broken. They had no water since the morning; they could talk only in whispers; their eyes were sunken; their knees trembled; some broke down and cried like children.'[16]

The British landing at Suvla Bay was under the command of Lieutenant General Sir Frederick Stopford, a 61-year-old regular soldier called out of retirement who had never commanded troops in action. His soldiers of the British 10th and 11th Divisions were mostly young recruits of Kitchener's New Army, lacking in training and many of poor physique. The aim of the attack was to secure Suvla Bay as a base for operations and capture the heights in order to draw away

Turkish forces and reduce pressure on the Sari Bair attacks. There was little co-ordination of the Suvla Bay attack with those of Birdwood's Anzacs. The operation failed and little headway was made. It is probably a canard, but it was said that the attacking British troops stopped for morning tea after landing. The Australians were well aware of the failure of the British operation and its consequences.

A very critical reference is made to the shortcomings of the British force and its commander in the diary of Douglas Marks, held in the Mitchell Library, Sydney. Marks was one of the remarkable 'boy colonels' of the AIF, rising from subaltern to lieutenant colonel in the 13th Battalion and commanding it at the age of 22 years. Murray had first met Marks during the early days after the landing. He wrote: 'I noted among them [the 13th] a particularly game and efficient subaltern [lieutenant] in charge of the platoon around our gun. Slight of figure, he was little more than a boy, but was the life of his men. Later I got to know him as Douglas Marks, one of the most brilliant and dashing soldiers on the Peninsula.'[17] Murray was later to transfer to the 13th Battalion, and served with Marks for nearly three years.

In his diary, Marks made an additional entry on 21 October next to his entry of 8 August: 'Note — the landing at Suvla will be the "black day" in the history of the campaign. We lost what was practically in our hands through their failure to "make good". STOPFORD [Marks's emphasis] will be a name I sha'n't forget.'

The assault on Hill 971, the highest point in the Sari Bair range, the 'left hook', was assigned to the Australian 4th Brigade under John Monash and the 29th Indian Brigade under Herbert Vaughan Cox, later GOC of the 4th Division AIF. The Brigades set off at 9.30 pm on 6 August, heading north along the beach road. Turning right, a 'short cut' was taken on the advice of a local Greek guide. Visibility was poor, the terrain was mountainous. Phillip Schuler, who had been on Gallipoli, wrote in 1916: 'I have been in the heart of all that mass of tangle of hills and ravines. The country resembled, on a less grand scale, that of the Buffalo Ranges of Victoria or the Blue Mountains near Sydney. It may be ideal bushranging country but the worst possible for an army fighting its way forwards to its heights; gullies and precipices barred the way.'[18]

The column came to a halt in the darkness and Monash, 'by dint of yelling and swearing',[19] directed the column across the Aghyl Dere, the ravine leading to Hill 971. The 4th Brigade regrouped on 7 August and dug in under continuous fire. Another attack was launched at 3 am on the following morning. The men were exhausted; the commanders did not really know where they were and the operation ended in tragedy. When daylight came the Brigade found itself under tremendous fire from Turkish machine-guns on the heights. It suffered 750 casualties during the morning, 500 of them in the 15th Battalion, which had to leave its wounded when it retreated. Withdrawal of the 4th Brigade was necessary and the battalions moved back. Once more the machine-gunners of the 4th Brigade showed their worth. Bean wrote:

At this moment there came up to the same point the magnificent machine-gun sections of the 4th Brigade under Captain Rose, Lieutenants Black and Blainey and Sergeant Murray, possibly the finest unit that ever existed in the AIF. They set up their guns on either side of the indentation in which was Pope's headquarters, and from that moment all anxiety as to the safety of the Brigade's retreat really ceased.[20]

In his Reminiscences, Murray again described a bayonet fight, on this occasion in the Sari Bair attack: 'I had to use my bayonet about the eighth of August, we charged a Turkish trench. I bayoneted a Turk and could not get my bayonet out, it stuck in his sternum. A Turk rushed at me with his bayonet. I thought he had me when I saw the top of his head jump in the air. A Gurkha with us threw his kookery [kukri] and cut his head in half.'[21]

In August 1986, Joseph Crumlin of Sydney, a master mariner and tugboat master with an absorbing interest in Gallipoli, spent nine days going over the area in which the 4th Brigade had operated 6–9 August 1915. Having studied maps not available in 1915, Crumlin followed the route taken by the 4th Brigade and found that it ended in an impassable ravine. He attempted to climb his way out as the 4th would have had to do but found it a 'task for a mountaineer'.[22]

Then a corporal, Murray was transferred to the 13th Battalion on Gallipoli on 13 August. On that day he received promotions, first to sergeant and then to second lieutenant. The 13th Battalion had lost its machine-gun officer and Murray's transfer was requested. Colonel H. Pope wrote: 'Herewith No. 315, L/C H.W. Murray, DCM as requested. I have no objection (beyond the natural objection to losing a most excellent man) to his being transferred to the 13th Battalion.' In 1934, an article in *Reveille* gave some background on Murray's transfer and promotion:

> *At Gallipoli, when casualties had deprived the British 29th Division of most of its officers, invitations were extended to non-coms in the AIF to apply for commissions in that famous division. Murray was amongst the number who sent in their names, and there was great consternation among his comrades when they heard that his transfer had been recommended. Colonel Tilney, who in the meantime had taken over command of the 13th Bn., shared in this anxiety and he at once saw the Brigadier [John Monash] and told him that his machine-gun officer had been knocked out the night previous, and requested that Murray be commissioned in his stead. This the Brigadier sanctioned and Murray walked into the 13th Bn. lines the next morning as a fully fledged machine-gun officer.[23]*

The British 29th Division had landed south of Anzac Cove, at Cape Helles on 25 April 1915. The division of regular soldiers suffered appalling losses and the Lancashire Fusiliers, to repeat a famous phrase, 'won six VCs before breakfast'. Murray thought highly of this British division, of whom he said: 'If all Allied troops had been as good as the 29th Division, the war would not have lasted long.'[24]

The commissioning of men from the ranks 'in the field' introduced a new type of soldier to officer rank in the AIF. Percy Black, a self-employed miner, was commissioned second lieutenant in May 1915. Murray, commissioned in August, had been leader of a gang of sleeper cutters. Jacka, commissioned on 29 April 1916, had been a forestry worker. Gallipoli had thrown up natural leaders; the pattern of officers belonging to the middle classes, all holding pre-war commissions in the militia, was being broken. In Dale James Blair's article, 'An Australian "Officer-Type",' in the military history journal *Sabretache*, a table appears of the occupations of original 1st Battalion lieutenants and sergeants. Sixty-nine per cent of the lieutenants are listed as having the occupations 'Professional, Clerical and Rural', the latter assumed to be property owners, managers, or gentlemen 'jackeroos'; 3.17 per cent of the original officers had been labourers, and the percentage listed as having mining as their background is nil. Blair states: 'Officers of the 1st Battalion were likely to be tall, Anglo-Celtic, educated at a private school or university and/or from the professional classes residing in the more affluent suburbs of Sydney.'[25] Black, Murray, Jacka and many officers of the AIF commissioned from the ranks as the war progressed differed greatly from that type.

HILL 60

Its capture would not have affected the issue of the campaign one iota.
— Major H.G. Loughran, Medical Officer, 14th Battalion[26]

During the attack on Hill 971, the 4th Brigade had secured a feature, Hill 60, but had relinquished it during the retreat. General Birdwood, however, considered it to be dominant ground and, despite the weariness of the Allied troops, ordered that it be recaptured. On 21 August, a composite force of British, New Zealand, Indian and Australian troops attacked the feature. The Australians were from the 13th and 14th Battalions of the depleted 4th Brigade, only 500 men in all. The first line of Turkish trenches was captured but then the hail of machine-gun fire was so great that the attacks stalled. The 18th Battalion from the Australian 2nd Division, which had landed on the peninsula as recently as 6 August, was thrown into another attack on Hill 60 on the 22nd. It was a terrible baptism of fire for the new battalion. In a few hours, 383 men of the attacking force of 750 became casualties; half of them killed. Douglas Marks was blunt in his diary entry for that day: '18th Battalion [5th Brigade] attacked Kaiakick Aghala but made a very poor showing … The 5th Brigade certainly aren't yet fit for this warfare.'

Amongst the soldiers of the 18th Battalion taking part in the assault on Hill 60 was Private Joseph Maxwell, a nineteen-year-old boilermaker's apprentice from Newcastle, New South Wales. 'Joey' Maxwell survived Hill 60 and later served in France and Belgium with the 18th, where he was awarded a Victoria Cross, Military Cross and Bar and a Distinguished Conduct Medal. Maxwell, who was commissioned at twenty-one, is, after Harry Murray, the most highly decorated Australian soldier ever. He led a disordered life after the war, plagued by alcoholism, losing his medals on at least two occasions and drifting from job to job. His autobiography, *Hells Bells and Mademoiselles*, ghostwritten by a journalist, Hugh Buggy, was published in 1932 and reprinted six times. He was frank about his reasons for enlisting: that as an apprentice he was earning eight shillings a week and that six shillings a day paid to the Diggers represented 'the wealth of the Indies'.[27]

Maxwell wrote of Hill 60:

> *Our first attack. We were to face it at dawn, Sunday 22 August … Out we went tripping and stumbling among the undergrowth. What a tragic morning it was! We had never seen*

a hand grenade, nor had our officers. Ridges sprang to life. They began to crackle. Turkish machine-gun bullets pelted us. Rockets of dust burst and flew. The rapid machine-gun rattle that we came to know so well raced up and down a ridge that loomed in the grey light ahead. Men fell in gullies and pockets. There were groans and thuds to the right and left. You just held your breath and stumbled or crawled on.[28]

Further attempts were made to secure Hill 60, without success. Major H.G. Loughran, medical officer of the 14th Battalion, later wrote of the action: 'For a few days afterwards, the New Zealanders and light horse did some heavy bomb fighting in the trenches to the left, but the actual summit of the hill was never taken — and it did not matter. Its capture would not have affected the issue of the campaign one iota. And yet, for that useless excrescence, brave men's blood was shed like water.'[29]

Harry Murray took part in the Hill 60 action with the 13th Battalion, which he had recently joined, and soon made his mark. In the Battalion history it was noted: 'Lt. Harry Murray looked thin and ill, but he remained full of spirits, watching and sniping all day with his Maxim. He worried the Turks tremendously and they retaliated but could never find his skilfully hidden gun. How he enjoyed it!'[30]

THE EVACUATION

I hope THEY won't hear us marching down the deres (gullies)
— Australian soldier to General Birdwood, December 1915

Murray, 'thin and ill', was suffering from dysentery, which caused his evacuation to Egypt on the Hospital Ship *Valdivia* on 26 September. He spent nearly six weeks in the 2nd Australian General Hospital at Ghezireh. On 29 September, in a depressed mood, he wrote to his sister Dot:

Just a few lines in a hurry as you will doubtless know that I have been sent from the front sick. I'm not at all very ill, although I had dysentery for nearly three weeks before I left Gallipoli. I had just about got rid of it when I left. More than anything I require a rest and change, both of climate and food, and the darned English authorities are sending all colonial officers to Cairo to rot on their arrival from Gallipoli. I have been 22 weeks at the front. I would give anything for a comparatively good climate away from sand, dust and disease. If ever I do get back I will not try to battle a day against wounds or sickness, but clear off the base at every opportunity, which is exactly what a lot of their officers do. The less said about some of them the better ... I don't suppose the censor will pass this now, but he can only defer, never suppress, the inevitable truth. I do absolutely detest the idea of Cairo. It has been a curse to our men from the first. Now I've had a growl, I feel somewhat ashamed of myself. Usually I accept all that comes along without comment and make my men do the same. But Cairo, and I'm not well! How I would love a few days in dear old Tasmania. A few days and I would be as keen as ever.

Murray rejoined the 13th on Gallipoli on 7 December 1915. In great secrecy, plans were then advanced for evacuation of the peninsula. The failure of the August offensive and lack of enthusiasm for further attacks, the poor state of health of the Allied forces on Gallipoli, the commitment of a British force to the Salonika campaign, depriving Gallipoli of reinforcements, and the approach of winter, all influenced the higher command to consider evacuation. An Australian journalist, Keith Murdoch, father of media tycoon Rupert, visited the Anzac positions in August and, appalled at the condition of the men, formed an adverse opinion of British leadership. A forceful personality, in London he made his views known to members of the British Cabinet and to the media, and wrote a long derogatory report to the Australian

Prime Minister, Andrew Fisher. Murdoch's intervention was effective. There had been growing dissatisfaction with the leadership of Hamilton and he was relieved of his command. Lord Kitchener visited Gallipoli on 9 November, made up his mind that the positions at Anzac and Cape Helles were untenable, and reported to the British War Cabinet, which ordered evacuation.

Plans for the evacuation were prepared by a brilliant Australian staff officer, Brigadier (later Lieutenant General) Cyril Brudenell-White. His plans were extraordinarily successful, as 40,000 men were evacuated without one fatality. 'Silent stunts' were introduced. For periods daily all gunfire ceased, then was resumed with intensity. The Turks, getting used to silence for periods, would take some time to realise that the Anzacs had finally left when the evacuation had been executed. A private of the 7th Battalion, William Scurry, who had landed on Gallipoli as late as 11 November, invented an ingenious self-firing rifle. This device was set up in all the Australian forward trenches and set off shots at intervals after the trenches emptied. Evacuation was carried out during the nights of 18, 19 and 20 December. The last lighter left Anzac at 4 am on the 20th. Perhaps the Turks were suspicious at the end, for they shelled the Anzac trenches at 6.45 am on the 20th and attacked at 7.15, only to find the trenches empty. The British position at Cape Helles was evacuated on the night of 8–9 January 1916, again with negligible losses.

When it became known that Anzac was to be evacuated, the remaining Australian soldiers were relieved but filled with bitterness that all the prodigious effort and bloodshed had been futile. In December, often under fire, graves were tidied up and crosses erected with the names and units of the dead. The withdrawal parties made their way down the deres with fabric packed around their boots to ensure silence. The cynical said that silence was needed so that their dead cobbers would not hear them leave.

Harry Murray and the machine-gunners of the 13th were amongst the last 170 of the 4th Brigade, proudly known as the 'diehards', to leave Gallipoli. Murray had been at the landing, and had spent 131 days on Gallipoli, under fire for every one of them. His absences from Anzac had been for the standard reasons: wounds and sickness. Murray's entry in the *Australian Dictionary of Biography* states: 'Cool, determined and confident', Murray remained 'a compelling, ubiquitous figure on Gallipoli'.[31]

Australia lost 7809 men on Gallipoli; New Zealand, 2701; Britain, 21,255; France, 9874; India, 7594; and Turkey (conservatively), 86,972. The memorial at Lone Pine lists the names of 4228 Australians and 708 New Zealanders who have no known grave on Gallipoli or were buried at sea. The 13th Battalion suffered 785 casualties; the 16th, 834. Approximately one-third of these were fatal.

It is an emotional experience to visit Gallipoli. Australian and New Zealand visitors fall silent when they see the tiny beach at Ari Burnu and the steep hills for the first time and try to visualise 16,000 men struggling up those hills under fire on 25 April. Later, 40,000 men were packed into a small area which, after a few weeks of incessant shelling, became devoid of vegetation and resembled a mining camp. In a letter to his wife dated 18 June 1915, Monash wrote:

When peace comes, and we are free to move about the country, no doubt the tourist of the future will come to inspect these parts. The Catacombs of Rome will be a baby compared to the extraordinary amount of digging and trenching and road making and tunnelling that we have done. I suppose that some day on some high plateau overlooking Anzac Beach, there will be a noble memorial to honour the memory of their fallen dead, who lie peacefully sleeping in the little cemeteries in the valleys all around.

How prophetic the last sentence was. In recent years, on 25 April the Anzac and Cape Helles sites are crowded with visitors, but on other days there is an eerie silence over the peaceful area, which has changed little since December 1915. Military historian Dr Peter Pedersen visited Gallipoli in 1981. Writing in the *Journal of the Australian War Memorial* he captured the spirit of the place:

It was 9 p.m. on my last night at Anzac. I walked a few yards from my hut on the beach and sat down on a small mound on which a few tufts of grass were struggling to grow. The sun was setting behind Imbros and Samothrace, colouring the waters of the Aegean with brilliant shades of gold and red. All was quiet, the only sound the gentle lapping of the water on the shingles. Ari Burnu rose from the sea, crowned by the slopes of Plugge's Plateau and Russell's Top. The cemeteries on the heights were faintly visible and watching vigilant over them was the eternally impassive face of the Sphinx. The silence was oppressive. Then suddenly it was shattered by the shouts of men climbing Ari Burnu, the rattle of machine-guns and rifles on Baby 700, the incessant explosion of bombs at Quinn's, the screams of hand-to-hand fighting at Lone Pine. I heard the crunch of feet on the road behind me as long columns of men marched on their way to attack Chunuk Bair and Hill 971 ... I was back at Anzac among the Australians and New Zealanders whose deeds had established the name of their nations sixty six years before.[32]

3

PRELUDE TO THE SOMME

During the night of 20 December 1915, Harry Murray and the other diehards of the 4th Brigade embarked in lighters off the beach at Ari Burnu, transferred to a transport and sailed to Mudros on the island of Lemnos. There they received a stirring reception from their comrades of the 4th Brigade. Ted Rule of the 14th Battalion described the scene: 'About midday the "diehards", as the last men to leave the Peninsula became known, marched into our camp. First came the band, blowing as they had never blown before, followed by a neatly dressed and very portly brigade major [Patrick John McGlinn, brigade major, 4th Brigade], and then a company of dirty ragamuffins who held themselves up like guardsmen. The hills echoed with the cheers.'[1]

There was true camaraderie amongst the Australian soldiers of World War I. It became routine for units leaving the line to be cheered by those marching in, and regimental bands played. There were emotional scenes in France and Belgium in 1918 and 1919 as contingents marched out for Australia and battalions were broken up. After the war a term was coined and used for decades — 'The Brotherhood of the AIF'. The scenes on Lemnos in December 1915 were the first mass demonstration of that brotherhood. Speaking at the 41st Annual Reunion of the 13th Battalion in 1966, Lieutenant

Colonel Alan Lilley said: 'I guess there never was, before or since, forged such a spirit of comradeship and affection for one's fellow man as was developed in the First AIF.'

The 13th Battalion spent a quiet week on Lemnos, being excused parades and indulging in sport, card playing and walks. No need now to scurry from trench to trench; no Suicide Corners, Jacko's Delights or Roads to Heaven, as mordant wits had named hot spots on Anzac. Above all there was silence; it was estimated that silence on Anzac lasted only ten seconds in between sniper, machine-gun and shell fire. Christmas 1915 was celebrated with a concert and the opening of 'billies' from home containing Christmas puddings, sweets and cigarettes. Some of the covers of these billies had drawings depicting a kangaroo kicking a Turkish soldier off Gallipoli. The irony of this was not lost on the Australians.

From Lemnos, the New Zealand and Australian Division gathered at Moascar Camp near Ismailia. The 1st and 2nd Divisions assembled at Tel el Kebir, west of Ismailia, the site of a famous British victory in 1882. The Gallipoli veterans were exhausted and in poor health and an attempt was made during those first weeks in Egypt to give them rest and improve their rations before intensive training commenced. A major reorganisation of these divisions and the creation of new divisions took place. Recruiting drives in Australia had gained masses of new recruits, as there was much motivation to enlist. The casualty lists stirred the public conscience; the deeds of the Anzacs had been romanticised — the Gallipoli VCs became household names — and for those of military age who did not volunteer, a new term, 'shirker', was invented; there was the risk of receiving a white feather from a patriotic female. In January 1916, 40,000 Australian and New Zealand reinforcements were in Egypt and many thousands more were in camps in Australia waiting for troopships to take them to the Middle East. General Godley now had enough New Zealanders under his command to create a separate New Zealand Division and the New Zealand Brigade of the NZ&A Division was transferred to it. New Zealand had a guaranteed source of recruits — it adopted conscription in June 1916. Australia rejected conscription in two bitter referendums in 1916 and 1917 and depended on volunteers throughout the war.

The parting of the New Zealanders was celebrated with lively parties as officers' and sergeants' messes bade each other farewell. Douglas Marks noted these in his dairy:

16 Feb. 1916. At Moascar. Canterbury battalion (NZ Inf. Brigade) gave farewell party to 13th officers — wild and woolly night.

18 Feb. 1916. Champagne supper as return to C's. Another such night.

Harry Murray later wrote warmly of the New Zealanders in *Reveille*: 'The New Zealanders were a body of men with whom anyone would be proud to be associated ... The conviction of the rank and file of the 16th Bn. [Australian] was that the New Zealanders were better men than the Aussies. Often I had been told by New Zealanders that they thought us better than themselves. There could be no doubt, however, of the mutual sentiment towards each other.'[2]

Two new divisions of the AIF, the 4th and the 5th, were created in Egypt early in 1916; another new division, the 3rd, was forming in Australia and, from July, was being transferred to England. To ensure that new battalions of the 4th and 5th Divisions were not made up of new recruits without frontline experience, half of the veterans of the sixteen 'old' battalions of the 1st Division and of the 4th Brigade were posted to the new battalions. The veterans were replaced by recruits. Thus men from the 1st, 2nd, 3rd and 4th Battalions were posted to the 53rd, 54th, 55th and 56th Battalions of the 14th Brigade of the newly raised 5th Division. Half of the strength of the 13th, 14th, 15th and 16th Battalions of Monash's 4th Brigade went to the 45th, 46th, 47th and 48th Battalions of the 12th Brigade of the 4th Division. Although there was logic in the decision to split the old battalions, it caused great dismay for the men transferred, who felt a deep attachment to their old units. To soften the blow, the new battalions wore on their sleeves, vertically, the colour patches of the parent battalion, which had previously been worn horizontally. Bert Jacka, VC, never one to hide his feelings, opposed the decision. Rule describes the scene, early in March 1916, as Jacka read out on parade the list of NCOs to be transferred from the 14th to the 46th: 'A few days later we were drawn up on parade, and the final stage of the great separation began. I can still see Jacka standing in front of the Company, his heels together, and disgust and rebellion written on his face, as he called out.'[3]

The 4th Division, which had moved from Moascar to Tel el Kebir during February 1916, moved to Serapeum in March to form part of the defences of the Suez Canal. Because of the absence of railway rolling stock, eleven battalions of the 4th Division and eight battalions of the 5th Division were ordered to take part in a forced march to Serapeum which ended in disaster. The distance was 44 miles in blazing heat with severe sandstorms and severely restricted water. Exhausted men suffering from thirst fell out from the marching columns, and there were several fatalities. The 4th Brigade suffered least because of a degree of planning by Monash, but the 15th Brigade 'virtually disintegrated'.[4] The commander of the 15th Brigade, Brigadier Godfrey Irving, was relieved of his command and returned to Australia.

On 25 April 1916 the first anniversary of the Gallipoli landing was celebrated throughout the Anzac forces in Egypt and in England, as it was in Australia and New Zealand. The Australian and New Zealand soldiers were clearly well aware of the significance of the day, and a tradition of commemoration was established which has lasted down the years. Monash held a parade of the entire 4th Brigade at 6.45 am on the 25th. The men who had served on Gallipoli wore a blue ribbon on the right breast; those who had taken part in the landing, a red ribbon also. Monash noted how few wore both. Sporting events and parties were held, and as ever with the Anzacs, high spirits prevailed. The tent of Major General H.V. Cox, newly appointed GOC of the 4th Division, was raided and his stock of whisky stolen. The General issued a furious order demanding return of his spirits. A band responded by marching round the divisional lines playing over and over a music hall song of the day: 'Hold Your Hand Out, Naughty Boy!'

That the original Anzacs had a special standing in the AIF is evidenced by the following poem written in 1916 by G.F.S. Donaldson, of the 2nd Field Company Engineers. Weymouth and Salisbury were training camps in England; the Western campaign was in France.

THE REAL ANZACS

There are plenty of slouch-hatted soldiers in town,
Doughty and debonair, stalwart and brown;
Some are from Weymouth or Salisbury Plain,
Others have 'pushed' in the Western campaign;
Call them 'overseas soldiers' or 'Down-under men'
Declare that each one is as daring as ten;
Call them 'Cornstalks' or 'Fernleaves' all out for a fight,
But don't call them ANZACS, for that isn't right.

The ANZACS, their ranks are but scanty all told,
Have a separate record illumined in gold;
Their blood on Gallipoli's ridges they poured,
Their souls with the scars of that struggle are scored,
Not many are left, and not many are sound,
And thousands lie buried in Turkish ground.
These are the ANZACS; the others may claim
Their zeal and their spirit, but never their name.

25 April was not celebrated only by the Anzacs. To the British forces who had endured so much at Cape Helles it was also a sacred day. Since April 1916, Gallipoli Sunday has been celebrated annually in

Bury, the garrison town of the Lancashire Fusiliers. In 1990, when the Rector of Bury was asked if the parade would be held when the last Gallipoli veteran had gone, he replied: 'If there are no survivors left there will always be something to remember. I am proud to remember them as long as the regiment wants us.'[5] Apart from the annual service at Bury, Gallipoli services are held at other sites in Great Britain, including the Cenotaph and Westminster Abbey.

Harry Murray received promotion to lieutenant on 20 January 1916 and to captain on 1 March 1916. His promotion to captain was influenced by officer vacancies in the 13th caused by the posting of so many officers to the 45th Battalion. His position as battalion machine-gun officer was now redundant. The value of the machine-guns had been shown on Gallipoli and it was decided that they would be more effective if their fire was concentrated. This was done by forming machine-gun companies, one to each brigade. Murray's machine-guns, and 37 men of the 13th, were transferred to the 4th Machine-Gun Company serving the 4th Brigade. To replace the Vickers guns in infantry battalions, a new machine-gun, the Lewis gun, was introduced. Lighter than the Vickers, weighing 26 pounds, a Lewis gun was issued to each infantry section, with 38 to a battalion. It could be carried and fired by one man and became very popular with Australian troops in France.

TO FRANCE

Late in February 1916, the 1st, 2nd, 4th and 5th Divisions of the AIF in Egypt were informed that they were to be deployed to France. The first battalion to move to France was the Victorian 21st Battalion of the 6th Brigade, 2nd Division. The Battalion landed at Marseilles on 24 March and was first into the line at Fleurbaix, south of Armentières, on 7 April 1916. Remarkably, it was the last battalion of the AIF to vacate the trenches in France on 6 October 1918, having fought in the final Australian action of the war, at Montbrehain.

The 13th Battalion, with the 14th and 15th, embarked at Alexandria for Marseilles on 1 June 1916 in the *Transylvania*, a passenger liner of 14,900 tons requisitioned from the Anchor Line.[6] At Marseilles, Harry Murray showed his determination and powers of command when a large crowd of 4th Brigade men tried to leave the docks and enter the city illegally. As the men attempted to force the gates to the docks, Murray confronted them with drawn pistol and ordered them to return to the wharf, which they did.

Every history of the AIF records the delight that the Australians felt on reaching France. They had spent months under fire on the ridges of Gallipoli or had endured the sandstorms of Egypt, in both places with a shortage of water. Their first view of France was described as 'heaven'. *The History of the Fourteenth Battalion, AIF* lyrically describes the train journey from Marseilles to the battlefields of the north of France:

> It was June. The air was sweet and balmy, and the sky seemed to vie with the landscape in adding to the beauty of the scene ... The enthusiasm of the inhabitants rivalled the charm of the landscape. Peasants left their work and waved salutations. The towns were crowded with onlookers, who cheered and waved handkerchiefs and flags as the troop trains swept past. The fair daughters of France flashed glances of admiration, whilst ragged urchins ran along the tracks shouting for bully beef and souvenirs, both of which were thrown to them in generous profusion. At the stopping places the residents crowded to the railway stations to supply refreshments and exchange compliments with the Anzacs ...
>
> The Australian is not emotional; at all events, his emotions are not on the surface, but our men would not have been human had they remained unmoved by the scenes of beauty and enthusiasm through which they were passing. Nor were they; indeed, they were intoxicated by it, and gave vent to their

feelings in boisterous Australian fashion. They crowded to the carriage windows; they sang 'The Marseillaise' and 'Australia Will Be There'; they cheered, laughed, yelled, and roared greetings and salutations to the French, and at all stopping places animated and spirited attempts at conversation with the inhabitant took place.[7]

The 4th Brigade spent 8–10 June on troop trains taking it to Bailleul in northern France, passing through such cities as Lyons, Dijon and Amiens. To the chagrin of the Australians, Paris was bypassed. At Amiens the big guns on the Somme could be heard, and at Bailleul the continuous rumble of gunfire on the British front from Armentières in northern France to Ypres in Belgium. The 13th Battalion now had its first experience of being billeted amongst a civilian population; other ranks occupied barns or sheds on French farms, officers lodged with monsieur and madame in farmhouses. These other ranks also gained a taste for wine in estaminets in villages; 'vino' — as they called it — was a drink few of the soldiers had ever tasted in Australia. As was the custom in the AIF, the 13th Battalion acquired a mascot, a small dog which had attached itself to a group of bombers. The dog was provided by the unit tailor with a khaki jacket and acquired rank, being eventually promoted to sergeant and 'awarded' a Military Medal. The mascot's name in the Battalion was 'Sergeant Toute de Suite MM'.

In mid-June, the 13th moved into trenches in a so-called 'quiet area', Bois Grenier, near Armentières. Battalion Headquarters was located at White City, between 'Queer Street' and 'New Queer Street'. For the first time, tin helmets, not available at Gallipoli, were worn. The Battalion received training, to some degree, in trench warfare, taking part in patrols and raids in No-Man's Land. The 14th Battalion learned a stern lesson in its first week in the line. General Godley, Commander of 2nd Anzac Corps, ordered a Company-size raid on the German trenches as an initiation for the newly arrived Australians. The 4th Brigade was selected and Monash chose A Company of the 14th

Battalion to carry out the raid. The attack was launched near midnight on 2 July, preceded by a bombardment. The attacking Company met heavy machine-gun fire from the well-entrenched and very experienced Germans in the area. Although it fought valiantly and captured part of a German forward trench, the raiding party was forced to retreat after nearly every man had become a casualty. Some of the wounded were left in No-Man's Land. The 14th Battalion history wrote of the raid: 'So ended the first engagement of the 14th in France — an operation that greatly enhanced the reputation of the battalion and caused it to be held up as an example to the whole of the 4th Division.'[8] In fact, it was a pointless, mindless slaughter which achieved nothing.'

In his first weeks in France, Murray commenced his patrol activities, often alone, in No-Man's Land for which he acquired a reputation for coolness and daring. In his Reminiscences he wrote:

Soon after getting into the trenches in France I encountered the first German I had seen. I was a bit too far out from our lines in No-Man's-Land. I saw a man, it was pretty dark and I could not tell if he was one of us or a German until I could just make out he had an overcoat on, and we had no overcoats in the front line. I was unarmed — someone had 'half inched' my revolver. This was the first German I had seen where I could get a chance at him. I determined to take him prisoner, he had not seen me. It was getting darker. He had his rifle slung from one shoulder only. I, crouching so as not to get on the sky line, felt about and picked up a piece of black mud that had dried very hard. I intended to bash him in the face with it and take his rifle from him. When about six feet from him and on his right side, I said in a savage voice 'hands up!' He dropped his rifle and put up his hands. What a wonderful feeling of relief it was to get it. I prodded him back to my outpost. They knew I was somewhere in front but did not expect to see me come in with a prisoner, so when I was about 15 yards off and I could see very dimly their outlines, I called out, not too loudly, 'Don't fire men, it's me.' I was only just in time for they had us covered and the sergeant was just about to give the order to fire. We found our prisoner was a sniper going out to take a position from where he could shoot at us in daylight. I was teased by my brother officers for taking our first prisoner with a fistful of mud.[9]

On display in the home of Douglas Murray, son of Harry, in Townsville, is a German pickelhaube helmet. These spiked helmets were much prized by Allied soldiers as souvenirs. Harry Murray acquired his in another display of reckless courage. On a two-man officers' patrol into No-Man's Land with Douglas Marks, he saw smoke rising from a chimney in a deep German dugout and heard German being spoken. He and Marks looked inside carefully and saw stairs leading to the depths of the dugout. On the first landing, on a hook, was a German helmet. Marks said to Murray: 'Bet you're not game to go down and get it?' Murray crept down the first flight of stairs and stole the helmet. In later years, he would say to his son: 'I wonder what the German who owned the helmet felt when he came up the stairs and found it gone!'

John Monash, early in July 1916, was appointed to command the new 3rd Division. He had raised the 4th Brigade in those innocent days of 1914 and, as was his way, trained it superbly, and led it on all its days on Gallipoli. From July 1916, his career in the AIF was marked by success after success. 'Feeding the troops on victory', he called it. In May 1918, on Birdwood's departure to the 5th Army, he was selected to command the Australian Corps when for the first time all five divisions fought alongside one another under one commander.

Monash's successor as GOC of the 4th Brigade was a Queensland regular soldier, Charles Henry Brand, who had served in the Boer War. He had excelled as brigade major of the 3rd Brigade at the landing and had commanded the 8th Battalion. Ted Rule wrote of the 4th Brigade's introduction to its new commander:

Colonel Brand came to take us over, and later he became a brigadier. From the first he began to show all hands that he was boss, and intended to be so … One morning the Brig. had the whole Brigade paraded on the top of a hill, and he laid down the law to us to some order … One part of it we all remember well: 'I won my D.S.O. before any of you were on Gallipoli.' This fairly 'broke up' the Brigade and no end of murmuring went round, for the old 4th Brigade had landed on Gallipoli only about six hours later than the 1st Division. When the parade was over, the old Brig. was just about the most unpopular man in France as far as our brigade was concerned.[10]

Brand commanded the 4th Brigade until the end of the war, leading it in engagement after engagement. Always known as 'The Old Brig' or 'Digger', and although abrasive, he resurrected his reputation with his men, showing bravery and concern for their needs.

The 13th left the Nursery Area on 13 July and entrained at Bailleul for the Somme. The horror of Pozières and Mouquet Farm lay ahead.

4

THE SOMME OFFENSIVE —
POZIÈRES AND MOUQUET FARM

The Windmill site [at Pozières] marks a ridge more densely sewn with Australian sacrifice than any other place on earth.

— C.E.W. Bean[1]

When the AIF came to France in 1916, the Allied forces — French, British and Belgian — occupied a trench system extending from the Belgian port of Nieuport on the English Channel to near Belfort on the Swiss–French border. From the Channel, Belgian troops and a French Army Corps held 20 miles; British, Canadian and Indian divisions held 80 miles from Ypres in Belgium to the Somme river; and the French held the final 400 miles finishing at the Swiss border.

The Allied offensive on the Somme had been originally planned for 60 divisions of Anglo-French troops on a front of 45 miles in July 1916. However, because the great German offensive on Verdun in February 1916 tied up so many French divisions, the plan was reduced to eighteen divisions on a front of 21 miles. The British were to attack with thirteen divisions north of the Somme and the French with five to its south. The Allied plan was for a breakthrough of the German defences to exploit open warfare. The breakthrough, it was hoped, might come immediately the offensive was launched — or later after continued pressure. As far as the history of the AIF in France is concerned, this notion of breakthrough is of critical importance. As is well known and well documented, there was no immediate break-through when the massive offensive was launched. While there were some advances, initially of less than a mile, in many cases there was little success and many casualties. The second phase of the Somme offensive developed into attacks on comparatively narrow fronts in attempts to outflank the strong points in the German line such as Fricourt, La Boisselle and, importantly for the future fortunes of the AIF, Thiepval.

Thiepval was on a commanding ridge in front of Bapaume, a principal objective, and was on the northern end of a ridge running down towards the Ancre River at Pozières. General Sir Douglas Haig, British Commander-in-Chief in France, felt that its capture was essential for future offensive operations in this area. The 4th Army, under General Sir Henry Rawlinson, began a series of attacks south of the Pozières ridge towards Bazentin and Delville Wood and captured so much ground that an attack on Pozières and northwards towards Mouquet Farm and behind Thiepval became a possibility; at least in the minds of Haig and General Hubert Gough, the newly appointed, adventurous commander of the Reserve Army (later to become the 5th Army), which was facing the Pozières–Thiepval Ridge.

From the commencement of Haig's blow on 1 July to 16 July, the British Army sustained 100,000 casualties. To the British, 'Somme' is one of the saddest and most evocative of words. Twenty thousand soldiers of Kitchener's New Armies died on 1 July 1916. In a memor-able phrase, it was said that the life story of the gilded youth of the upper classes of that World War I generation, the subalterns who died in their thousands on the Western Front, could be summed up as: 'Eton, Oxford and the Somme'.

The 1st, 2nd and 4th Australian Divisions had been moved south to Picardy early in July and encamped there west of the Amiens–Doullens road, within reach of the Pozières area. The 1st Australian Division attacked Pozières from the south-west on 1 July, and thus began the Australian involvement in six weeks of horrendous struggle to advance the British line northwestwards behind Thiepval via Pozières and Mouquet Farm.

These three divisions sustained 23,000 casualties between 21 July and the end of August. The 1st Division suffered 7700 casualties, the 2nd 8100, and the 4th 7700. The Pozières battle was a terrible example of the tremendously destructive power of massed heavy artillery and machine-guns. Many historians and soldier eyewitnesses have written about this battle and all of them accentuate the artillery barrages. The village of Pozières disappeared; nothing of its natural features was recognisable; objectives were unidentifiable; trenches were obliterated and men disappeared in the ferocious slugging match presided over by Haig, Gough, Birdwood and Brudenell-White. It is not the purpose of this book to describe the work of the 1st and 2nd Divisions at Pozières, but suffice it to say that they launched bloody assault after bloody assault to creep the British line up to and beyond Pozières and to point north towards Thiepval, the strong point which was the object of Haig's plans.

Ultimately, it was decided to drive a salient behind Thiepval by attacking towards Mouquet Farm. Thiepval would thus be isolated and must fall. This was the task confronting the 4th Australian Division when it relieved the worn-out 2nd Division on 5 August. Since Harry Murray was in the 13th Battalion of the 4th Brigade of the 4th Division, this is the part of the Pozières–Mouquet Farm holocaust with which this book is largely concerned.

The three brigadiers of the 4th Division were Charles Brand of the 4th, Duncan Glasfurd of the 12th, and William Glasgow of the 13th. The Division, as previously noted, was commanded by Major General H.V. Cox, an Indian Army general who had commanded the column, which included the 4th Brigade, in the failed attempt on the heights of Sari Bair on Gallipoli. No sooner had the 4th Brigade relieved the 7th Brigade of the 2nd Division than it was subjected to a tremendous German barrage that was the prelude to a strong German counterattack. The 14th and the 48th Battalions were most affected. The 14th was occupying OG1 (Old German Trench No. 1); its deep dugouts offered some protection although losses were heavy.

The German attack overran the dugout in which Lieutenant Jacka of the 14th and some of his men were sheltering. The Germans had previously captured about 50 Australians of the 48th Battalion. Jacka emerged from the dugout and led his men in a savage attack on the German rear. Bean states: 'Jacka's counter-attack ... stands as the most dramatic and effective act of individual audacity in the history of the AIF.'[2] Against all the odds, and largely due to his single-minded purpose, he released a group of prisoners, defeated a determined German attack, and restored the line to OG1. The hand-to-hand fighting into which the action developed was viewed by Sergeant Ted Rule as a melee of men fighting with bayonet, rifle butt or any other available weapon. Jacka's seven wounds included three hits at point blank range. One bullet passed through his body. Finally, he collapsed. Rule saw a line of stretchers being carried out and asked a bearer: '"Who've you got there?" The reply was "I don't know who I've got, but the bravest man in the Aussie Army is on that stretcher just ahead. It's Bert Jacka and I wouldn't give a Gyppo piastre for him; he is knocked about dreadfully."'[3] Jacka was reported as dead, but he recovered to fight more battles in 1917 and 1918.

The 4th Brigade was to begin its offensive towards Mouquet Farm on 8 August, supported by heavy artillery. Gough planned to take Mouquet Farm by the 14th or 15th. Bean wrote:

> *The series of battles which ensued, repeating as they did within a narrower area most of the horrors of the Pozières fighting, cannot be described with the minuteness hitherto employed. The*

*reader must take for granted many of the conditions — the
flayed land, shell-hole bordering shell-hole, corpses of young men
lying against the trench walls or in shell holes; some — except
for the dust settling on them — seemed to sleep; others torn in
half; others rotting, swollen, and discoloured ... the air fetid
with their stench or at times pungent with the chemical reek of
high explosive; the troops of both sides — always in desperate
need of sleep — working or fighting by night and living by day
in niches scooped in the trench sides — dangerous places
perilously shaken with the crashing thump of each heavy shell
whose burst might all too easily shovel them on top of their
occupants.*[4]

Stretcher-bearers, runners, food carriers, ammunition carriers, all had
to work in these hellish conditions. Casualties were continuous and
mostly impersonal, from shells and machine-guns and bombs
(grenades). As the salient deepened, these conditions became more
acute. The attacks were delivered on ever narrowing fronts in the
salient, which meant more concentration of shelling from both sides.

The Pozières–Thiepval ridge resembled a stretch of featureless
ploughed ground. Supplies and ammunition had to be dragged up to
the salient in spite of enfilading fire. The 4th Brigade made six attacks
on consecutive nights as it gnawed its way towards Mouquet Farm foot
by foot. Almost 90 years later it is difficult to come to terms with the
mental processes of the High Command at army and corps (and
central command) levels. Their mathematics were accurate; they could
calculate expected casualties and exhaustion rates of units very well.
They knew when battalions were finished and fresh ones needed to be
thrown in. It seems opposed to common sense and good military
practice to throw troops in on a narrowing front, getting ever
narrower, to be slaughtered by enfilading fire of all kinds and where
defence could be concentrated. Surely there could be nothing worse
for morale than troops attacking night after night in the same way on

the same front. The few yards won by the 4th Brigade at Mouquet Farm were at a prohibitive cost to the AIF and the Australian nation as a whole.

Haig tended to excuse the cost of his Somme offensive as either a 'wearing down' process or at least keeping the Germans engaged, thus relieving the French at Verdun. One might ask which side was being worn down at Mouquet Farm. There was no concept of a breakthrough here. Indeed, the Australians never took Mouquet Farm.

On 13 August, orders were written for the 13th Brigade to attack Mouquet Farm. The 50th Battalion of the 13th Brigade on the left was joined by the 13th Battalion (lent by the 4th Brigade) in the centre, and the 51st Battalion on the right. The 50th was under heavy artillery attack before the proposed attack, timed for 10.30 pm, and its CO warned that his unit might not be able to reach its objective. The CO of the 51st Battalion, Lieutenant Colonel A.M. Ross, sent the following message to his brigadier, Glasgow:

> *Both 13th C.O. thinks, and it is my genuine (not depressed) opinion that it would be a mistake to press the offensive further locally in this salient. We are heavily shelled from due E. right round to N.W., and the communications are simply awful. It really requires some days' solid work. Water- and ration-carrying is most precarious. The boys are sticking it well, but are so congested that it will be most difficult to deploy tonight. Do not worry about us, but we need WATER and digging tools always.*
>
> *Our artillery are bombarding our own front trenches (heavies!!!).*[5]

Despite the obvious signs of nearly certain failure, the battalions were ordered to attack. The barrage fell at 10.30 pm and the assault began. Since the objective of the Fabeck Graben trench system was 400 yards away, the 13th Battalion attacked from a jumping-off position about halfway between the lines. The 50th Battalion could not advance and the 51st Battalion on the right was cut to pieces by enfilading machine-gun fire and could only reach the jumping-off point.

The 13th Battalion, led by Captain Harry Murray, advanced superbly and took the Fabeck Graben Line. It had cleared about 200 yards of trench when Murray found he could not find support on either flank. He sent a messenger for news but, realising he was in danger of being outflanked and captured, he ordered a fighting withdrawal. His decision was a difficult one to make as the trench had been dearly won with casualties.

Murray's soldierly instincts were probably never better displayed than here. He sent the wounded back through strong points that he had established in the OG1 trench down which he planned to retreat. With his Lewis gunners sweeping above the trench, the Germans were forced to pursue him down the bends of OG1. By the sparing use of their dwindling supply of grenades, Murray and his men kept the enemy at bay long enough to carry their wounded and reach each strong point. Ultimately they had only six grenades left and were in desperate straits. They were saved by the appearance of Lieutenant R.J. (Bob) Henderson with a bombing party of the 13th and a plentiful supply of bombs. Murray and his survivors reached safety. Bean wrote: 'So just before dawn, after one of the most skilfully conducted fights in the history of the AIF, Murray's men returned across the old No-Man's Land entirely unmolested.'[6]

This action was the 4th Brigade's last in this period in the line. After this the 4th Division was withdrawn. It suffered 4649 casualties; the 13th Battalion had 386 officers and men killed or wounded.

In 1935, Harry Murray, upon request, wrote for *Reveille* an account of this action. His article philosophises on the nature of cowardice, fear and discipline. He wrote of the need for a controlled retreat, holding the enemy in check whilst under 'hostile pressure'. The Germans, 'cool, courageous men' as he called them, were aware that the Australians were short of grenades. Murray organised holding actions at no fewer than seven successive points, groups of his men leapfrogging their way back, Murray himself being the last man to leave each point. He would wait until he heard 'guttural voices with the rattle of enemy accoutrements' and hurl his grenades; although torn by a desire to flee helter skelter, 'the discipline of the AIF enabled me to see it out'. Just before he reached the fifth post, he found a badly wounded man. 'His leg was doubled and twisted and although he did not speak his eyes were eloquent. It was then I fought the hardest battle of my life between an almost insane desire to continue running and save my own life, or to comply with the sacred traditions of the AIF.' Murray carried the man on his back to the next post. Finally he had support. Murray continues:

> It looked as if we were to be reduced to our last resort — the bayonet — but then I heard dear old Bob Henderson's voice calling for me. He was our bombing officer and I called out promptly, 'Here I am Bob — have you any bombs?' and back came his reply, like a returning wave, and couched in strong Australianese, 'ANY BLOODY AMOUNT! THROWERS TO THE FRONT!' [Sadly, Lieutenant Henderson, 'dear old Bob', died on 13 May 1918 of wounds received at Villers-Bretonneux.] …
>
> The whole incident impressed upon me, as never before, the supreme value of strict discipline coupled with the force of accepted traditions. I am not ashamed to confess that it was these things that enabled me to do what, after all, was merely my job, and being done all along the front line on both sides day after day. The ability to do such things depends largely upon discipline.[7]

Harry Murray used his experience at Mouquet Farm to write in didactic style about the force of discipline; however, his account was most modest. His skilful handling of the whole advance and the fighting withdrawal, all carefully thought out, are evidence of his tactical ability and, above all, his extraordinary presence of mind and courage. In the 13th Battalion history, Thomas White writes of Murray at Mouquet Farm: 'Captain H.W. Murray was one of the decisive factors in the successes of the following days. He seemed to sense the dangerous points and got there always in time to help save or regain them. He was already the 13th's hero, the one spontaneously regarded as the ideal leader in actions requiring coolness, thought, initiative, personality and gallantry. So quiet and unassuming, too, but always there.'[8]

White's *The Fighting Thirteenth* gives the facts of Murray's advance to Fabeck Graben and withdrawal in great detail. However, it should be noted that the trench names given there are different from Bean's. For example, Fabeck Graben becomes the Murray System, OG1 becomes Bob's Trench. But there are no major differences in their accounts of the actions, except that White gives a more detailed and personal account. What should be added to his account is that Murray not only thoroughly reconnoitred the area of Mouquet Farm before the action, but after his escape went out at dawn with Bob Henderson and fearlessly scouted for wounded men to bring in from No-Man's Land.

Murray's A Company had gone into this action with five officers and 180 men; it came out with one officer (Murray) and 60 men. The 4th Brigade losses for this period of action were 49 officers and 1714 others.

There was little rest for Murray and the 13th, however. The Battalion took in reinforcements and the 4th Division was recalled to the front on 26 August. There the 4th Brigade was required again to attack Mouquet Farm. Orders were written for it to attack the Fabeck Graben trench system (Murray System) again and with the 16th Battalion on its left, to attack Mouquet Farm directly on 29 August.

The front line had not changed much. The 1st and 2nd Division assaults had not been successful and the left of the line had been advanced a few yards. However, the conditions in which the 4th

Brigade was required to attack had altered considerably. It had been raining constantly and the front was a quagmire, a sea of mud. White wrote: 'The trenches, crumbling under the constant soaking rain, were nowhere less than knee deep in "sticky mud or soup". Crashing salvos smashed them still more and their occupants too; and the bearers were wearied even before the line was reached.'[9]

The task with which the 4th Brigade was confronted was a formidable one in any conditions, but in the gluey, slimy, clogging mud it was even more difficult. The strength of the Mouquet Farm defences has never been disputed. The deep, reinforced, large dugout system of the Germans was impervious to the heaviest shelling, and the complicated trench systems around it were protected by machine-gun nests with fixed sightings to sweep away any attacking force even in the dark. Also, German artillery had long ago ranged accurately on the trenches used for jumping off purposes by the Australians, and also on to No-Man's Land.

With the 13th and 16th Battalions in the line for the evening attack of the 29th, the German barrage was accurate, heavy and frightful all day. Murray and the other Company commander spread their men out into shell holes to lessen the casualties, but A Company had 32 men killed or wounded. The difficulty was increased by the fact that the Australian artillery was dropping shells short on to the Australian trenches.

Murray and Captain R.H. Browning reconnoitred the ground over which they would have to lead their men. Then, just as the Battalion was massing for the attack — zero hour was to be 11 pm — another shell landed in A Company, killing nine men. Murray had but three officers and 60 men left for the attack.[10] The conditions were worsened by rifles and Lewis guns, and even the pins in grenades, becoming clogged with mud. Accurate throwing of bombs was made difficult because of muddy hands and slippery bombs.

The attack by the 16th Battalion directly into Mouquet Farm was led with dash by Percy Black and reached its objective, where Black seized and destroyed a machine-gun. A terrific bomb fight ensued as the enemy emerged from their shelters. Black was stunned and wounded, the attack was beaten back, and the 16th was unable to link with the left flank of the 13th Battalion's attack. Murray's A Company, following closely behind the barrage, again captured the Fabeck Graben trench and linked up with R.K. Henderson's bombing section on the right to hold about 150 yards of trench. It had been a costly advance and fight, however, and Murray had only 28 men left to control about 150 yards of frontage which, with saps (deep, narrow trenches) and posts, added up to 300 yards.

Once again, Murray's tactical sense and determination were apparent. He divided his 28 men into seven posts of three men each and organised a group of five bombers with a roving commission to support any point being counterattacked. Both defence and offence in this struggle were largely done by bombs. Two strong German attacks were beaten off before Murray took two men and went left to try and make contact with the 16th Battalion on that flank. All he found was a German patrol which bombed his group. One of his men had a foot blown off, the other was wounded in the eye, and Murray was also wounded. In an unofficial account of what happened next, Murray, describing himself only as 'the officer', wrote: 'The officer sprang ahead and jumped on top of a German patrol who were lying on the ground. They jumped up and attacked him with knobkerries. One hit him on the steel helmet and another hit at his revolver … he shot both. The three others cleared. He threw a Mills bomb at them and, with the man whose eye was wounded, helped the third man back.'[11]

The Germans launched two more attacks on the Fabeck Graben trench, which were beaten off. The account of the rest of Murray's action that night is worth quoting in full from White's history:

On his return Murray found the enemy attacking 94 [a reference point], Lt. Marper, now 'A's' only unwounded officer, setting a cheerful example of cheerful and gallant leadership. Again an

*enemy repulse. Still again came another attack, this time against
73 [reference point]. Murray's men now were only 16 and were
consequently scattered in ones and twos, each fighting grimly in
the mud and darkness without knowing what was happening
five yards from him; knowing only that he was going to fight to
the last. Murray moved rapidly from man to man, fighting
alongside one after another, or encouraging the lonely man. Not
one but would gladly have died for such a leader.* [12]

After 30 hours of shelling, mud, rain, and bomb fighting, now twice
wounded and with a wide open flank, Murray reluctantly had, once
again, to send back the wounded and withdraw. It must have been a
bitter decision; his Company had virtually been wiped out in the
attack.

The attack of the 13th and 16th Battalions had been a costly
failure that gained the troops who survived it nothing but bitter
experience. The 13th Battalion history makes a restrained criticism of
the planning for this attack, which had insufficient force to achieve the
set objectives and hold them. It questions whether the attack should
have been attempted in the weather conditions. The 16th Battalion
lost nine officers and 219 men killed or wounded; the 13th Battalion,
ten officers and 221 men.

When listing the men who had distinguished themselves in this
fight, the Battalion history refers to Sergeant B. Marlin, who was
confronted by nine Germans. Marlin defended himself but would
undoubtedly have been killed had not the ubiquitous Murray rushed
into the fight. Four Germans fell and the others fled in the darkness.
Captains Wells, Browning and Harry Murray were all seriously
wounded, but all had to be ordered to evacuate. Murray's wounds were
to his back, with damage to a lung and a thigh. He fainted through
loss of blood before he could be persuaded to receive treatment.

Murray was awarded a Distinguished Service Order for his part in
the attack and Captains Browning, Wells and Mills all received

Military Crosses. The citation for Murray's DSO reads: 'Although twice wounded, he commanded his Company with the greatest courage and initiative, beating off four enemy attacks. Later, when an enemy bullet started a man's equipment exploding he tore the man's equipment off at great personal risk. He set a splendid example throughout.'

Apart from the rarely awarded Victoria Cross, the usual gallantry award for junior officers in the Australian army, prior to the abandonment of Imperial honours, was the Military Cross. The DSO was usually awarded to officers above the rank of major, mostly to lieutenant colonels. The award of a DSO to a more junior officer indicated recognition of a particularly gallant deed. Murray was to win a bar to his DSO at Bullecourt in 1917. The only other officer in the Australian Army to win two DSOs as a captain was Walter Duncan of the 33rd Battalion, First AIF.

Despite all their efforts, the Australians were never to occupy and hold Mouquet Farm, although they had entered parts of it and Murray had twice gone past it in attacks. They had made at least seven attacks on this formidable objective, each one launched by forces neither numerous enough nor supported well enough for the task to be successfully completed. The losses and the wastage in human life need only to be mentioned to be regretted. The 1st, 2nd and 4th Australian Divisions were worn out by the time the final assault failed.

Mouquet Farm, in September, was captured and then lost again by Canadian forces. Finally it fell to fresh, stronger British forces, but the idea of a salient to isolate Thiepval was never really successful.

On 9 September 1916, Murray was evacuated on the hospital ship *Asturias* from Le Havre to England and admitted to the 4th General Hospital, London. With him in the hospital were Albert Jacka and Percy Black, also being treated for their wounds, received at Pozières and Mouquet Farm respectively. While Murray was in hospital, the award of a DSO to him was announced. Douglas Marks wrote to him from France:

Many many congratulations, never was an honour more justly deserved. You know that we are proud of you and that no one begrudges you the distinction. I will say though, that not all the honours in the world could have made us think more of you than we always have thought.

Having shared a dugout with you I know what a cuss you are. If you aren't wearing that ribbon when you come back, there'll be some rough house.

Murray was convalescing in Plymouth at the Grand Hotel when he wrote to his sister, Dot, on 29 September. He was glad to be in the south of England, he wrote, as London fogs 'are not too good for the old lung yet'. As ever, he was disparaging of his honours. He had torn up one congratulatory card sent to him and was thinking of doing the same to a card received from General Cox: 'I don't like General Cox and don't value his card.' But, Murray told Dot, he was proud to receive a letter from Colonel Durrant: 'I think a terrible lot of him; he is, as we say, some soldier and some man.' Further in the letter, Murray displayed his own confidence and his pride in the fighting qualities of his fellow Australians and, unusually for him, denigrated Germans, something he did not do in his *Reveille* writings:

They [the Germans] cannot fight in hand-to-hand. A determined man could beat half a dozen with his hat — so long as the Germans thought the hat was a weapon that would hurt. I had a hand-to-hand struggle with five of them after they had wounded me and knocked my two companions out with two grenades. My shell helmet saved me from one at the outset of the struggle. He hit me on the head with a knobkerrie but I had a revolver and he did not get time to hit twice and the other four tried to escape after they saw their comrade fall. Fancy five of our fellows running from, even five, Germans. There's no fear of anything like that.

Seventeen days later, on 19 October, Murray was back in France with his battalion.

THE EFFECTS OF POZIÈRES AND MOUQUET FARM

The Australian 1st, 2nd and 4th Divisions suffered over 23,000 casualties in six weeks in the Pozières–Mouquet Farm attacks. In yet another disastrous feint attack at Fromelles, on the night of 19–20 July 1916, the 5th Division had 5500 men killed, wounded or captured. It became a vexed consideration as to whether the Australian government could continue to maintain five divisions of infantry plus reinforcements at this rate of loss. Ultimately, this led to the first conscription referendum being put to the Australian people, on 28 October 1916. It was rejected. Another effect of the Pozières bloodbath was seen in the attitude of the Australian troops who survived. Bean in his *Official History*, in his usual restrained way, expressed his criticism of Generals Haig, Gough, Birdwood and Brudenell-White for the relentless using up of the three Australian divisions on narrow fronts with unachievable goals, all in the interest of Haig's stated policy of 'keeping the Germans under pressure'.[13] Readers must make their own assessment of the value of this strategy in view of the later exhaustion of the British forces in 1917 after 'keeping pressure up' through 1916–17.

It is possible to see the strategic sense of trying to isolate Thiepval by means of the salient, especially since costly frontal attacks by General Hunter-Weston's 8 Corps had failed disastrously early in the Somme battle. However, the tactical problems which had to be overcome by brigadiers, battalion commanders and junior officers in a series of murderous, smallish attacks on narrow fronts do not seem to have been appreciated, or were ignored, by senior command, with the possible exception of Brudenell-White, who was always concerned to widen the salient.

Bean observes that properly prepared assaults with sufficient planning and preparation, broad enough fronts and adequate manpower would have been more of a problem to the Germans than the costly hacking and mincing machine process which had gone on. A later attack by the 13th Battalion at Gueudecourt in February 1917 was an example of preparation and planning for a relatively small attack. This will be dealt with in a later chapter.

Gough became extremely unpopular with the Australians and Bean later wrote: 'The Australian troops, who learned to hate the reiteration of attacks on narrow fronts, not unfairly attributed to him the responsibility, and their aversion from serving under him, which became pronounced in the following year, dated from this time.'[14] Birdwood, a beloved figure, also suffered some loss of popularity with the Australians.

Haig claimed, after the Somme battle, that the three main objectives of the offensive had been achieved: Verdun had been relieved, German forces had not been released for other fronts, and German forces had been considerably worn down. The force of Bean's argument against this statement is that the wearing down was never Haig's intention and was added as an objective forced on him when no breakthrough was achieved. Bean presents evidence to support the idea that Haig, essentially, aimed at a breakthrough. Bean does not mention it, but if Haig was trying only to wear down the Germans on the Somme, why were cavalry divisions brought up close to the front? The notion that cavalry might exploit infantry breakthroughs was still — staggeringly — adhered to by Haig and Gough at Bullecourt in 1917. Apparently, the notion that horseflesh against machine-guns, shrapnel and gas was passé had not occurred to them even after two and a half years of slaughter.

The argument advanced in favour of the success of wearing down in the Somme battles needs to be considered. Undoubtedly the German army was worn down in the huge battles, but so too and to a far greater extent was the attacking force. Bean gives the British losses between July and November 1916 as about 410,000 and the German as 180,000.[15] However, there is considerable controversy about these figures. A.H. Farrer-Hockley claims that the casualties/losses were about 600,000 on each side,[16] and John Keegan more or less supports these figures,[17] which represent an average of about one in three soldiers on the Allied side as casualties.

Whichever of these figures is nearest to correct, Germans and Allied soldiers clearly suffered alike and some kind of lunacy must have been abroad in the world at that time. The other aspect of the debate, of course, is which side could better *afford* to be worn down and which could muster the strength through men and resources to prevail. On the face of it, it appears that there was considerable doubt about this in 1917, with the exhaustion of the French Army after Nivelle's offensive, and then of the British after the 'wearing down' at Third Ypres, ending at Passchendaele. After the entry of the USA into the conflict in 1917, the question of men and resources formed a different equation.

Ted Rule of the 14th Battalion, in his diary, gives the point of view of the frontline soldier: 'There were not many men who hunted around and saw as much of the old Somme battlefield as I did; and one thing that always struck me forcibly was the scarcity of dead Huns and the abundance of English dead. Without counting, or trying to collect details at the time, I have since put it at three to one, and that's low to my way of thinking.'[18]

Rule may be considered a reliable reporter. His book on the 14th Battalion, *Jacka's Mob*, is well known and was well received. In any case, Haig's desire for the offensive was not deterred by the Somme results or casualties in 1916. His mind was already concentrated on the next blood-letting blow at Arras or Messines.

5

STORMY TRENCH —
WINNING THE VICTORIA CROSS

After Mouquet Farm, the 13th spent three months in 'quiet' trenches or behind the lines working on road or trench building. The Battalion was restored to full strength, 1028 men. A count showed that of the original 1100 who had left Melbourne in 1914, only 144 were still serving with the Battalion. On 27 November 1916, the Battalion moved into the front line near Gueudecourt as 'the cruellest winter in 50 years' set in.[1] Murray's A Company occupied Grease Trench and Goodwin's Post, the latter a difficult position facing Germans on three sides. The Battalion history states that: 'Being so dangerous it was naturally given to Capt. Harry Murray, and within two days most splendid work was done in strengthening it from the enemy, and improving it for the accommodation of our men.'[2]

Then followed a period of active patrol work and aggressive trench raids. On 6 December, the 13th was relieved by the 5th Battalion of the 2nd Brigade and marched back to Ribemont. Their casualties for this period in the line amounted to 21. During this spell in the line, Murray had taken the opportunity to scout through the village of Gueudecourt and furnish Headquarters with maps and sketches of water and gun positions.

It was not all military matters which concerned Harry Murray at this time, however. The diary of his friend, Douglas Marks, records:

22 Oct. 1916. Rode into Cassel with Murray for tea.

31 Oct. 1916. During the afternoon rode across to Warloy-Baillon to see the estimable M. Domon, le Notaire, but more importantly, to see Jeanne. Promised to have dinner with them the following night and bring Harry Murray.

12 Nov. 1916. Rode over to Warloy (six miles) with Harry Murray through an icy head wind and driving rain. Nevertheless, Madame's cuisine is well worth the trouble and we had a pleasant evening.

Murray had a spell of leave in London in December 1916 and enjoyed his time in the West End with Douglas Marks, who reported in his diary:

25 Dec. 1916. Afterwards went to London Opera House with Harry Murray and Henleys. A very good show.

27 Dec. 1916. Dinner at 'Troc' and then to Bing Boys *with Murray and Howden.*

The 13th was fortunate that it did not return to the front line until February 1917, thus partially avoiding the terrible conditions in the trenches endured by other units in that bitter, wet winter. Men had to stand in the trenches, almost freezing, night and day whilst the rain came down unceasingly. They could not build niches in which to shelter in the sides of the trenches for fear of cave-ins. Bean stated that: 'Captain Morgan Jones has recorded that he saw one of the 20th Battalion standing with his feet deep in mud, his back against the trench wall, shaken by shivering fits from head to foot, but fast asleep.'[3] Later, the Australians, when comparing conditions in France and Belgium, would say that nothing was as bad as the trenches of the winter of 1916–17.

The 13th relieved the 15th Battalion on 2 February 1917 at Gueudecourt. The 15th had attacked Stormy Trench on 1 February with some success at first, but when the Germans counterattacked from three sides in great strength the Battalion was forced to retire. Capture of Stormy Trench would give a view over a depression which was obscured at that time from observation from the Australian front line. Colonel Durrant, CO of the 13th Battalion, received orders to re-attack Stormy Trench on the evening of 4 February. He immediately assembled his Company commanders, explained their tasks and objectives, and wrote the orders later. All of the Company commanders, Captains D.P. Wells, N. McDonald, W.S. Bone and Murray, scouted No-Man's Land that night. Although by the usual standards, the coming attack was a relatively small one, it stands favourable comparison with the disastrous failures at Mouquet Farm. It formed a part of a series of engagements suggested by General Birdwood in response to General Rawlinson's request for a more aggressive attitude from his 4th Army. Also, it would 'keep up the pressure' on the Germans. The trench to be taken was about 330 yards long and a whole battalion was entrusted with the attack, which was to be preceded by a barrage.

On moving into the line, immediately after posting his men, Murray and some of his scouts, as in December, crawled over the area and examined the wire where he knew he would be leading his men soon in an attack. The 13th Battalion history states: 'He was never the man to leave anything undone that would help save his men or make victory surer. Before dawn on the 3rd February, he was familiar with every shell-hole and strand of wire in No Man's Land, and every possible route back to Battalion Headquarters, and several of his officers, scouts and nco's were almost as familiar.'[4]

Colonel Durrant, in his planning of the attack, left as little as possible to chance. A barrage was laid down by two Australian Field Artillery Brigades, the 6th and the 10th. Since a German counter-attack was certain, an extremely plentiful supply of bombs was requested by Durrant; 12,000 were to be carried to the jumping-off point and another 8000 were stored at battalion headquarters, the Chalk Pit, close behind the line. There were 36 bombers with each Company, each bomber carrying twenty bombs or more forward. Each Company was followed by twenty carriers, each of whom carried 24 bombs. The infantry were all wearing greatcoats in the freezing cold and were able to carry extra bombs in their greatcoat pockets. In Murray's Company, each man carried six bombs, the whole Company carrying 2040 into action. As it turned out they were all needed. In addition, because the German egg-bombs might outrange the British Mills bombs, 1000 rifle grenades were also carried forward. A massive 'bomb fight' was expected. Because of the scouting and preparation of Murray and others, the troops were well tutored as to their tasks and objectives. The final aid (and maybe not the least important) was in the form of a rum issue against the bitter cold.

The four rifle companies of the 13th were to advance in a single wave. When they moved forward, a supporting Company of the 14th Battalion was to occupy the jumping-off trench as they left it. Murray's A Company was on the right hand end of the attack, a flank regarded by Colonel Durrant as the most difficult and dangerous area.

The barrage fell at 9.58 pm and was effective. The advance under a full moon made good ground and the larger part of the objective was quickly taken. Murray knew that in his sector the German wire was still intact, so he led his men left around it and then bombed his way to the right. After gaining a good length of the trench, Murray blocked it off, reasoning that to go further into a maze of complicated old saps in that area would be too difficult and not worth the risk. To this stage, the attack had been highly successful. Sixty-six prisoners were sent back and, within an hour, battalion HQ knew the results.

The inevitable barrage preceding a counterattack from the Germans fell heavily and accurately behind the line newly captured by the Australians and on the support trench. The carriers and the 14th Battalion reserve suffered heavily, while those of the 13th were later mentioned as being heroic in continuing their vital work under intense shelling and despite heavy losses.

The Germans counterattacked on Murray's trench block. In the dark they were initially thought to be supporting Australian troops, and so got close enough to shower bombs on Murray's men. The bombing caused the withdrawal of the Australians. A signal rocket was fired and the Australian barrage came down immediately. Of this stage of the action Bean wrote: 'Murray flung himself into the most famous fight of his life. He was a leader whose presence always raised other men to heights of valour and energy.'[5]

Private MD Robertson, a 35-year-old from Bungendore, NSW, although wounded, held the Germans at bay firing rifle grenades while Murray brought up 20 more bombers to attack the Germans, who were in a trench just out of range of the bomb throwers. Lance Corporal Withers, a 24-year-old from Leichhardt, NSW, wounded in the knee, also distinguished himself in this attack.

Fearing further counterattacks, Colonel Durrant arranged for a protective barrage to be laid on the depression beyond Stormy Trench and kept a gun firing down the German trench on Murray's right all through the night. Murray, in the lull that ensued, scouted the maze of saps on his right and was ready for any attack from that direction. He now had too few men left to occupy any more trench but the area he had was strongly held. With his Company strength down to only 48 men out of the original 140, he was relieved by a Company from the 16th Battalion. When the 16th had heard that Murray's force needed relief, every man of his old battalion volunteered. Later, the 16th sent a message to Durrant: 'Heartiest congratulations. Tell Murray we are delighted he got through safely.'

Bean wrote that the success of the operation was largely due to Murray's magnificent leadership but also very much to the careful planning and the good artillery work. The history of the 13th Battalion gives much detail of the attack. It stresses the care taken by Durrant in ensuring that all officers and men were informed of their tasks and his insistence on warning Murray of the certainty of strong counterattacks on his most dangerous section. Murray is alleged to have said to Durrant: 'If the enemy ever get my trenches back, they will only find a cemetery.'

The 13th Battalion history also describes in detail the attack undertaken by Murray and Withers and Robertson, previously mentioned:

> *Withers, a big strong lad, who could hurl our bombs 60 yards, stood on top (of a trench) and threw bomb after bomb, exposing himself recklessly. Murray again charged over the top to get at the enemy in bomb-posts on three sides of him. He jumped into six Germans, shot three of them within a second and captured the other three. This made one side safe. Returning to the trench, he found three wounded Diggers who had followed him and carried them to safety one after the other. His uniform was torn by bullets in several places ...*
>
> *From 1 to 3 a.m. there was a period of comparative calm, and Murray erected two bomb-stops and trench-blocks made from timber and frozen earth, on his Right.*[6]

At about 2.40 am Murray realised that there was another counter-attack massing, as German mortar attacks began. He was correct, as the enemy attacked in large numbers at 3 am. Not waiting for the main German rush, Murray with a lacerated hand, Withers with his painful knee and Robertson with a wounded face — all with bullet-torn clothes — led charges in three different directions from the extreme right, and Lieutenant Marper towards the front. There was fierce hand-to-hand fighting, the enemy slowly but surely giving way.

The German reports of the action support the notion of the meticulous planning and a well-organised and well-led attack. The failure of the earlier attack by the 15th Battalion is attributed, by the Germans of the Guard Reserve Corps, to having had an inadequate barrage which proved too weak to prevent the successful German counterattack, although the reports refer to what a stiff fight it was to eject the Australians. The German account of the 13th Battalion's successful attack states that the barrage before their attack was good. 'The success of the invader had been complete; he had won a trench, taken prisoners, and lost nothing which afforded the Germans any information about himself.'[7] The report makes mention of the counterattacks being repelled (though not of the bomb fight) and puts the German losses at 250, of whom 100 were prisoners.

The 13th Battalion's casualties at Stormy Trench were seven officers and 226 men, which is about the same as the Germans suffered, but the German barrage on the supporting battalion had caused 93 casualties, including Captain S.M. Hansen, an experienced and highly thought of officer.

In his official report, Colonel Durrant wrote of the Stormy Trench action:

> *Then followed the severest fighting in the history of the 13th, and I am sure that the position could not have been held and our efforts crowned with victory but for the wonderful work of this officer [Murray]. His Company beat off one counter-attack after another — three big attacks in all — although one consisted of no less than five separate bombing attacks. All through the night the enemy concentrated the fire of many 4.2's and 5.9's on the sector held by the Coy., and in 24 hours the fighting strength dwindled from 140 to 48 — 92 casualties including one officer killed and two wounded. On one occasion the men gave ground for 20 yards, but Murray rushed to the front and rallied them by sheer valor, his revolver in one hand and a bomb in the other. He shot three Germans and took three others prisoner single-handed. From one end of the line to the other he was ubiquitous, cheering his men, heading bombing parties, leading bayonet charges, or carrying wounded from the*

dangerously-shelled zones. So great was his power of inspiration, so great his example, that not a single man in his Company reported shell-shocked, although the shelling was frightful and the trench at times a shambles that beggars description.

The attack had taken 700 yards of trench, which afforded a good view for observation for future operations. Murray, Withers and Robertson were all recommended for Victoria Crosses. Only Murray received the coveted honour; Withers and Robertson were awarded DCMs. The following decorations were awarded to the 13th Battalion for Stormy Trench: 1 Victoria Cross, 3 Military Crosses, 3 Distinguished Conduct Medals and 14 Military Medals. Of Murray's VC, T.A. White noted: 'Not only was the 13th proud of him, but the whole Brigade was, from General to Digger. And his unconscious modesty won him greater admiration. He told of the deeds of his men, but would give no information about his own doings ... No VC was ever more truly merited.'[8]

The comment on his modesty is verified by Murray's words in a letter he wrote to Cyril Longmore, author of *The Old 16th*: 'My getting the VC was all rot and I'm seriously annoyed about it. I hate people booming a chap that is in no way entitled to it, and for God's sake, if you see any more about me in the press don't believe a single word of it.'[9]

The recommendation for and approval of Harry Murray's VC was processed rapidly. General Holmes, commanding the 4th Division, submitted his citation on 7 February 1917. Murray's deeds were performed on 4–5 February, so Colonel Durrant must have submitted his citation almost immediately after the Stormy Trench action. Then, within five weeks, the *London Gazette* of 16 March 1917 announced that:

Captain H.W. Murray DSO, DCM.

His Majesty the King has been graciously pleased to approve of the award of the Victoria Cross to the above mentioned officer. The citation reads:

For most conspicuous bravery when in command of the right flank Company in attack. He led his Company to the assault with great skill and courage, and the position was quickly captured. Fighting of a very severe nature followed, and three heavy counter-attacks were beaten back, these successes being due to Captain Murray's wonderful work. Throughout the night his Company suffered heavy casualties through concentrated enemy shell fire, and on one occasion gave ground for a short way. This gallant officer rallied his command and saved the situation by sheer valour. He made his presence felt throughout the line, encouraging his men, heading bombing parties, leading bayonet charges, and carrying wounded to places of safety. His magnificent example inspired his men throughout.

George Stanley McDowell, a young officer in the 13th, wrote to his father on 20 March describing the celebration in the officers' mess of the 13th for Murray's VC:

Had a banquet in honour of the new VC and had a variety show to entertain us after the speechifying was over. The show was good and some speeches went along swimmingly. Towards the end of the night the wine got in and the wit out and, of course, there were the usual thick heads in the morning after they had seen others to bed. That is the worst of these shows — the [Catholic Irish] padre was looking after the liquor; he is caterer in our mess and always makes SHURE there is plenty of grog.[10]

An extraordinary feature of Murray's superb effort at Stormy Trench was that he was suffering from a severe bout of influenza at the time. Before the attack, Major R.C. Winn, then acting Regimental Medical Officer of the 13th, attended Murray, found that he had a temperature of 103 degrees and made arrangements to evacuate him. The following conversation ensued:

> *Murray: You can cut that out. I'm not going away.*
> *RMO: Not going. You'll get pneumonia if you don't. In fact I'm not too certain you haven't got it already.*
> *Murray: Pneumonia or not, I'm not going to hospital. I'm going to take Stormy Trench tomorrow.*
> *RMO: Don't be silly. You're not fit.*
> *Murray: I tell you I'm going to take Stormy Trench; and what's more let me tell you, I'm going to keep it.*[11]

Murray's fever was accompanied by continuous violent shivering which continued throughout the action. Dr Winn wrote: 'I've wondered since whether this VC winner was suspected of being uncontrollably frightened that night!'

In 1996, a diary was discovered written during World War I by Sergeant Eric Evans of the 13th Battalion. (It was published as *So Far From Home* by Kangaroo Press in 2002.) Evans had been evacuated to Australia from Gallipoli and on recovery from wounds was sent back to the Battalion. On Salisbury Plain he heard of Murray's Victoria Cross and wrote in his diary, on 11 April 1917:

> *'Mad Harry' as he is affectionately known was awarded the VC for his part. He is quite some soldier. From being a lance corporal at Gallipoli he must have been promoted faster than anybody in the Allied Army and his list of decorations goes on forever. By all accounts Murray led the hand-to-hand fighting and carried three wounded Diggers to safety while besieged by incessant shelling. He and his men then succeeded in repelling wave after wave of German attacks (one consisted of no less than five separate bombing attacks.) His Company's fighting strength dwindled from 140 to 40 and it looked as if they were going to*

be forced to give ground, but he rallied his men and revolver in hand, shot three Germans and captured three others in the process. Some dog![12]

The Stormy Trench attack by the 13th Battalion surely reflects great credit on Colonel Durrant, the battalion commander, for his meticulous planning. The Australian artillery support, also, was excellent for its attacking barrage and its quick and accurate response to SOS signals. The planning allowed for good support efforts from carriers and the troops involved were sufficient in number, and had the courage, for the objective involved. Of prime importance, however, was the fact that the objective set was achievable; it was not, as so often was the case, beyond the capacity of the attacking unit. In almost every way, except for the courage of the men in both actions, it was the very antithesis of the costly, failed attacks at Mouquet Farm. The planning allowed the talents and valour of Company commanders, junior officers and Diggers to respond successfully with a complete victory. At least their losses were sustained in a victorious, well-organised attack, and this is probably as much as a soldier can really expect. Sadly, in World War I, soldiers very often received much less than this chance.

The whole of Murray's efforts at Stormy Trench, together with his exploits at Mouquet Farm, give a quite comprehensive view of this extraordinary soldier's abilities and character. There seem to have been two Harry Murrays. First, the careful planner, the scout who wanted to know all about the landscape and the likely difficulties involved; the first-class Company commander who had the faith and loyalty of his men because they knew he would do all he could for them in preparation for an attack or in defence. The fact that some of his men deferred leave to England to take part in the Stormy Trench attack speaks volumes.

The tactical decisions that he made, for example, his concerns with flanks and the risks he took to secure them or find out where they were, seem to have been militarily correct. His decisions about retreat and his disposal of his troops and resources to make the withdrawals as secure as possible and to evacuate the wounded all indicate his worth as a Company commander. His cheerfulness and morale-boosting support of his men in action helped to ensure their loyalty and effectiveness in the desperate actions in which they became involved.

All of the foregoing qualities add up to a Company commander who accepted the full responsibility of the position and carried out his duties at a level of excellence not often equalled or excelled. Proof of this is provided by the fact that General Holmes, Colonel Durrant and others refer to the fact that he was usually placed to lead in the most difficult, demanding and dangerous positions and situations.

The other Harry Murray who emerges from the actions at Mouquet Farm and Stormy Trench is the warrior. His extraordinary hand-to-hand fights with the enemy in both these engagements, his hurling of himself, against odds which appear overwhelming, into fights with revolver, bomb and bayonet, are evidence of the warrior in action, the hyped-up red-blooded man whose courage and fire were such an example to others.

Murray's own view of bravery, courage and fear is discussed by him in several of his writings and will be dealt with fully later. It is sufficient to say here that all who knew him in his soldiering days comment on his modesty and refusal to seek praise or indulge in self-aggrandisement.

Edward Kennedy Murray, father of
Harry Murray.
Murray family

Clarissa Murray (née Littler),
mother of Harry Murray.
Murray family

Harry Murray, Launceston Artillery
c. 1905.
Murray family

Harry Murray, gold courier, WA, 1908. *Murray family*

Some of the original 16th Battalion machine gun section, Blackboy Hill, 1914. Harry Murray is second from right, back row. Percy Black is in the centre of the front row. From *The Old Sixteenth* by Capt. C. Longmore

Second lieutenant Harry Murray recovering from dysentery, Alexandria September 1915.
J. Cocker

Captain Harry Murray
with Littler relatives,
England 1916.
Right: Keith Murray
Adams R.N. (cousin)
Centre: Capt. William
Littler (uncle).
J. Cocker

Charles Littler, DSO, 'The Duke of
Anzac', cousin of Harry Murray, K.I.A.
Mouquet Farm, 3 September 1916.
J. Cocker

Major Percy Black DSO DCM CdeG
16 Bn K.I.A. Bullecourt, 11 April 1917.
From *The Old Sixteenth* by Capt. C.
Longmore.

Top: Lieut-Col. Douglas
Marks DSO MC 'The
Boy Colonel' C.O. 13 Bn
1917–18.
AWM H00010
Middle: Lieut-Col. John
Durrant CMG DSO
C.O. 13 Bn. 1916–1917.
AWM H00008
Bottom: Joseph Maxwell,
VC MC and Bar DCM,
Australia's second most
decorated soldier.
AWM P00171.002

4th Brigade Battalion Commanders, May 1917. *Left to right*: Lt. Col E
Drake-Brockman; Lt. Col J M A Durrant; Lt Col T P McSharry and Lt Col
J H Peck. ('Those iron men ...' see p.101.)
AWM E00642

Lieutenant
Colonel Harry
Murray, 1919.
J. Cocker

Nell Murray with Douglas and
baby Clem, 1934
Murray family

The Hon. Clementine Montgomery
Murray family

Lieutenant Colonel Harry Murray with young soldiers of the
26th Battalion c. 1941
Murray family

Harry and Nell Murray at the wedding of daughter Clem to Ian Kelman, 1953
Murray family

Harry and Nell Murray in Sydney 1956 en route to the centenary celebration
of Victoria Cross, London.
Murray family

'The Old Bushie' Harry Murray at 80. *Murray family*

Annie (Dot) Cocker,
sister of Harry Murray.
J. Cocker

Nell Waugh (Murray) with her children Clem Sutherland and
Douglas Murray, 1989 *Murray family*

MAPS

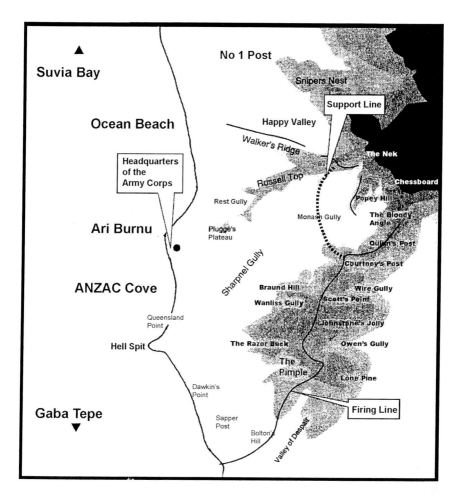

Gallipoli Anzac area

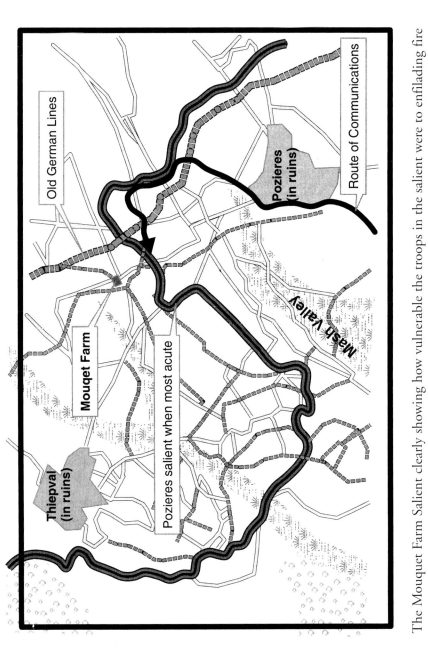

The Mouquet Farm Salient clearly showing how vulnerable the troops in the salient were to enfilading fire and how open to attack the supply route along Mash Valley was. The map shows the old German trenches down which Murray retreated in his hair-raising effort to extricate his men from danger

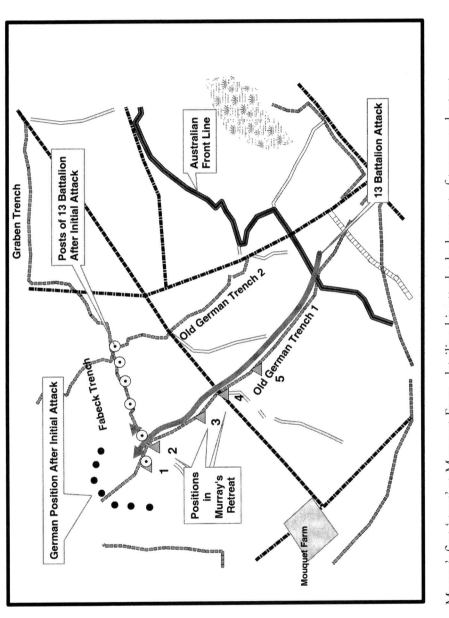

Murray's first 'stunt' at Mouquet Farm, detailing his attack, deployment of troops and retreat

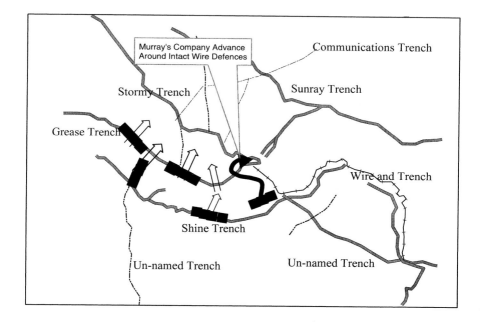

The attack on Stormy Trench by the 13th Battalion. The black right hand
arrow shows Murray's difficult approach route

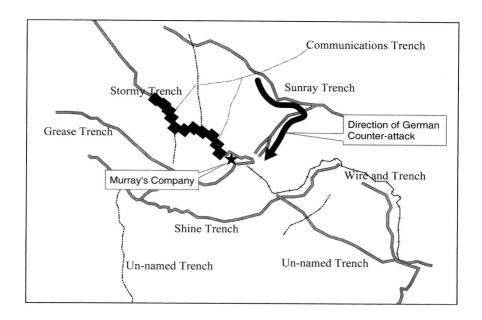

The captured section of Stormy Trench (in black) and the direction of the
German counter-attack

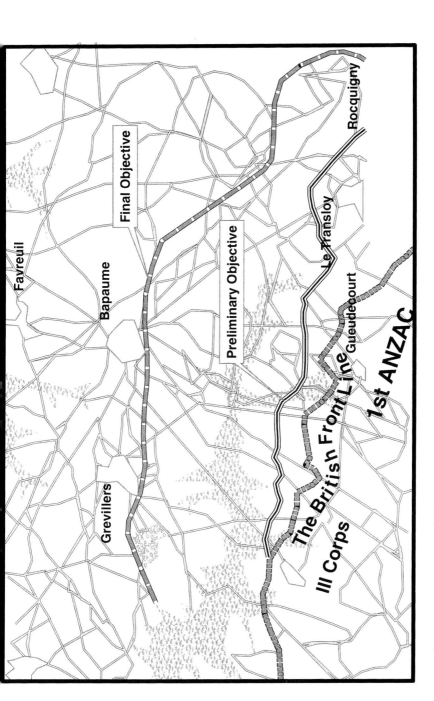

Map showing an overview of the Gueudecourt Battle

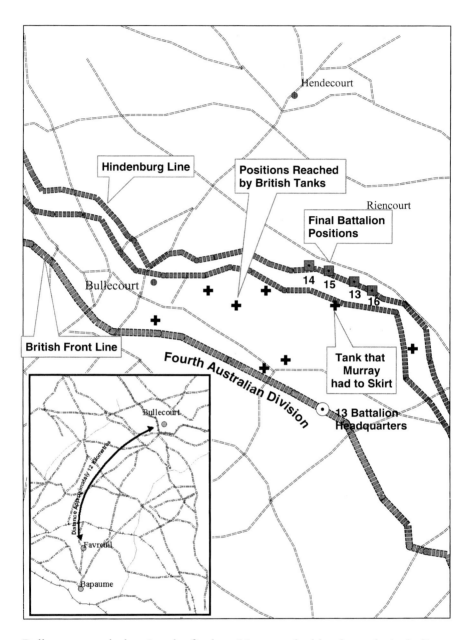

Bullecourt attack showing the final positions reached by the tanks including the tank that Murray had to skirt around to get into the German trenches. *Inset*: The distance from Bullecourt to Favreuil which Murray's 13th Battalion had to twice march over before they launched their attack

6

THE FIRST BATTLE OF BULLECOURT

What passing bells for those who die as cattle?
   Only the monstrous anger of the guns.
   Only the stuttering rifles' rapid rattle
Can patter out their hasty orisons.
No mockeries now for them; no prayers nor bells,
   Nor any choice of mourning save the choirs,
The shrill, demented choirs of wailing shells;
   And bugles calling for them from sad shires.

What candles may be held to speed them all?
   Not in the hands of boys, but in their eyes
Shall shine the holy glimmers of good-byes.
   The pallor of girls' brows shall be their pall;
Their flowers the tenderness of patient minds,
And each slow dusk a drawing-down of blinds.

— Wilfred Owen, *Anthem for Doomed Youth*

On 11 April 1917 at 4.45 am, the 4th and 12th Brigades of the 4th Australian Division launched an infantry assault on the Hindenburg Line between the villages of Bullecourt and Quéant. The attack was supported by twelve Mark I tanks of the 11th Company of D Battalion. The newly raised British tank units were organised in battalions, of which A, B, C and D were in France. The Hindenburg Line was a defence system prepared by the Germans to which they had made a strategic withdrawal in March.

Ludendorff and Hindenburg, the German leaders, had reached an overall strategy by which they intended to fight on the defensive in 1917 and bring Britain to her knees by the resumption of unrestricted submarine attacks on shipping supplying her needs. The withdrawal also meant that the German reserves of men could be built up — the new defence line was shorter and could be held by fewer men.

The original strategic justification for the attack was to support the offensive of General Edmund Allenby's British 3rd Army at Arras. It was thought that a breakthrough at Arras would bring the 3rd Army on a line of advance deep behind the Hindenburg Line defences in the Bullecourt region, and that an attack in this area might jam the retreating Germans between the two attacking armies. General Hubert Gough's 5th Army, of which 1 Anzac Corps was a part, would be the one to attack in the Bullecourt–Quéant area.

Looking back, one can assume that to be successful, any offensive in 1917 would require as a prerequisite a heavy concentration of artillery with plenty of reserves of ammunition for the guns. After two and a half years of trench warfare, just about every soldier knew that no infantry attack could succeed against barbed wire entanglements which had not been well cut by artillery barrage, without incurring horrific casualties. This lesson had been learned at the cost of massive casualties on the Somme in 1916, if nowhere else. Any British attacks that succeeded in 1917 did so because their artillery was superior, at that time, to that of their German counterpart, both in numbers of guns and supply of ammunition. The step-by-step advance of the infantry, after huge, destructive bombardments and with a protective creeping barrage, had become the most feasible method to cross No-Man's Land.

The second prerequisite, for the original Bullecourt plan to be successful, was that the 3rd Army's offensive break through on the German front. The plan was then to pass several divisions of cavalry through the gap so as to exploit the advantage of the breakthrough. Since no breakthrough had been achieved (or even nearly achieved) in over two and a half years of warfare, and cavalry had not been used successfully against machine-guns and artillery since 1914, one must assume that the prospects for the second prerequisite being present were, to say the least, highly unlikely.

The Australian 4th Division was to attack the strongest defence system ever seen on the Western Front battlefields, create a gap, and pass a cavalry division through that gap to link up with the (hopefully rampaging) cavalry from the 3rd Army's breakthrough at Arras. C.E.W. Bean wrote that:

> The wire entanglement of the Hindenburg Line was known to be the most formidable ever constructed; aeroplane photographs showed its broad belts, three deep, the last of them 50 yards out from the first trench, and a single strong belt before the second trench. The front wire was in many places triangular so that machine-guns could fire along its edges, and an attack would split and lose direction. The wire alone — not to speak of the two well-dug trenches 150 or 200 yards apart, would require protracted bombardment, and to any close reader of the records of that period, it is evident that the sufficiency of time, guns, and ammunition was from the first so uncertain that GHQ regarded the possibility of any stroke by the Fifth Army as doubtful.[1]

Writing in *Reveille* in 1936, Harry Murray also commented on the strength of the German barbed wire: 'The entanglement was just too high to straddle, and so crossed and intertwisted that it formed an 8 ft mesh netting of barbed wire, on which the enemy fire, converging from all points, sang a ceaseless death song, thinning our already fearfully depleted ranks.'[2]

Added to the obvious difficulties already mentioned, it was decided to make the attack in a re-entrant between the village of Bullecourt, which jutted out in a heavily defended projection, and Quéant to the east, which also projected out and was also heavily defended. In effect, the two Australian brigades of the 4th Division were to attack into a re-entrant shaped like a large flattened letter 'U' and, obviously, unless its two advanced horns could be neutralised, from these projections the Germans would be able to enfilade the ranks of the attacking troops with machine-guns and artillery.

Another difficulty for the attacking troops was that No-Man's Land here was up to 1000 yards wide and mostly quite flat, so that the infantry, if discovered, would be exposed to heavy fire long before they got anywhere near the barbed wire. In brief, then, for the strategy of the Bullecourt plan to work masses of artillery, plenty of shells, a creeping barrage, surprise, neutralised ends of the re-entrant and, of course, first-class officers and soldiers were needed. These were the problems that confronted the staff officers of the 4th Australian Division and the 5th Army.

The first difficulty was with the artillery, which had problems of access caused by the devastation that the retreating Germans had left behind them. Railways were destroyed, bridges blown, and road tarmacs damaged; to bring the heavy guns through this terrain took time, and if the 5th Army attack was to coincide with the 3rd Army's Arras offensive, time was something it did not have in abundance. Also, Haig had directed that some of the 5th Army's artillery was to be switched to the 3rd Army for the attack at Arras. All of this meant that General Gough did not have enough artillery in place in time for his plans for the Bullecourt attack.

In front of the Hindenburg Line was a series of villages, usually referred to by historians as the Hindenburg Line Outpost Villages. Before Allenby or Gough could launch their offensives, these villages had to be attacked and taken. The Australian 1st, 2nd and 5th Divisions were involved in these attacks, with the addition of the 13th Brigade of the 4th Division. It is not within the scope of this book to discuss these successful operations in detail, but the attacks proved costly in casualties — the 1st Division alone suffered 649. There were three Victoria Crosses won by Australians in these actions, by Captain P.H. Cherry at Lagnicourt, Corporal Bede Kenny at Hermies, and Captain J.E. Newland at Boursies.

Impatient as usual to get to grips with the enemy, Gough congratulated 1 Anzac Corps for its good work but sacked the commander of the British 7th Division, Major General G. de S. Barrow, for what he regarded as lack of energy. The truth was probably that in his haste to prepare his masterstroke, Gough failed to understand Barrow's problems.[3]

Most unfortunately for the fortunes of the 4th and 12th Brigades of the Australian 4th Division, Gough seems to have believed that the German withdrawal was a sign of defeat and weakness, and that the Hindenburg Line was being held by only a rearguard for the German retreat. This aspect of Gough's mental approach to the Bullecourt attack is of crucial importance in understanding his subsequent decisions.

By 20 March, Gough appears to have decided to order an infantry attack at Bullecourt in lieu of the artillery bombardment originally envisaged by Haig. He warned the Corps Commanders of 1 Anzac and 5 British that he would attack when the Outpost Villages had been taken. Clearly the first change of plan had already occurred. Three days later, GHQ issued, through Gough, orders for an attack between Bullecourt and Quéant. Bean states:

> On the 24th at a conference at GHQ Gough again stated his
> belief that the Germans were occupying the Hindenburg Line

merely as a rear-guard position, and affirmed his readiness to attack it with two divisions on a front of 3,000 to 4,000 yards by April 8th. He was doubtful, however, whether the strength of his artillery would allow him to include in his objective Quéant, in front of which the Germans were hurriedly digging an advanced line apparently almost as strong as the Hindenburg Line itself. Haig decided *that Gough's task should be limited to seizing a section of the Hindenburg Line* — he was not to push further; *but through the gap opened by his troops the 4th Cavalry Division was to pass into the area in front of the Drocourt–Quéant switch, where it would join the 1st, 2nd, and 3rd Cavalry Divisions, which would have passed through the main breach between Arras and Vimy*[4]. *(emphases added)*

One might well say, as did Robert Burns, 'the best laid schemes o' mice an' men Gang aft a-gley'.

Haig, apparently initially lukewarm about the attack, became more enthusiastic when cavalry was introduced into the equation. He therefore made available no fewer than twelve of the new experimental weapon — tanks — to assist Gough in crushing the barbed wire in his attack. This proved to be a fateful decision.

According to the diary of the 5th Army General Staff, General Birdwood 'agreed with the general plan'.[5] On 31 March Major General Brudenell-White, Chief of Staff to Birdwood, wrote a staff appreciation of the projected attack in which he stated that any attack into the Bullecourt–Quéant re-entrant, without attacking Quéant, would be unwise, because of the probability of enfilading fire from Quéant.[6]

Gough wanted the Bullecourt attack to coincide with the Arras breakthrough, which was set for 8 April. It was therefore necessary for his artillery to have cut the wire entanglements of the Hindenburg Line by bombardment by then. This proved to be impossible because his artillery was delayed in being emplaced.

Allenby's attack was postponed until 9 April, so Gough's Bullecourt attack was set for the 10th. At a conference with Gough, Birdwood and White said that the attack could not go ahead until the wire was effectively cut, which would take at least eight more days with the available artillery. Shocked, but nevertheless partially accepting the advice, Gough informed GHQ that he could not attack until the 12th. Allenby's offensive was launched on the 9th with masses of artillery (twice as many guns per yard as the Somme) and effective creeping barrages for the infantry attacks. Significantly for the coming Australian attack, 48 tanks were used at Arras, but two-thirds of them did not reach the line. However, the advance, by World War I standards, was good. Allenby's success seems to increased Gough's sense of urgency about his own attack.[7]

Actually, the 3rd Army's initial success was illusionary; it petered out when the Germans were able to bring up reserves. This result was typical of offensives in France, at least up to 1918. Because he felt time was of the essence, Gough was vulnerable to a 'wild plan' submitted to him by Lieutenant Colonel J.H. Lloyd and Major W. Watson of the 11th Company of D tank battalion, which had been committed to the attack. These officers claimed their tanks could crush the wire of the Hindenburg Line by stealing up on it without a barrage. It is difficult, however, to imagine how anyone thought these ponderous, huge, roaring, steel monsters could steal up on anything.

Gough, apparently still clinging to the idea that the Hindenburg Line was not heavily defended, ordered patrols to report on the condition of the wire and the strength of the defence forces. Captain Albert Jacka, who at this time was intelligence officer of the 14th Battalion, led an officers' patrol and reported that the line was held in strength and that the wire was not well enough cut for an infantry attack to be successful. Meanwhile, the news from the 3rd Army was that the breakthrough had not succeeded on its right flank. In view of the patrol reports and those from the 3rd Army, an apprehensive General Birdwood telephoned Gough's HQ and questioned forcibly whether the attack should go ahead. But Gough insisted on the attack 'as the Commander-in-Chief wished'.[8] General White telephoned three-quarters of an hour later and, as Bean records it, noted 'that the patrol reports now to hand showed that the Hindenburg Line was strongly held. Moreover, information received, through the V [British] Corps that the 21st Division and the right of the 3rd Army had been driven back "materially changed the situation and made a haphazard attack hard to justify."'[9]

White further pointed out that the arrangements had been hasty and the tanks were an uncertain factor. Gough, however, through his Chief-of-Staff, Major General Neil Malcolm, refused to cancel or defer the attack, which left Birdwood and White little alternative but to obey orders. It should be noted, importantly, that Gough's plans had been expanded and the Australian brigades were now not only to take two trenches of the Hindenburg Line but were to continue on and capture the village of Riencourt, half a mile further ahead. Gough had even more ambitious plans, but Birdwood objected and Riencourt remained the final objective. (In any case, this objective was well beyond the capacity of the attacking forces in the manner laid down by the plan.) The bane of a soldier's life in World War I was ad hoc, unplanned, or badly planned attacks on objectives that were utterly unachievable by the forces involved.

One could be forgiven for thinking that the prelude to the Bullecourt attack was some strange black comedy, but of course what happened was stark tragedy. The strategic purposes of the attack had changed several times. Artillery support was always going to be inadequate; no cavalry was passed through at Arras; the tactical plans had undergone several drastic changes (including the changed role for tanks), even up to within a few hours of the attack; there was little time for thorough briefing of officers and troops; and, finally, the objectives set were absurdly unachievable.

The final plan was full of ifs. If the tanks failed, what would happen? If German strongposts in Bullecourt and Quéant could not be silenced by the artillery, what would happen? If the attack was discovered while advancing over 1200 yards of open ground, without a barrage, what would happen? If the Australian counter-battery fire was not effective against the German barrage, what would happen?

The opening scene of the tragedy of the First Battle of Bullecourt was set to begin, and the ifs all worked in the Germans' favour. The advancing brigades were the victims of the appalling command blundering. The tanks failed almost totally (only one got to the wire with the 4th Brigade), the wire was not cut, the attacking infantry were enfiladed from Bullecourt and Quéant and fired on heavily from Riencourt in front of them. The troops were cut to pieces in the wire by a hail of rifle and machine-gun fire. The 13th Battalion alone lost 510 men out of 750 who took part in the attack.

On the evidence of Captain Harry Murray and other survivors, the gas mortar bombing and HE (high explosive) shelling of Bullecourt and the HE and smoke shelling of Quéant did not stop firing from these flanks. The problems of the attack were compounded by the fact that once it was under way, the protective bombardment of the flanks had to cease or the tanks assigned to attack these positions would be endangered.

On the night of 10 April, the attacking battalions assembled. In the 4th Brigade, the 14th and 16th Battalions were to lead the attack and take the two German trenches, OG1 and OG2. The 13th and 15th Battalions were to pass through them and take Riencourt without a barrage. The 12th Brigade, on the left, was to attack with the 48th and 46th Battalions, with the 47th in reserve. They were to enter Bullecourt and link up with the 15th, thus closing the gap between the two brigades for the advance on Riencourt. Tragically, as it turned out, the staff plans allowed for a 400-yard gap between the right flank of the 12th Brigade and the left of the 4th. This was because there was a depression in No-Man's Land at that point, which was deemed to be difficult for an infantry attack. Four tanks were assigned to cover this gap, which would close as the advance towards Riencourt continued.

The 13th Battalion was bivouacked at Favreuil, eight miles behind the jumping off position at a railway cutting about 1200 yards from the Hindenburg Line. The Battalion left Favreuil at 10.30 pm on the 9th and was in position at the railway cutting, ready to attack, at 4.30 am the next morning. The 14th Battalion, with the 16th on its right, was lying out in No-Man's Land in a sunken road 700 yards from the Hindenburg Line. All was in readiness, but where were the tanks? They failed to materialise due to a combination of factors, including technical problems and going astray in the snow and darkness.

At 5 am, with dawn breaking, a hasty decision was made to abort the attack before the German artillery found the brigades. Under the cover of a sudden, fortuitous snow storm, the 3000 men fell back in any order. Lieutenant Colonel Durrant of the 13th Battalion, realising that sending messages to his men ordering withdrawal would take time, ran out to inform his Company commanders personally, shouting, 'Get back for your lives. Back to Noreuil.'

The 13th Battalion marched back to Favreuil. At 6 pm orders were received to return to the railway cutting as the attack would now be made at 4.45 am. The Battalion left Favreuil at 10 pm and marched straight to the cutting again, arriving there at 3 am. The Battalion had little sleep on the night of 9–10 April, advancing at 4.40 am on the 10th and then withdrawing. It had marched for five hours from 10 pm on the evening of the 10th. At 4.30 am on the 11th, after two near sleepless nights, it was to launch a full-scale attack. One wonders what the men's physical condition would have been by this time.

At 4.30 am the battalions were in their positions again, ready to attack. Only three of the allotted six tanks for the 4th Brigade arrived on time to move off at 4.30. Captain Albert Jacka, whose task it was to get the tanks onto their starting points, after a discussion with a tank commander realised that the infantry would reach the enemy line before the tanks could possibly get there. Jacka tried desperately to have the infantry attack delayed but, although he was supported by Lieutenant Colonel Drake-Brockman and Brigadier General Brand, the orders from General Holmes were that the attack must proceed as planned.

The 4th Brigade, at this time, was at the peak of its fighting efficiency. The four battalions were commanded by first-class colonels: Drake-Brockman of the 16th; Peck, the 14th; McSharry, the 15th; and Durrant, the 13th. All were experienced officers from Gallipoli on. The Company commanders formed an elite group. Bean claimed that those of the 14th Battalion, 'as a team can never have been surpassed in the AIF'. They were Captains Williamson, Stanton, Wadsworth and Orr. Sadly, only Wadsworth survived Bullecourt.

Major Percy Black was a Company commander in the 16th Battalion. He had a well-earned reputation as possibly the best fighting leader in the AIF. A veteran of Gallipoli and Mouquet Farm, he had never failed. After a midnight conference with Colonels Drake-Brockman and Peck, Black is reported to have said: 'Well good-bye Colonel — I mayn't come back but we'll get the Hindenburg Line.'[10] His words were to prove tragically accurate.

Of course, Captain Harry Murray led A Company in the 13th Battalion, which was at full strength and in great condition following a rare extended rest. The veterans of McSharry's 15th Battalion had earned their spurs at Quinn's Post at Gallipoli and at Pozières and Stormy Trench; no other recommendation is necessary. The attack was no surprise to the Germans. Captain D.P. Wells, captured at Bullecourt, confirmed later that the Hindenburg Line had been reinforced with extra men and machine-guns after the fiasco on the 10th.

Also, Captain Jacka, in his intelligence report on the tanks, wrote that they blazed away with their guns when well short of the objective, which immediately drew fire on them. The small arms fire in front of the barbed wire was murderous from both flanks, and through the wire from Riencourt.

Bullecourt, to Harry Murray, was the 'worst stunt' that he was ever in. He wrote at length on the battle in *Reveille* in 1936, and his passionate descriptions reflect his memories of the horror.[11] On the morning of 11 April, his Company assembled in the 'sunken road', uncertain as to whether they were to attack. At first, the tanks could be seen but were not going well. Terrific rifle and machine-gun fire enveloped the Australians as they advanced, 'a blended roar sounding like the crackle of a bush fire fanned by the wind and racing though a field of ripe wheat — and, like wheat stalks our men were collapsing before it'. In front of him, Murray could see the rear Company of the 16th 'were getting unshirted hell'. They had reached the wire and 'were being cut to pieces'. A Company, 'a pitiable remnant', also reached 'the mighty Hindenburg Line'; 'there was a fierce bitter fight for a few seconds with bayonet and bomb and the trench was ours'. At that moment Percy Black, 'the bravest man in the AIF, who had been gallantly leading the remnants of the 16th, threw up his hands and dropped ... Another of our best men gone.'

Murray and the survivors took the second trench. He believed there had already been about 60 per cent casualties. Sadly, too, they had not come prepared for lengthy trench warfare. The plan had called for the 13th and 15th Battalions to pass through the 14th and 16th and make the long advance to Riencourt; consequently they had not carried large quantities of bombs and small arms ammunition with them.

Murray and the surviving officers set about organising the defence of what they had taken — about 825 metres of frontage. Clearly, because of the casualties already taken, no further advance was possible. Murray now quickly visited all of the captured positions in the second trench (OG11), advised all, and placed blocks, posts and gun positions.[12] At 7.15 am he sent a runner, who miraculously survived and reached HQ at 8.45 with a comprehensive message of the situation in the Hindenburg Line. The message read:

We hold first objective and part of the second. Have established blocks on right of both objectives. In touch with 14th on left. Expect heavy bomb fighting in evening. There are six tanks at a standstill, apparently damaged — just behind the first objective are four, and two near second. Quite impossible to attack village. 'A' Company 13th badly cut about by machine-gun fire in wire, some of all other 13th companies here O.K. We will require as many rifle and hand grenades as you can possibly send, also small arms ammunition. Most of Lewis machine-guns are O.K. Have four Vickers guns. Fear Major Black killed. Several officers killed and wounded ... Have plenty men. Have about 30 prisoners of 124 Regt. Will send them over at dusk. Look out for S.O.S. signals. Send white flares (as many as possible). With artillery support we can keep the position till the cows come home.[13]

Unfortunately for the 4th Brigade, the artillery support did not come. In keeping with the complete shambles that was the organisation at Bullecourt, absurdly optimistic and hopelessly erroneous reports of sightings of Australians and tanks being in Riencourt and Bullecourt, and even Hendecourt (which was not even an objective) from artillery observation officers, aeroplanes, and even one from the British V Corps on the left, convinced senior command from Birdwood up, as well as the artillery officers, that the guns should not fire.

There were no fewer than eighteen SOS flares sent up by Murray and the 4th Brigade in OG2, calling for an artillery barrage. These were ignored — not by the battalion commanders or Brigadier Brand and Brigadier General Robertson of the 12th Brigade, who were certain that Murray's comprehensive message represented the true state of the attack — but by senior command and senior artillery officers. The ensuing disaster is a terrible indictment of the lack of coordination in the command structure. Murray's message, clear and comprehensive, arrived at 8.45 am. Clearly the attack had stopped at OG2, yet for four long hours nothing happened. Perhaps, as far as Gough was concerned, the wish was father to the thought; he may have preferred to believe the vague reports rather than the concrete, written evidence of a highly respected officer of proven tactical understanding and great experience. That is, if Gough ever got the message.

Black comedy appears again as Gough ordered up the 4th Cavalry Division, apparently in the belief that the horses could pass through. Obviously, a few HE shells and a few bursts of machine-gun fire were all that was necessary to stop this attempt at archaic warfare. It was, however, no comedy for the cavalrymen involved.

The situation of Murray and the survivors of the four battalions was by now desperate; the murderous crossfire behind them meant that communication to and from them was, if not impossible, highly hazardous. Their only chance of being resupplied was if the artillery would lay down a barrage, which it refused to do. The gap between the two brigades was never closed and a German communication trench emptied into this gap, which meant that four extra flanks were created to be defended while ammunition and bombs were running out. The most determined German counterattacks were mounted from here and, by attacking along OG1, threatened to isolate Murray and his men. The remnants of the four battalions were faced with either surrender or a desperately dangerous retreat through a hail of machine-gun fire and artillery bombardment. The 12th Brigade, on the left of the 4th, retreated at 11.30, suffering terribly in doing so.

Because they were in OG2, Murray and his group of men were in danger of being captured. Murray, Sergeants T. Gilday and A. Oswald and Corporal G.W. Hickling, who had carried Stoke's shells, and Private C.H. Knight were cut off several times and called upon to surrender, but their reply was always to fight. At one stage someone in OG1 raised a white flag and Murray ordered it to be shot down, which it was. The desperate fight for seven hours to hold the trenches can barely be imagined. Eventually, with absolutely no alternative, Murray said to the few survivors: 'There are two things now — capture or go into that.' Casualties among those who elected to run the gauntlet were heavy; Murray himself was the last of his group to leave.

The history of the 13th describes events:

After crossing the wire, those left rested in shellholes awhile before continuing. Murray jumped into one of these holes. The remnant of the glorious 4th Bde. was still being cut down. It was too much for Murray. 'This is not war; it is murder,' he exclaimed. 'Some of those men helped me to get my VC, and I must help them now.' With these words he ran out into the hail to advise in order to try to save his men. And our artillery was still silent, allowing the enemy to pour his lead into us at his sweet will. Thus it was that, after fighting heroically for seven hours, dozens of splendid men were killed returning.[14]

The 4th Brigade losses for the First Battle of Bullecourt as given in the 13th Battalion History were:

UNIT	OFFICERS	OTHER RANKS
13th	21	489
14th	19	582
15th	20	380
16th	13	623
4MG Co	5	99
Trench Mortar Bty	1	30
Details		57
TOTALS	79	2260

These figures probably represent about 75 to 80 per cent of those engaged, killed, wounded and missing. Over a thousand became prisoners of war; this was the largest number of Australians captured in one action in World War I.

In his *Reveille* article of December 1936, Harry Murray emotionally described his return to Battalion HQ via shell holes in No-Man's Land. Of the men who accompanied him, only four survived. Miraculously, he was aided by a German mistake; in the general confusion, his German pursuers were gunned down by their own machine-gunners. Completely exhausted on his return, Murray was able to go only a few steps at a time. Even in his over-modest description of his condition, it is obvious that his mental and physical endurance were just about at their end:

There is not much more to tell. We were relieved at dusk. Colonel Durrant saw to it personally that every man got a feed, and that all had left before he took me along that same narrow track by which had come forward — was it yesterday, or last year? No, only this morning. I was still so exhausted that I could only walk a few yards at a time. The Germans were still sending over a lot of big stuff, anticipating that supports would be moving to the front, but Durrie would not leave me (as I wanted him to), and let me come along in my own time. There was a strong likelihood of one of those plunging, ripping, tearing 5.9's getting us. What did it matter. What did anything matter? It was surely coming to us sometime or other.

I wanted to lie down and sleep; sleep above all things, and let Durrant get away from the shelling, but not he. Somebody from the relieving battalion had given him a flask of whisky, and he gave me several nips. As a rule a little spirits affects me, but that night it had no more effect than water ...

I have mentioned some names in passing, picking out a few deeds from that grim phantasmagoria of struggling fighting men, but, of course, hundreds of other fine actions were performed that day. Every man who followed his officer through those shrieking fields of fire was a hero. The whole battle was as hopeless as the charge of the Light Brigade at Balaclava, and the effort was sustained far beyond the limits usually assigned to human endurance. Clinging automatically to the discipline of the AIF, the few survivors had to hang on, when, by all the laws, human resources should have been completely expended, and when even mind and body seem to be divorced by a ceaseless succession of stunning and stupendous events. It is only necessary to mention that in our Company alone there were 17 unwounded survivors; this will give an idea of the losses as a whole.[15]

Harry Murray went on to criticise the military blunder of the Bullecourt planning. The use of unproven tanks; infantry assault without artillery; then he finally made the point that the worst mistake of all was 'over-estimating our infantry and under estimating the German, and it was fatal to underrate such men'. It seems to this writer, as to Murray, that this was the fatal flaw that underwrote most of General Hubert Gough's plans at Bullecourt.

Murray's final words on Bullecourt need to be quoted because they seem to sum up, most profoundly, the whole disaster:

I then witnessed the meeting of the four colonels of the 4th Brigade with General Brand, who was waiting in his advanced HQ to see the last of his men come out. The CO's came last, and exchanged one long look. Weary to death as I was, I flinched at their expression, laden with bitter condemnation of those responsible for the ghastly blunder. Behind those burning eyes, and stern set lips, one could sense the dammed-back floods of denunciation which might break forth at any moment, but no word issued from those iron men. The High Command had blundered, and men had had to pay the price; that was all. Had I been responsible, I would sooner have gone through another Bullecourt than have faced those men, although their lips were sealed. They seemed to epitomise in their stern silence all the tragic horror and heroic futility of Bullecourt — bitter grief and stern indignation at the recollection of their men, torn, dismembered, and blown to shreds on that fatal barrier; then the hand-to-hand fighting, the temporary advantage, and finally the grim hanging-on and waiting for the barrage and munitions that never came.[16]

In January 1937, Major General Brand, who commanded the 4th Infantry Brigade at Bullecourt, commented in *Reveille* on Murray's article:

Murray's is a graphic story of an unparalleled Infantry adventure, which resulted in the loss, in the 4th Brigade alone, of 75 officers and 2661 other ranks killed, wounded and missing [the numbers differ slightly from those given in the Battalion history]. It was a terrible price to pay to prove to the Higher Command that tanks are not substitutes for artillery in support of infantry … I prefer not to open up the argument as to why the guns were silent at the most critical stage of the battle. I hold the same view now as I did at the time.[17]

Murray's account of the battle was also favourably commented on by two men who were colonels at Bullecourt; R.L. Leane (48th Bn) and J.M. Durrant (13th Bn). They wrote in *Reveille*, also in January 1937, stressing the accuracy of the article and praising, unstintingly, Murray himself and the men of their battalions.

Bert Knowles was a lance corporal in Murray's A Company at Bullecourt. In 1931, he too wrote an excellent article in *Reveille* which needs to be quoted. Writing about his Company's advance across No-Man's Land on 11 April 1917, he said:

As L/Cpl, I had charge of six men and a Lewis gun section behind them. In front, and slightly to my left, was Captain Harry Murray, VC. He was strolling along as if death was something which only came with old age.

After we had crossed the sunken road from which the 16th had started, our right flank seemed to come in towards the centre; owing to a road slanting inward across the front. Murray, seeing the danger of our getting too close together, strode across and simply said, 'Right incline 13th' and it was done without any fuss. A few yards further on we walked into a barrage of machine-gun fire from the village of Quéant, on our right. Glancing in that direction, I saw rows of men in the semi-darkness crumple up. My own section now comprised two men and myself.

Out of the gloom ahead came the same quiet voice, 'Get down, 13th until it passes' ...

I was brought back to realities by the same wonderful voice in front, 'Come on 13th! The 16th are getting hell,' and we did the next 200 yards or so at a jog trot. It was now almost daylight, and although there was still a mist, the drizzle of snow had ceased, also our artillery fire, and the enemy machine-guns were having it all their own way. Anywhere, where men were grouped together trying to penetrate the barbed wire, the machine-guns simply wiped out 50 per cent with a swish; but men lay on their sides and hacked at the wire with their bayonets. Some few had cutters; others tried to cross the top, leaping from one strand to another. Many slipped and became hopelessly entangled in the loosely bunched wire. Many were shot down half-way through, and hung upon the wire in various attitudes ...

... My clothes were in rags and thighs and arms were scratched with barbed wire. We had come up from Favreuil on the night of the 9th, gone back on the 10th (as 'someone had blundered') in the teeth of a blizzard, and started back again the same night to carry out the attack which had just subsided — about 30 miles altogether, 20 of which were done in the night. I fell into a kind of doze.[18]

Bert Knowles was captured, but his story is typical of Bullecourt. The 'doze' took place in a shell hole with two wounded mates, as they tried to retreat. His experiences throw an interesting cross-reference on Murray's own story of the advance and give some idea of why he was so highly regarded as a leader by his men and fellow officers.

Murray was promoted to major (temporary) immediately after Bullecourt and on 15 May 1917 was awarded a bar to his DSO. The commendation for which he received the bar, signed by Lieutenant Colonel Durrant and Major General William Holmes (CO of 4th Division), reads:

He rendered conspicuous service for the attack near Bullecourt on 11-4-17. He led his Company with great courage and skill through 1,200 yards of shell and machine-gun fire and he and his Company still kept on although they lost 75% of their strength before reaching the second objective. Captain Murray being the senior officer of the 4th Brigade in the 1st and 2nd objectives went along the whole frontage, 900 yards, directing the defence, always encouraging the men of all units by his cheerfulness and bravery and always moving to the points of danger.

When the bomb supply was running out and the men gave ground he rallied them time after time and fought back the Germans over and over again. When there was no alternative but to surrender or withdraw through the heavy machine-gun fire, Captain Murray was the last to leave the position. He is not only brave and daring but a skilful soldier possessing tactical instinct of the highest order. He has already been awarded VC, DSO, DCM.

In his Reminiscences, Murray stated: 'I was given a bar to my DSO, Birdwood personally told me it would have been a bar to my VC had we won the battle. It is not the practice to give the VC to a man who had been in a losing battle.'

Murray's deeds in OG1 and OG2 trenches, and his subsequent return to the jumping-off point, are certainly the actions of 'no ordinary man'. His extraordinary optimism and cheerfulness are very apparent in his message back to headquarters after occupying OG2 with the pitiful remnants of four battalions. He is going to send the German prisoners back at dusk and expects heavy evening bombing attacks. But he does not mention any doubt about his and the men's ability to hold the position all day and night. Once again his tactical instincts are apparent — blocking trenches, deciding not to advance further, ensuring the 14th were covering his left flank, siting his machine-guns and strong points, and so on.

Of course Murray did not know that the guns would not fire. A full analysis of his message would fill a booklet. He located six of the twelve tanks (enough to clearly indicate their failure). He also clearly indicated that there had been no advance beyond OG2, that the two tanks assigned to blank out their right flank towards Quéant had failed to do so, as he had had to order the trenches to be blocked on that flank. Competent army intelligence officers should have gleaned much from this comprehensive message, written and delivered in the most harrowing of circumstances. It offers a large window on Murray's extraordinary ability as an officer and leader.

C.E.W. Bean is scathing in his attack on both Gough and Haig, a rare departure from his usual restraint. Of Gough he says:

> But, with almost boyish eagerness to deliver a death blow, the army commander broke at every stage through rules recognised even by platoon commanders. He attempted a deep penetration on a narrow front, and that at the head of a deep re-entrant. When, despite impetuous efforts, he was unable to bring forward his artillery and ammunition in time to cut the wire, he adopted, on the spur of the moment, a scheme devised by an inexperienced officer of an experimental arm, and called the attack on again for the following morning. Finally, after the tanks, on the first trial, had confirmed the worst fears of his subordinates, he insisted on repeating the identical operation the

next day. Within two hours of the attack being delivered every one of his impetuous predictions were being paid for by the crushing of the magnificent force which had been given to him to handle.[19]

Certainly, no one who writes about the Australian 4th Division at Bullecourt fails to say that the men of the Division achieved, heroically, what was believed to be impossible; without the aid of a barrage they temporarily occupied a strongly defended position behind barbed wire defended by a first-class enemy, even while suffering horrendous losses. Like many military disasters, the most memorable thing about it is the courage and discipline of the men involved. The attack did not gain any ground; it also gave the Germans a morale boost, and cost the Australians dearly. Similarly to Mouquet Farm, all that the soldiers who survived gained was bitter experience at the loss of so many comrades.

The following poem is included because, written in France by Edmund Sambell of the 14th Battalion, it undoubtedly expresses views and attitudes held by many men of the AIF. Sambell died on 29 January 1918 as a result of gas poisoning received at Ypres in 1917. (Blue was the 4th Brigade colour patch.)

Bullecourt

You boasted a wall of granite strength,
Which nothing on earth could take,
The skill you learned in forty years,
You defied us blokes to break.

Four thousand men from the 'Southern Seas,'
In War but infants yet,
They crept grey-eyed from a sunken road,
And through your barbed wire swept.

No guns to aid, no barrage long
　To sweep the wire away,
But a headlong charge of a thousand yards
　And the blues they paved the way.

The first line through, the second held,
　They fought as strong men do,
'Hindenburg's Line' with its vaunted strength
　Was smashed by an Anzac crew.

No bombs to throw, no guns to speak,
　Nothing but lives to sell,
The 'Dark Blues' like a quivering wave,
　Fought through this eternal hell.

'Officers this way, the men go there!'
　The Hun O.C. called out,
But the men hung back as men will do,
　They broke — and a few got out.

There's a tale that is told in history,
　It's large on the scroll of fame,
Of a charge they made in Crimea —
　'Balaclava' is the name.

But the charge we know and the charge we've seen
　Never from our minds will fade,
God speed the day we'll avenge those boys
　Who fell with the Blue Brigade.[20]

Bullecourt is now a tiny place with only about 250 inhabitants, but the Australian soldiers of World War I are still honoured there. Anzac Day has been celebrated there, and at nearby Hendecourt, since 1919. A museum with memorabilia of the AIF has been developed in the village in rooms provided by the mayor. As a bicentennial gift in 1988, the Australian War Memorial donated one of its best-known paintings, James Scott's *The Battle of the Somme (Death of Major Percy Black)* to the museum. In 1992, the Australian government also donated a 2.4 metre bronze statue of a Digger designed by an Australian artist, Peter Corlett, which was erected on a memorial cairn in the middle of the village.

7

MESSINES AND PASSCHENDAELE

The winter, and now Bullecourt, were just behind us, memories fresh, vivid and terrible. The future was flame-racked gloom, not good to contemplate. It was a strange calm time of utter peace. Never is the day so restful as when the cyclone has passed. Never do the birds sing so sweetly as amid the wreckage of the trees ... But we thought much, and said very little of those faces that were gone, of those voices that were first in banter and song and that we would hear no more.

— G.D. Mitchell, *Backs to the Wall*[1]

After Bullecourt, the remnants of the 4th Brigade were withdrawn from the line, marched to Favreuil, thence entrained in rain and snow for Albert, where General Birdwood, overcome with emotion, addressed them, 'grieved as perhaps never before or since'.[2] Finally, they reached familiar surroundings at Ribemont, where the locals showed their horror at the so obvious losses of the 'beautiful battalions', amongst whom they had made many friends. G.D. Mitchell, MC, DCM (48 Bn), in his work *Backs to the Wall* describes a 'catechism' from the villagers after Bullecourt:

'Where is Monsieur Zhack?'
'Mort.'
'Ah, Mon Dieu! Le pauvre garçon. Quel malheur! C'est la
guerre terrible. Et Monsieur Blue?'
[Dead. Ah, My God. The poor boy. What bad luck. It
is the terrible war. And Mr. Blue?][3]

A sad, standard duty for officers after battles such as Bullecourt was to
write to the next of kin of those killed in action. In kindly fashion, the
writers used a set formula: the dead man was most popular with all in
his unit; he had always been a gallant soldier; he died instantly; his loss
was most keenly felt by all. Colonel Burford Sampson, writing to
relatives of men of the 15th, used a standard phrase: 'May the Father
of all help and comfort you.' Never did they say that the body could
not be found, as was the case for over 11,000 Australians killed in
France and Flanders. Simpler letters were written by the dead man's
comrades: we had been mates since Gallipoli; he was the best of pals;
we had some good times on leave together; he often spoke of you; I
will miss him a lot. These letters were to be treasured by the loved ones
of the dead; kept for long years in drawers in sideboards with the
medals which arrived after the war and the scroll which read:

> *He whom this scroll commemorates was numbered among those*
> *who, at the call of King and Country, left all that was dear to*
> *them, endured hardness, faced danger and finally passed out if*
> *the sight of men by the path of duty and self-sacrifice, giving up*
> *their own lives that others might have freedom.*
>
> *Let those who come after see to it that his name be not*
> *forgotten.*

In the *Sydney Morning Herald* of 11 April 1997, next to the Death and
In Memoriam notices, there appeared an entry under the heading 'On
Active Service':

NOBLET — *in memory of Private Charles Emil Noblet, 13th Battalion AIF, killed at Bullecourt, France, April 11 1917, and in memory of all those Australian soldiers of 4th Brigade, comprising 13th, 14th, 15th and 16th Battalions who were killed on that fateful and memorable day of the first attack on The Hindenburg Line.*
April 11, 1917   80 Years on.

Someone still remembered Bullecourt.

The sorely depleted battalions of the 4th Brigade were made up to strength with reinforcements rushed from the training depots on Salisbury Plain. At this time, mid-1917, there were enough new soldiers to do this, although plans for establishing a 6th Division of the AIF were abandoned. After the remaining battles of 1917, there were not enough reinforcements to restore units to full strength. Two conscription referendums had been lost, casualties continued to be suffered at a high rate and the pool of young men willing to enlist was drying up. At the end of 1917 there was even talk of disbanding the 4th Division, whose numbers were so depleted. In the great battles of 1918 — Villers-Bretonneux, Hamel, Mont St Quentin, to name some — the battalions of the AIF went into action at half strength.

'To get his mind off Bullecourt', as the 13th Battalion History notes,[4] in April 1917, Colonel Durrant placed Murray in charge of musketry training. It was said that: 'he trained the battalion to as perfect a state of proficiency with the rifle as any battalion was ever trained'.[5] Murray trained the soldiers for active service conditions. Platoons charged forward across rough country, took cover, fixed sights and opened up on to a target within seconds. It was a repeat of the super efficiency of the old 16th's machine-gun section at Blackboy Hill in 1914.

The Brigade enjoyed fine weather in May. Inter unit football matches were played and morale-boosting medal presentation ceremonies held. The 13th's history noted the discrepancy between the number of decorations which the Brigade had won in eight months on Gallipoli (42) and the number won in a year's fighting in France (359). For example, seven Military Medals had been awarded on Gallipoli; 241 in France. The history stated: 'One feels that the deeds of heroism on Gallipoli in the case of Company Officers and lower ranks were practically unconsidered. The war became more democratic as it proceeded.'[6]

Murray's friend, Douglas Marks, who had been badly wounded at Bullecourt, made a retrospective entry in his diary for 12 April: 'They tell me I wasn't expected to live through the 12th.' On 15 April, Colonel Durrant and Murray rode fifteen miles to visit Marks in hospital, only being allowed to see him for two minutes. By mid-May, the durable Marks was enjoying convalescent leave in London and was joined by Murray. On the 28th, they and three other officers from the 13th dined at Romano's with five chorus girls from the stage show *High Jinks*. What a picture — decorated Australian officers in their best uniforms, elegant surroundings, pretty girls, fine wine and food. It was such a contrast to the horrors they had just endured.

On 2 June, Harry Murray was decorated with his Victoria Cross by King George V in a large investiture in Hyde Park. The *Melbourne Herald* of 21 July 1917 reported that:

Not since the days of the Crimea had such an historic gathering been held as that which took place at Hyde Park on Saturday, June 2, when the King invested a number of British and Australian war heroes ...

Soon after 2 o'clock a guard of honour of Scots Guards marched into the arena. They wore service uniforms but the massed bands were in all the bravery of the gorgeous scarlet and gold which has so seldom been seen since the piping days of peace. Shortly before a quarter to three a resounding cheer broke from the direction of Hyde Park Corner heralding the coming of the King and Queen and Princess Mary. The spectators around the arena had a fleeting vision of rapidly moving khaki-clad Life Guards with flashes of steel and flashes of scarlet. Then the Royal Standard was broken from a mast in the centre of the arena, the National Anthem was played by the massed bands and the King in service uniform was seen standing at the front of the dais taking the salute of the guard of honour.

The first officer to mount the dais was Major Murray who wore the broad-rimmed slouch hat of the Australian Infantry and who was heartily applauded as, with loose swinging step, he passed back to his seat.

An unknown fellow officer staying at the Hotel Windsor with Murray wrote how he assisted him before the presentation: 'Murray was an untidy dresser, if you know what I mean, like a lot of very good soldiers. He was a sleeper cutter and anything would do with him. He would just throw his Sam Browne [officer's belt with shoulder strap] on. It wouldn't matter if the buckle was in the right place or around the back, or where it was. He wasn't a man who went in for ceremony at all. But we were putting him on public display, so I smartened him up a bit.'

That day, 351 decorations were awarded, including 11 Victoria Crosses, four of which were posthumous. It was the biggest public investiture held since the first presentation of VCs, again at Hyde Park, by Queen Victoria on 26 June 1857. Murray was the most prominent recipient of decorations at the investiture, for in addition to his Victoria Cross he received two DSOs to join his earlier awarded DCM. King George V spoke to Murray for some time and the King's mother, the Dowager Queen Alexandra, stood for that whole period listening to the conversation.

In his Reminiscences, Murray stated that the King did not pin the decorations to his chest but attached them to hooks that had been put in place by an official before the ceremony. The official instructed Murray, with some firmness, to return the hooks after the investiture.

'Evidently he had heard of Ned Kelly,' wrote Murray, who also remembered an incident after the presentation. Elsie Henley, the sister of Leslie Henley of the 13th who was killed at Pozières, was in London at the time of Murray's presentation and had asked him if she could be the first to shake his hand after he left the dais. Murray agreed. However:

> She did not realise what she asked for, dozens wanted to shake after the investiture, many of them pretty girls almost too wonderful to be true, but Leslie Henley was my friend and so through him was his sister, Elsie. I could see the bevy of beauties awaiting as I went down the exit from the dais and thought furiously how I could keep my promise to Elsie, though I might kiss them instead of shaking hands. Then came a flash of intelligence. Why not pose as a wounded hero and carry my right hand thrust into my coat? This I did and got extra sympathy as a poor wounded chap and kept my promise to Elsie. Her thanks, when she met and shook hands, was 'Harry you're a sport.'

With Marks and others, on 3 June Murray took a train trip, first to Nottingham, and then by the Great Northern to Scotland. The Australians in World War I received a warm reception from the hospitable Scots: Glasgow and Edinburgh were the most popular leave destinations for them after London. Perhaps it was on this, his first trip to Scotland, that he stayed at Glenlyon in Perthshire, the home of Lord and Lady Montgomery, who held 'open house' for soldiers. Murray became attached to the Montgomerys and, his family believes, had a romance with Clementine, a daughter of the house who became a lifelong friend and after whom he named his daughter, who was born in 1934. By coincidence, the property outside Richmond, Queensland, on which he finally settled in 1928, was named Glenlyon. He also visited the estate of the Duke of Athol, whose family name was Murray, and was very proud when, during a ball, the

Duke invited him to dance on the section of the dance floor reserved for bearers of the Murray name. A photo is said to exist which shows Murray with the Duke, and family members claim there is a resemblance, thus reviving the claim that the original Kennedy Murray was connected with the 3rd Duke.[7]

Back in France later in June, Murray rejoined the 13th, which was about to take a minor part in a major engagement at Messines, where three British Corps, including II Anzac and its 3rd Division AIF, were required to take strategic ground as a preliminary to the attacks in the Passchendaele region later in the year. The attack commenced on 7 June with the detonation of nineteen large mines that had been placed under the German front line after months of tunnelling by the British. The explosions were 'the largest man-made explosion in recorded history' and were heard in London as a muffled roar.[8] It is reputed that 10,000 Germans were killed in the explosions. The 3rd Division performed well in its first major action at Messines, where Monash showed his capacity for meticulous planning. Three of the mines exploded were in front of the 3rd Division's attacking position, and the Division made good ground despite heavy shelling with gas shells. The 4th Division, after its terrible mauling at Bullecourt, was kept in first reserve. Monash appreciated having the 4th in this role, describing it as his 'star turn'.[9] The Battalion history records, in a matter of fact way, the 13th's part in the battle: 'It was a quick and lively period indeed. In 25 hours we marched in, relieved a front line battalion, advanced 400 yards, dug in, handed over and were on our way out.'

Returned to the support area, the men of the 13th 'enjoyed a bath and a change';[10] these were much needed, as in the trenches the soldiers never changed their uniforms, shirts or underclothing, sometimes for weeks. The only hygiene observed was shaving when possible. Captain James Churchill Dunn, DSO, MC and Bar, DCM, medical officer of the 2nd Battalion of the Royal Welch Fusiliers, wrote in his diary on 25 April 1918: 'Even I am lousy. The men have had one bath in five weeks and no change of underclothing.'[11] Body waste was collected in tins and emptied into shell holes or over the sandbags into No-Man's Land. Apart from a bath and a change when first out of the line, soldiers were also passed through delousing sprays in an attempt to rid them of lice. In the rear area, at this time, the Battalion was employed in road making or cable burying, 400 men being engaged in the latter task. The summer sun was drying out the boggy trenches and the battalion enjoyed a 'Flanders Forest in July';[12] leafy canopies with wildflowers, buttercups and daisies growing in profusion. The area, however, had been occupied with trenches for years. In the trenches, lice and huge rats abounded, a foul smell pervaded and the earth oozed foul liquid. 'It was a medical miracle,' notes White, 'that whole divisions were not exterminated by such conditions.'[13]

George Stanley McDowell, MC, wrote to his father in Australia of this quiet time in reserve: 'Harry Murray and I have a walk every evening in the twilight and yarn about all kinds of things — he is a wonderful character, brave to a fault, keen and quick in thought and action, gentle as a woman, a born gentleman.'

At Bailleul on 27 June, the 67-year-old Duke of Connaught, third son of Queen Victoria and an old soldier, inspected the 3rd and 4th Divisions. How incongruous it was that the Duke of Connaught, a brother of the mother of Kaiser Wilhelm II of Germany, had himself married a German princess, and that his nephew, King George V of Great Britain and the Empire, was the Kaiser's first cousin. Murray, Jacka and O'Meara, the VCs of the 4th Brigade, were presented to the Duke, not by their divisional commander, General Holmes, but by General Monash, commander of the 3rd. This caused a serious rift between Monash and Holmes, who considered that he should have been given the honour. Monash's explanation was that General Godley, his corps commander, had motioned him forward to carry out the introduction.[14] A few days later, on 2 July, Holmes was killed by a stray shell when escorting W.A. Holman, Premier of New South Wales, around a rear area of the Messines battlefield.

Martin O'Meara of the 16th Battalion won his VC at Pozières

where for four days he repeatedly carried out wounded men under intense artillery and machine-gun fire. An Irishman from County Tipperary, O'Meara had the saddest of fates. After Pozières he was wounded three times and returned to Australia in September 1918. Shortly after discharge from the AIF on 30 November 1919 he was admitted to Claremont Mental Hospital, near Perth. He remained there for the rest of his life and his records state that his death, on 20 December 1935, was caused by his war service.

In early July 1917 the 13th spent a few weeks in the line, occupying trenches between Ploegstreert Wood and Warneton on the River Lys. Extensive patrolling was carried out, with Murray, as usual, prominent. Eric Evans's diary entry for 9 July 1917 states: 'Tonight there is to be a raid led by "Mad Harry" Murray on the "possie" which opened on one of our patrols a few days ago. The mission involves ten men from the fighting patrol and their objective, I understand, is a blockhouse about 800 yards ahead. It is a dangerous operation and I feel extremely relieved not to be included.' Evans's diary entry four days later reports further on Murray's activities: 'Word is going round that "Mad Harry" made his way through the enemy posts to examine the river [Lys] last night. Some are even saying that he swam across it to examine the other side. Nothing surprises me about the man. He is the most complete soldier I have ever encountered.'[15]

This remarkable man never spared himself, even after all the 'stunts' in which he had been involved and the numerous wounds he had suffered. He was promoted to the rank of major on 24 July 1917 in place of his friend, Major Marks, who temporarily assumed command of the 13th after Lieutenant Colonel Durrant was wounded. On several occasions, when Durrant or Marks was absent, Murray assumed command of the Battalion. Murray's friend, McDowell, in a letter to his father dated 5 August 1917, wrote the only derogatory comment about Murray's service in World War I that research for this book has found: 'Major Murray is in command for the time being — he will do well I am sure, although administration is not his strong point.'

In late August and early September, the 13th had a few weeks in reserve. It was the Battalion's first close encounter with Flemish peasants, whom they found to be even more dour than the phlegmatic northern French. At Lisbourg, the locals had not previously met Australians and were suspicious of them. The village schoolmaster had informed them about Australians, associating them with negroes, boomerangs, kangaroos, emus and alligators. 'No wonder the dear simple souls were terrified,' noted the Battalion history. The men of the 13th soon established friendly relations: 'Bonjour, Madame; it's all right; we've got Beaucoup Money and want beaucoup oeufs and pommes-de-terres and très vin blanc' (much money and want many eggs and potatoes and white wine).[16]

After a few weeks respite from the front line, the 13th, with the rest of the 4th Division, was involved in the battle of Passchendaele, also known as Third Ypres. The aim of the battles of Passchendaele, which lasted from 31 July to mid-November 1917, was to advance to the German-held Belgian ports, neutralise the U-boat bases there and take the German-held high ground which gave them such a strategic advantage. Another motivation for the offensive was to take pressure off the French, the morale of whose soldiers was at a low point after the failure of General Nivelle's offensive on the Aisne in April 1917, which had incurred huge losses. Some regiments had mutinied. The mutinies were put down with severity. A number of mutineers were shot, 'pour encourager les autres [to encourage the others]', as the famous phrase has it.

Passchendaele, which ranks with the Somme as one of the two most tragic names for the British in World War I, had its special horror — mud. The area was low-lying and boggy. Massive barrages destroyed the man-made drainage systems of the area and rain fell steadily during the campaign. Shell holes filled with water and mud. The only means of passage in the frontal areas was by duckboards, often narrow. To fall off them was to risk drowning in the mud, which was the fate of many soldiers. Bringing up rations and ammunition could only be done by exhausting hand carriage along the duckboards. Getting food to the forward trenches took hours. Sergeant McKay, of a British field ambulance, noted in his diary: 'Bringing the wounded down from the front line today. Conditions terrible, the ground ... is simply a quagmire and shell holes filled with water. There is neither the appearance of a road or path and it requires six men to every stretcher, two of those being constantly employed helping the others out of holes; the mud in some places is up to our waists. A couple of journeys and the strongest men are ready to collapse.'[17]

The first attack in which the Australians were involved, usually known as the Battle of the Menin Road, was launched on a fifteen-mile front on 20 September 1917 by the 2nd and 5th British Armies and the French 1st; twenty Divisions in all, of which only two were French. The 1st and 2nd Australian Divisions, fighting side by side, the first occasion for Australian Divisions, joined the successful attack. Here for the first time a German system of fortifications, known as blockhouses, was encountered. These were made of concrete, resisted heavy shelling and were manned by German machine-gunners who were described in the 14th Battalion history as 'picked men, the flower of their army, who frequently fought to the death'.[18] After Menin Road, the 1st and 2nd Divisions were relieved by the 4th and 5th, who continued the series of attacks at Polygon Wood, Broodseinde, Poelcappelle and finally Passchendaele.

Harry Murray's 13th took part in all these actions. On 15 October 1917, the battalion suffered its first heavy barrage with gas shells. It was to endure a gas attack for a week, and its history notes that Passchendaele 'was almost as disastrous as Bullecourt'.[19] There were 309 cases of gas poisoning in a week; throats, eyes and skin were raw, lungs were affected, and 'sneezing and acute vomiting could be heard on all sides'. The Battalion history, published in 1924, declared with foreboding: 'It would have been better had several of these gas casualties paid the full price up there on the foggy, soaked and poisonous Passchendaele Swamps.'[20] Many of the victims of gas were to endure years of suffering, and Australians who can recall the 1920s and 1930s still shudder at the whispered tales of gas cases in hospitals, such as Randwick Military Hospital, Sydney, reputedly kept permanently in chemical baths because of the horrendous effect of mustard gas on skin. Let us hope that those tales were untrue.

In the 14th Battalion history, Newton Wanliss summed up the horror of the Passchendaele campaign:

> *It may be fairly claimed that the work of the Australians in the third battle of Ypres and the staggering blows they struck their opponents had been outstanding without in any way disparaging the fine work of the British and French troops who participated in the prolonged battle. This campaign, comparatively short as it was, had been the bloodiest of the many bloody campaigns in which the Australians participated during the Great War, while the hardships endured — everlasting mud, bitter cold, almost continual rain and waterlogged trenches — had tried the nerve and strength of all ranks.*[21]

The Australian casualties from 20 September to the end of October averaged nearly 1000 per day. Nor was the campaign 'comparatively short', as stated above. Newton Wanliss lost his son, Captain Harold Boyd Wanliss, DSO, at Passchendaele.

For his services at Passchendaele, Murray was mentioned in Haig's despatch of 7 November 1917 for 'distinguished and gallant services and devotion to duty'.

Colonel Durrant left the 13th in December 1917 on his promotion to AA & QMG of the 2nd Division and Douglas Marks, aged 22 years and 9 months, assumed command. Durrant had been an original officer of the Battalion and had first assumed command, temporarily, in May 1915 on Gallipoli after Colonel Granville Burnage, the original CO and 'the Gamest Old Man', as his soldiers admiringly called him, was wounded and returned to Australia. Durrant, who replaced Colonel Tilney as commanding officer in 1916, was a cool and inspiring leader who appealed to his soldiers' pride in their unit. When a soldier appeared before him charged with a serious offence he would say: 'You — a 13th man? A 13th? Surely you forgot you belonged to the 13th when you did that?' Or 'An A Company man? Captain Murray's Company? Do you want to be transferred?'[22] In World War II, Durrant reached the rank of major general.

Following Passchendaele, the 13th and the rest of the 4th Brigade at last enjoyed a lengthy period, three months, out of the line. After a long march and train journey the Battalion arrived at Fontaine-Les-Boulans, between Abbeville and Dieppe. As second in command, Murray searched widely in the district for baths, stables and straw. Thomas White, historian of the 13th, in his first book, *Diggers Abroad*, describes Murray's encounter with the mayor of a village:

> *The Maire, a very important, stout, old gent refused to believe Murray was a major and acting CO of the battalion, but took him for a sergeant. When enlightened, he was astonished and full of unwanted apologies, saying that an English sergeant-major once billeted there had far more shiny buttons, stripes and badges than Murray, who was dressed like a Digger except for the dark crown on each shoulder, a Sam Browne, and his VC, DSO (bar) and DCM ribbons. The Maire's idea of rank was the amount of shine, colour and gold braid.*[23]

Murray had leave in Paris from 12 January to 2 February 1918. At that time, he was under consideration for secondment to a special force of picked officers and men from all the British forces whose role was to organise and lead Russian forces in Trans-Caucasia. The force was to go to Tiflis, the capital of Georgia. A British officer, Brigadier General J.J. Byron, was given the task of organising the force, and on 3 January

1918 approached General Birdwood requesting outstanding officers 'for a very important and difficult mission'.[24] Birdwood wrote to each of his five divisional commanders proposing that four names from each division be put forward and suggesting men of 'exactly' the class of Harry Murray. From the 4th Division, Murray, Jacka and the brothers, Captains A.M. and D.S. Maxwell, were suggested. Murray and Jacka were interviewed by Byron on 8 January and, it is believed, accepted the posting. Birdwood, however, changed his mind on the secondment of these officers, although twenty officers and as many NCOs from the AIF were eventually posted to 'Dunsterforce', named for its commander, Lieutenant General Lionel Dunsterville. Rudyard Kipling was a schoolmate of Dunsterville, who is said to have been the model for Stalky in his *Stalky and Co.*

In March 1918, Murray's long service with the 13th Battalion ended as he was promoted to lieutenant colonel to command the newly raised 4th Machine-Gun Battalion. In its last mention of Murray, the Battalion history eulogised him:

> *On the 15th March Major Harry Murray, VC, DSO (and Bar), DCM, had been appointed to command, as Lt.-Col., the 4th Machine-Gun Battalion, being sincerely congratulated by the rank and file without exception on this well-merited distinction. He had still higher honors to gain, but we were proud to know that it was in the 13th that he had risen from the ranks through sheer merit to the command of a battalion, with a record for gallantry unexcelled by that of any other member, not only of the AIF, but of the Allied Armies. In our pride at possessing such a man as Murray, we had not thought of the fact that he was not a New South Welshman. He was an Australian, and that sufficed.*[25]

Eric Evans, on leave in London in April when he heard the news of Murray's promotion, wrote in his diary: '"Mad Harry" Murray has been made commanding officer of the 4th Machine Gun Battalion. He will be a sad loss to the 13th as he is undoubtedly our greatest-ever soldier, with a record for gallantry that no one in the AIF nor in the rest of the Allied armies can rival.'[26]

MAD HARRY

Murray's nickname throughout the AIF was 'Mad Harry'. He was well aware of the name and was not irritated or offended by it.[27] All the accounts of his actions, however, show his care in planning and his cool, tactical ability under enormous stress. In the trenches he insisted that his men wear their steel helmets at all times and he carried out inspections of rifles and equipment daily. The history of the 13th says:

Murray's courage was not a reckless exposure to danger like that of Jacka or Sexton, who didn't know fear. His courage was a deliberately formed quality derived from a fervent loyalty, an earnest sense of duty, a thorough confidence in himself and his men, and a firm belief in the justice of his cause.

Some VC winners aimed at death; Murray always at victory. The knowledge that death was the probability never deterred nor held him from his main aim.[28]

(Gerald Sexton, or Maurice Buckley, was the only other VC winner of the 13th Battalion. He enlisted in 1914 under his correct name, Buckley, and was posted to the 13th Light Horse Regiment. He was returned to Australia from Egypt in 1915 and in September was admitted to Langwarrin Hospital in Victoria, where cases of venereal disease were treated. He deserted from the hospital early in 1916 and re-enlisted in the AIF under the alias Gerald Sexton, Sexton being his mother's maiden name. Posted to the 13th Battalion, he served with great distinction on the Western Front. Already a DCM winner, he was awarded a Victoria Cross for an action on 18 September 1918 at

Le Verguier. An expert Lewis gunner, he rushed at least six machine-gun posts, captured a field gun and 100 prisoners. On the award of the VC he disclosed his correct name. Sadly, he did not survive the war for long, dying after a riding accident in January 1921.)

8

LIEUTENANT COLONEL
H.W. MURRAY — 1918

The War Diary of the Australian 4th Brigade for the 15th of March 1918 states as follows: 'Dull morning clearing as day proceeds, strong Easterly winds, Bailleul shelled in morning about 9 o'clock with H.V. [high velocity] shells. Few civilian casualties. Major H.W. Murray, VC, DSO, DCM, 13th Btn. appointed to command 4th Div. Machine Gun Battalion.' Harry Murray's official record states that he was transferred to command the 4th Machine-Gun Battalion with the temporary rank of lieutenant colonel. It had taken a little over three years to rise from private to lieutenant colonel; in the same period Murray had been awarded four gallantry medals, including the highest award of all, the Victoria Cross.

In April the War Diary of the 4th Division recorded: 'The Battalion organisation of the machine-gun units of this Division will come into force on the 14th inst. From and including that date the 4th, 12th, 13th and 24th machine-gun Companies will be administered by the CO. 4th Australian machine-gun Battalion. Major/temp. Lt. Col. H.W. Murray VC, DSO, DCM, has been appointed to command the Battalion.' The MG Battalion was attached directly to Divisional Command, and the CO of the battalion controlled all of the Vickers machine-guns of the division. This meant that Murray controlled no fewer than 64 guns. In action, machine-guns were usually allocated in companies or sections to infantry units, as they were required, whether in attack or defence.

Between 15 March and 14 April, Murray's movements are not noted in any of the relevant war diaries. The diary of the 4th Machine-Gun Battalion only commences in May. On 21 March, the great German 'Michael' offensive was launched. This spectacularly successful attack fell on the fronts of the British 3rd and 5th Armies; surprise was achieved by means of only a short, but heavy, bombardment and the providential closing in of a heavy mist. The 5th Army front was only thinly held and, arguably, had not fully recovered from the exhausting attacks it had been required to make at Passchendaele in late 1917. As a result of the quick early breakthrough by the Germans, the units of the 5th Army, in order to maintain some kind of defensive line, began a retreat that was in danger of becoming a rout. The details of the 30-mile retreat and the heroic defence of some of the British units, desperately holding on until reserves could be organised, is not in the province of this book to record. This has been written about in countless books and military memoirs of relevant generals and leaders of the Allied armies. C.E.W. Bean finds some excuses for Haig and General Gough, who commanded the 5th Army, but other writers are most critical of them.

The German success, significantly, led to the appointment of an Allied Commander-in-Chief to take charge of the whole Western Front; General Ferdinand Foch was chosen for this vitally important role. It also led to the sacking of Gough, rightly or wrongly, by Haig. Another result of the success of the German offensive, of more immediate relevance to this book, was that it brought about the hurried movement of the 4th, 3rd and 5th Divisions of the AIF to confront the German advance.

The 4th Division was positioned at Hébuterne, which was regarded as a critical sector. In particular, the 4th Brigade distinguished itself in the staunch defence in this sector. The battalions of the 4th Brigade, as they marched up towards their allotted defence positions, encountered sights not seen by them before. The local French inhabitants were hastily packing their belongings and quitting the area. Retreating British troops were straggling back past the Australians. Bean quotes the following comments from the commanding officer of the 13th Battalion, Lieutenant Colonel Marks: 'Evidences of rout were not wanting, and along the road to Humbercamp we passed an endless stream of retreating transport and refugees. At times we passed staff officers retreating in great haste, and some of these warned us that the enemy were in Souastre with armoured cars.'[1]

With wild rumours being repeated about the enemy being close behind and including tanks in their force, temporary Lieutenant Colonel Harry Murray of the 4th Machine-Gun Battalion took it upon himself to investigate. He borrowed a platoon from his old Battalion, the 13th, and hurried up the road to Souastre down which the Germans were allegedly advancing in numbers with tanks. Eventually, Murray sighted a red car some distance ahead that was followed by some type of machinery. He prepared an ambush on both sides of the road but hastily stopped his men firing as the 'tanks' turned out to be farm machinery being moved by members of the French Agricultural Corps who were proudly saving their equipment.[2]

Harry Murray's situation between 21 March and 14 April is obscure, apart from this episode. The only direct reference to him in this crisis period by Bean, or that research has revealed, concerns the part played by machine-guns in the desperate defence by the 47th Battalion of the 12th Brigade in the second battle of Dernancourt. It can only be assumed that he was busy with the four machine-gun companies of his new command, even though, officially, the new unit was only effective from 14 April. It must also be assumed that these four companies, the 4th, 12th, 13th and 24th, were very active in the defensive actions fought by the 4th Division.

At Dernancourt, the 12th and 13th Brigades of the 4th Division were deployed to oppose the expected German attack on that front. It was a difficult area to defend. The colonels of the 47th and 48th Battalions, A.P. Imlay and R.L. Leane, had set forward defence lines on a railway which ran through the valley in front of Dernancourt village which the enemy held. Unfortunately, the support lines were, of necessity, nearly three-quarters of a mile behind them on the top of a hill. To counteract this difficulty, a number of machine-guns had been placed halfway up the slope behind the forward defence. Obviously, these machine-guns were of critical importance in the event of German pressure on the forward defence being too strong. Four of the guns were in a quarry in the middle of the slope while four more were in a trench on the left of the quarry. Because of the exposed nature of the positions, the gun crews were instructed not to fire in daylight except in an emergency. During the day the guns were dismantled to avoid detection. When the German attack was finally launched behind a heavy barrage and machine-gun fire, the Australian machine-gunners did not have time to assemble their weapons and were captured without firing a shot.

Because machine-gun fire had been heard well after the enemy had overrun the positions, Harry Murray made considerable claims to war correspondents that his gunners had fought to the death. The truth was discovered later when two of the captured machine-gunners escaped. Apparently, it was felt by some that the failure of the machine-guns was crucial in the German success against the 47th Battalion. Research has not revealed any other information on this incident, which is recorded in Bean.[3]

There is a mention of an activity of Harry Murray's during those spring days of 1918 in G.D. Mitchell's *Backs to the Wall*, which shows in a light-hearted way his coolness and skill with weapons:

> *Close to our position was a large farm with its shell-gapped buildings. Hundreds of pigeons lived there. Each time a shell burst near, the pigeons rose in alarm ...*

Several times I watched Colonel Harry Murray, VC, enjoying himself. He would wait in the courtyard with a shotgun he had salvaged from somewhere. He would not shoot at the pigeons as they strutted and preened themselves on the roof-ridges, but wait until a close bursting five-point-nine would send them into the air. Then, 'crack-crack' would go his gun. Buckshee for the mess.[4]

The German offensive in the Somme area ended with the AIF holding sixteen miles of the front line behind which lay the important city of Amiens. The Germans were anxious to occupy this key transport centre. After much shuffling of his 4th Army units, General Rawlinson, who commanded the area occupied by the Australians, was able to record in his diary: 'I feel happier about the general situation … and I now have three brigades of Australians in reserve, so I think we shall be able to keep the Boche out of Amiens.'

One of the key places in the British defence line on the Somme was Villers-Bretonneux, a village just behind the front line. General Rawlinson regarded the holding of this village as crucial to the defence of Amiens, as did the local senior commanders. So when the Germans successfully attacked Villers-Bretonneux and occupied it on 24 April, the reaction from the British was one of extreme urgency to mount a strong counterattack. The rumble of the German success was felt even at Foch's HQ, and he ordered Rawlinson, through Haig, to retake the village. One interesting point about the German attack was that it was made with the aid of tanks; this was one of the main reasons for its success. The British had tanks in the area and three of these engaged the enemy tanks in what must have been one of the earliest tank to tank battles. The British won the contest.

Rawlinson ordered that the counterattack had to take place that day (24 April), as was expected by Haig. The details of the recapture of Villers-Bretonneux need not be given here. Suffice it to say that the 15th Brigade of the 5th Australian Division and the 13th Brigade of the 4th Division made brilliant but costly attacks either side of the village, which led to its recapture. The attacks were made on 25 April, the third anniversary of Anzac Day. The brigades attacked at night over unknown ground without the aid of artillery and succeeded, despite grievous casualties, in freeing the town, as the enemy was forced to withdraw.

The Australian casualties for this, the Second Battle of Villers-Bretonneux, were 2473; the Germans lost 10,400; the French 3500 and, apart from the Australians, the British lost 9529. The 13th Machine-Gun Company of Harry Murray's 4th Machine-Gun Battalion, which was attached to the 13th Brigade for its attack, lost two officers and 28 men in the battle.

By 26 April the crisis at Villers-Bretonneux was over, as Douglas Marks' diary entry for that date reads: 'With Harry Murray and Colonel Durrant to Amiens and lunch with Charlie Boccard in the basement of Hotel de Ville.' Amiens retained its restaurants and estaminets for most of the war and was a favourite leave resort for the British forces in northern France. To this day, Australians are fêted by the citizens of Villers-Bretonneux for the defence of their village so long ago, and the main memorial and cemetery for Australian dead in France are also placed there.

On 21 April, a few days before the second Battle of Villers-Bretonneux, Rittmeister Manfred von Richtofen, the legendary Red Baron, credited with 80 kills on the Western Front, was shot down over the Australian lines near Corbie. Argument has persisted ever since as to who was responsible for shooting him down. As recently as 1998, an article appeared in *Sabretache*, the journal of the Military History Society of Australia, entitled 'The Death of Manfred von Richtofen: Who Fired the Fatal Shot?'[5] Several theories are held concerning his death — namely that he was shot down by a Canadian pilot, Captain A.R. Brown, or by Australian machine-gun fire from Sergeant C.B. Popkin, 24th Australian Machine-Gun Company, or by Gunner R. Buie, 53rd Battery, Australian Field Artillery. Harry

Murray informed his son that one of his sergeants shot down the Red Baron — an obvious reference to Popkin, whose Company was in the 4th Division. He did not believe that the Canadian pilot could have been responsible as he was too far away from von Richtofen's plane when it came down.[6]

The War Diary of the 4th Machine-Gun Battalion for 1 May records that two of its companies were in the line at Villers-Bretonneux and that they covered the exits of the village. The diary also records that Harry Murray personally sited the guns for the interior defence of the village; the battalion maintained three companies in the line with one in reserve until 22 May, when it was relieved. After bathing in the Somme, the unit went into billets around Allonville.

The diary finishes the month with an interesting entry. Murray called a conference of his Company commanders at 10 am on the 28th. Captain W.M. Cory forgot to attend. There is no further comment in the diary, but speculation over what Murray's attitude might have been creates quite an image, especially in view of his often stated belief in the value of discipline in the AIF. Cory went on in the unit and gave excellent service until the end of the war.

During May, Harry Murray wrote a report on the effectiveness of armour-piercing bullets fired by his machine-guns against a derelict British tank which was being used by the Germans as an observation and machine-gun post. The ammunition penetrated the tank's armour and forced its evacuation. This report is interesting in view of a later directive issued from higher command that will be discussed later. The battalion diary also states that, in May, the unit claimed to have shot down three enemy aircraft using ammunition that included armour-piercing bullets. The unit diary, from this time on, indicates an increase in the amount of ammunition expended on anti-aircraft shooting, sure evidence that the aeroplane was becoming increasingly important in warfare. Evidence of Murray's diligence as CO of the unit is recorded in the diary by the number of times mention is made of him inspecting his companies in the line and doing such things as checking gun sitings and camouflaging. In June, five officers and ten NCOs of the United States Army were attached to the unit for training.

On 25 June, Murray was called to a conference at 4th Divisional Headquarters, where the proposed attack at Hamel was discussed for the first time by anyone below senior command. The proposed attack had been in the pipeline for some time; Commander in Chief Foch had been trying to hold back reserves throughout the crisis days of the German offensives so that he could go on the offensive as soon as possible. Hamel was one of the sites suitable for a smallish attack and suited Foch's aggressive intentions. General Rawlinson, the 4th Army Commander, agreed with the idea, as did Haig.

In May 1918, important changes had taken place in the command structure of the AIF in France. General Birdwood, who had commanded the Australian force from Gallipoli on, was high on the seniority list of the British Army, and Haig wished to appoint him to command a revamped 5th Army. After much consultation — in which, of course, the Australian government was involved — it was decided that Birdwood would go to the 5th Army but would retain administrative control of the Australian forces; his replacement as commander of the AIF in France was finally settled on — John Monash, who was promoted to lieutenant general. Major General Brudenell-White, Birdwood's Chief of Staff, went to the 5th Army with him and Colonel Thomas Blamey became Monash's chief of staff, with promotion to brigadier general. Of course, these moves caused considerable changes to be made in divisional commands. By 31 May, the date that Monash assumed command, the five Australian divisions were to be commanded by General Glasgow, 1st Division; Rosenthal, the 2nd; Gellibrand, the 3rd; Sinclair-Maclagan, the 4th; and Hobbs, the 5th. All these changes meant that when the planning for the Hamel attack began, it was to be an all-Australian affair. Obviously, for Monash it was a demanding task for his baptism as GOC Australian Corps. The history of the Battle of Hamel leaves little doubt that Monash was the right choice for the job.

Monash had shown at Messines his skill and talent for meticulous planning, and his brilliance in the exposition of his plans. The Battle of Hamel was to show his masterful ability to blend the attacking potential of the various branches of the forces under his command into an organisation that achieved its objectives in the attack with an efficiency unfortunately rarely seen in France.

When Harry Murray attended the conference on 25 June he was destined to play his part in this careful planning. He was required to submit a plan for the machine-guns, and on the next day he submitted one which was approved. Apparently his plan had been to include two machine-gun battalions, but on the 29th Murray was told that the extra battalion was not available; however, three sections from the 5th Machine-Gun Battalion and two from the 3rd were to be attached for the operation. Representatives from these battalions had to be briefed and the necessary adjustments made. At 1.15 pm on the 30th, armed with the machine-gun task map, Murray attended the Corps HQ conference on the offensive. On 3 July, the eve of the attack, he visited all of the machine-gun positions of the sections engaged in the attack and synchronised watches and checked sitings. The attack, which began on time at 3.10 am, was a brilliant success, with very few errors made. The objectives were reached at all points. The 4th Machine-Gun Battalion fired 373,000 rounds of small arms ammunition over two days and suffered casualties of two officers and 31 men.

The Battle of Hamel, as it is usually known, was remarkable for a number of reasons. After much consultation between Monash and Brigadier General A. Courage, the commander of the tanks engaged in the operation, and giving due weight to the objections of the brigadiers and battalion commanders, who all too well remembered the Bullecourt disaster of 1917 and were adamant about the need for a barrage despite Courage's contrary opinion, Monash had ordered the barrage. Monash was prepared to confer with men who were experienced and expert in their particular fields, and at Hamel, infantry, tanks, aircraft, artillery, machine-guns and the supply teams were fully informed and trained for their tasks; nothing was left to chance in terms of what could be foreseen. Monash also decreed that there would be no last minute changes after 1 July.[7]

After negotiations between Rawlinson, Monash and Major General Read, the commander of II American Army Corps, Read gave his approval and gained the approval of his superior officer for four companies of American troops to be added to the Australian units in the battle. Monash, however, asked for ten companies and this was approved. In the event, General Pershing, the American commander in chief, raised objections with Haig and six of the companies were withdrawn; the four others took part in the battle because of the claim that it was too late to withdraw them.

Monash was determined to achieve surprise with his attack and ordered that no observable unusual activity was to take place in daylight hours. For example, Harry Murray recorded that in order to avoid concentrated movement in the last few days, the sites for eight machine gun batteries of four guns each, which were to fire in enfilade in the attack, had been chosen by 26 June; the camouflage netting and 500,000 rounds of ammunition had been brought up by the night of the 28th. By the 30th, the posts had been dug, covered with netting, and 8000 rounds, a tin of water, and a base for the tripod were in position for each gun. It had been necessary to employ 60 transport teams, but excessive movement near to zero day had been avoided. This achievement is an excellent example, not only of the efficiency of Murray and his men, but of the excellent preparation of the whole of Monash's staff and command.

The victory at Hamel came at a time, after the successes of the German offensives of March and April, when leaders of both the political and military kind were thirsting for good news. It also came at a time when leaders had gathered in France for a meeting of the Supreme War Council at Versailles, and congratulations poured in to Monash's HQ at Bertangles from there. Clemenceau, the French

Premier, actually visited the Australian area and delivered what is now recognised as a famous speech to a selected group of Australian soldiers. Inter alia, he said:

When the Australians came to France we expected a great deal of you. First, because we had heard of what you had done in war at Gallipoli; secondly because we had heard a great deal of what you had accomplished in peace in your own country. The French people expected that when you came to France to fight in this great struggle, which, after all, is the same for the French, the English, the Australians and all those who have fought this great war out in the cause of freedom, which is the same for all, they expected a good deal of you and I should not like to say that they have been surprised that you have fulfilled that expectation.

Hamel — after all, that is not such a very great battle; but I am ready to hold that in a comparatively small battle the man, the fighting man, who goes in to give all he has — his home, his hopes, his life itself — in a small battle his qualities show in all the brighter light, the action of each individual man having more influence in the final result. In a very big action, it is not possible to notice so well the qualities of particular men who came from far away. Well in this battle the Germans saw that they had before them men who came from far away to attest that wherever free people lived, in England, in France, in Australia, New Zealand, Canada and all free countries, these were not ready to give way to the Boche who has acted with such barbarity — who wounded and killed not only men in battle, but women and old men and little children — who ruined and destroyed our country, our houses, our fruit trees, even our gardens.

I have come here just for the very purpose of seeing the Australians. I am going back tomorrow to see my countrymen and tell them, 'I have seen the Australians. I have looked in their eyes.' I know that these men have fought great battles

*beside us in the cause of freedom [and] will fight alongside us
again until the cause of freedom for which we are battling is safe
for us and for our children.*

Full details of the battle have been given in Volume 6 of Bean's *Official
History of Australia in the War of 1914–1918* and by the prolific
Australian military historian, John Laffin, in *The Battle of Hamel*. It is
not proposed here to do more than give the casualties and consider the
battle's main effects. The casualties for the battle were about 1400: the
4th Brigade, 504; 11th, 312; 6th, 131; and the 7th, 115. The
American casualties were 176. It is of interest that an American,
Corporal Thomas A. Pope of the 33rd Division AEF (American
Expeditionary Force), won the United States' highest award, the
Congressional Medal of Honor, at Hamel when attached to the 44th
Battalion AIF. He was also awarded the British DCM, a remarkable
pair of decorations to be awarded to one soldier.

According to Bean: 'Haig noted that the battle greatly
strengthened the British position on the Villers-Bretonneux ridge. It
also weakened the German position. The German prisoners exceeded
1,600, with two anti-tank machine-guns, 177 machine-guns, 32
trench mortars, and a new anti-tank weapon of the German infantry.'[8]

Perhaps the most important effects of Hamel on the Australians
were their morale boost in gaining a complete victory with modest
casualties, the establishment of their confidence in fighting with tanks,
and their success, fighting under their own Corps Commander, in
inflicting a defeat on the enemy with tactics which could serve as a
pattern for the future battles. Hamel bore little resemblance to the
horrors of the slugging matches of trench warfare of 1916 and 1917,
when so little was achieved at so horrendous a cost.

It should be noted, also, that Hamel coincided with a turning
point in the war. It is drawing too long a bow to suggest that Hamel
caused that turn, but it certainly signalled that the time had arrived for
the beginning of the Allied offensives which brought to an end the

bloodiest war in recorded history. The AIF was a part of these offensives until the Hindenburg Line was finally breached in September. Hamel is now commemorated by the Australian Corps Memorial Park, a handsome and elaborate structure that was officially dedicated on 4 July 1998 by the Australian Minister for Veterans Affairs, Bruce Scott.

The fighting between July and September assumed a different character as the new weapons came into use and older ones were improved. Artillery barrages became more effective as ranging devices helped to minimise the telltale registering shoots; the fusing of shells effectively reduced the importance of barbed wire as an impediment to infantry attacks; improved quality of aircraft meant more effective strafing and bombing and, above all, better intelligence of enemy movements. Probably the tanks, more than any other weapon, changed the nature of war. The Mark V tanks were a vast improvement on the earlier machines of 1917, although mechanical reliability remained a problem, and the tank crews were better trained and military planners understood their use more clearly. Tanks also played an important part in the improvement of transport to and from the battlefield; even at Hamel tanks had been used to transport wounded back as the machines returned after finishing their tasks. Later, Harry Murray's machine-guns and crews were taken into battle by these steel monsters and ammunition and supplies were also delivered by them. One of Monash's innovations at Hamel had been the dropping of ammunition and supplies from aircraft, which met with varying degrees of success. The foregoing innovations all contributed to the mobility of the armies and lessened the number of men needed in laborious tasks during which they were liable to be shelled.

In *The Australian Victories in France in 1918*, Monash acknowledges the importance of the tanks:

These extraordinary products of the war underwent a
remarkable evolution during the two years which followed their

first introduction on the battlefield in the Somme campaign of 1916. The standard of efficiency which had been reached by the early summer of 1918, in the most developed types of these curious monsters, as far outclassed that of the earlier types in both mechanical and fighting properties as the modern service rifle compared with the old Brown Bess of the Peninsular War. The tank crews had improved in like proportion, both in skill, enterprise and adaptability.

Nothing can be more unstinted than the acknowledgement which the Australian Corps makes of its obligation to the Tank Corps for its powerful assistance throughout the whole of the great offensive. Commencing with the battle of Hamel, a large contingent of tanks participated in every important 'set piece' engagement which the corps undertook. The tanks were organised into brigades, each of three battalions, each of three companies, each of twelve tanks. During the opening phases, early in August, the tank contingent comprised a whole brigade of Mark-V tanks, a battalion of Mark-V (Star) tanks, and a battalion of fast armoured cars; in the later phases, during the assault on the Hindenburg Line, a second brigade of Mark-V tanks and a battalion of whippets also co-operated.[9]

On 3 August, Harry Murray attended a conference at 4th Division Headquarters on the coming offensive, set for 4.20 am on the 8th, which was planned to drive the enemy clear of Amiens. The origin of the offensive lay in Foch's aggressive intention to turn the Allied armies to offensive actions as soon as possible. An attack in this area had been discussed on and off since April, firstly by Rawlinson, Birdwood and Brudenell-White, and later by Rawlinson and Monash. Haig agreed with the idea sufficiently to promise Rawlinson the four divisions of Canadians which had had the benefit of a long rest after their exhausting efforts at Passchendaele in 1917. The attack was designed for a deep penetration of some miles, and the French to the south and the British to the north were to form part of the offensive. Bean should be quoted here, as he expresses the importance of the roles of the Australians and the Canadians as shock troops spearheading the attack:

> *Rawlinson's scheme was for an attack by three British corps. Foch's intervention added four French corps on the right — and later stages four others, so that an operation, which Rawlinson planned as exclusively British, became, so far as the forces engaged were concerned, preponderatingly French. But the whole project admittedly hung on the success of the first surprise blow to be struck on August 8th between the Somme and the Luce by eight divisions of British overseas troops. These would be assisted by the British Cavalry Corps, and British tanks, and air force, and their flanks would be protected by two divisions of the III British Corps north of the Somme and the XXXI French Corps with three divisions south of the Luce; and the main blow would be accompanied and followed by other important operations. But the whole issue depended upon the shock to be dealt by this mass of overseas infantry — an instrument never before employed in this manner — to the portion of the German Second Army between the Somme and the Luce.*[10]

The preparation for this attack again showed Monash at his best, giving detailed directions to the various arms of the services involved. The organisation in the 4th Machine-Gun Battalion was complicated by the fact that some of the companies were to send officers, men and guns and ammunition forward in Mark V tanks. This involved very early starts to load the tanks at their assembly points in the dark. Once again, surprise was paramount in the success of the offensive.

At 9.00 am on the 8th, Harry Murray, with his second in command, were seen riding bicycles forward to establish a forward HQ. The 4th Company of Murray's Battalion was to support the 13th and 16th Battalions in the attack in the Mourcourt sector; eight tanks were to carry men, machine-guns and ammunition into action. Only four turned up on time, but the others eventually arrived. In the advance, most of the tanks were hit, but they had done good work and silenced several enemy machine-gun posts. The operations of this Company continued until the 11th, in which time it had casualties of three officers and 24 other ranks. The 12th Company supported the 48th Battalion and were also transported in tanks; they fired 60,000 rounds of ammunition in the action. The 13th and 24th Companies supported the 45th and 46th Battalions without the aid of tanks and reported successful results.

Murray wrote a lengthy report on his Battalion's actions dated 18 August in which he strongly recommended that there should be one despatch rider with each Company to ensure good communication. The tank radios, he said, were unreliable; he was silent on the tank transport of his units and wrote that the equipment and limbers were still the best way to bring the equipment into action. The 4th Machine-Gun Battalion was relieved on the 24th and 25th for a rest.[11]

On 30 August, the unit's diary records that the 4th Machine-Gun Battalion held a parade for the first time in its history! The unit was inspected by Major General Sinclair-Maclagan, GOC of the 4th Division. What is not clear is whether the lack of parades was due to lack of time or lack of will. The diary is silent in this regard. The total casualties for the battalion in August were 177, including sixteen killed.

The offensive of 8 August had been a complete success; the 4th and 5th Division troops reached the final objective having advanced three miles after passing through the 2nd and 3rd Divisions, who had made the initial attack. Monash's plans and attention to detail had triumphed again. Before the battle he sent a message, to be read to the whole Australian Corps, which is well worth quoting in full:

For the first time in the history of this Corps all five Australian Divisions will to-morrow engage in the largest and most important battle operation ever undertaken by the Corps. They will be supported by an exceptionally powerful artillery, and by tanks and aeroplanes on a scale never previously attempted. The full resources of our sister Dominion, the Canadian Corps, will also operate on our right, while two British Divisions will guard our left.

The many successful offensives which the Brigades and Battalions of this Corps have so brilliantly executed during the past four months have been but the prelude to, and preparation for, this greatest and culminating effort.

Because of the completeness of our plans and dispositions, of the magnitude of the operations, of the number of troops employed, and of the depth to which we intend to overrun the enemy's positions, this battle will be one of the most memorable of the whole war; and there can be no doubt that, by capturing our objectives, we shall inflict blows upon the enemy which will make him stagger, and will bring the end appreciably nearer. I entertain no sort of doubt that every Australian will worthily rise to so great an occasion, and that every man, imbued with the spirit of victory, will, in spite of every difficulty that may confront him, be animated by no other resolve than a grim determination to see through, to a clean finish, whatever his task may be.

The work to be done tomorrow will perhaps make heavy demands upon the endurance and staying powers of many of you; but I am confident that, in spite of excitement, fatigue, and physical strain, every man will carry on to the utmost of his

*powers until his goal is won, for the sake of AUSTRALIA, the
Empire, and our cause.*

*I earnestly wish every soldier of the Corps the best of good
fortune and a glorious and decisive victory, the story of which
will re-echo around the world, and will forever live in the
history of our home land.*

There is, in Bean, an implied criticism of the failure to exploit the
confused state of the German defenders after the successful deep
penetration of their lines.[12] However, Ludendorff called 8 August the
'black day' of the German Army. It also should be noted that the
victories of the Australian Corps did not come cheaply in human
terms; between 7 and 14 August the Corps suffered casualties to 339
officers and 5652 other ranks.[13]

The Australian Corps was in continuous action throughout
August and September, their efforts culminating in the assault on the
Hindenburg Line from 29 September to 5 October, after which the
exhausted divisions were relieved for an overdue rest period. The 4th
Division was relieved after its attacks on the Hindenburg Outpost Line
from 10 to 22 September.

Harry Murray's last battle of World War I was spent with the
Americans. The War Diary of the 4th Machine-Gun Battalion
laconically states that on 24 September the CO was seconded to the
II American Corps HQ and rejoined his unit on 3 October. The
American unit, made up of the 27th and 30th National Guard
Divisions, was offered to Monash for the assault on the Bellicourt
Tunnel of the Hindenburg Line. Monash decided to send an
Australian Mission of 83 officers and 127 NCOs to the American
units to help overcome their lack of experience. Major General
Sinclair-Maclagan led the mission and he and Lieutenant Colonels
Harry Murray and A.M. Ross went to II American Corps, while
Brigadier General Brand, Lieutenant Colonels Crowther and
Salisbury, and 106 others went to the 27th Division. This was the

group from the 4th Division AIF. There was also a contingent from the 1st Division.[14]

The Australians found the Americans to be brave soldiers but, in their first actions, foolhardy through inexperience. A rapport did develop between the two armies, however, Alfred Pollard, an English VC winner, wrote scathingly and unkindly of them in his book, *Fire-Eater: The Memoirs of a V.C.*: 'They [the Americans] had come in with the avowed intention of helping us to win the War, yet they were too proud or too pig-headed to let us help them ... They had to pay very dearly for their mistakes when they came up against such an intrepid and experienced fighter as Fritz. The two divisions to which I was temporarily attached were decimated in their first action.'[15] Harry Murray's view of the Doughboys, as the Americans were called, differed from that of Pollard: 'I found them amongst the bravest troops I have ever met,' he later wrote. 'They lacked experience but were very willing to learn and were eager for advice from anyone who had had previous experience. Too much cannot be said for their bravery.'[16]

Murray was recommended for an award of the American Distinguished Service Medal (DSM) by Major General John O'Ryan, GOC of the 27th Division. The citation, headed 'Award of D.S.M. to British Officers', and dated 25 November 1918, reads:

Lieutenant Colonel H. Murray, V.C., D.S.O., D.C.M.,
commanding 4th Australian MG. Bn.,
4th Australian Division.

Attached to unit of the 27th Division as liaison officer with the 27th Division, A.E.F., September 29th–October 1st 1918, while the division was affiliated with the Australian corps, B.E.F., for the attack on the HINDENBURG LINE. Lt. Colonel Murray was of the very greatest assistance to the machine-gun units of the division in the attack. He was most active in accompanying officers to the front, securing and bringing in information. His knowledge, activity and fearlessness were of inestimable value to the Division and assisted materially in the control of the attacking forces by battalion and brigade commanders.

Although recommended for the award, Murray did not receive it. If he had he would have received seven decorations in World War I.

The 27th and 30th Divisions' assault on the Hindenburg Line, especially their capture of the Bellicourt Tunnel on the Cambrai — Mont St Quentin Canal, was costly. The 27th Division suffered 7400 casualties and the 30th, 8000; on a scale with the Australian losses at Pozières in 1916. The 30th Division won twelve Congressional Medals of Honor in World War I, more than any other American Division. All were gained in its assault on the Hindenburg Line in September and October 1918.

The War Diary of Murray's Battalion records that in October the unit trained and enjoyed sport and recreation. On the 4th, Harry Murray left the unit on special leave. The next day, the announcement was made that Brigadier General R.L. Leane and Lieutenant Colonel H.W. Murray had been awarded the Croix de Guerre avec Etoile de Vermeil by the French. The first announcement of Murray's Croix de Guerre appeared in 'Ordre du Corps d'Armée No. 297' issued by the General Commandant of the 31st Corps of the French Army. A translation of the citation reads:

Lieutenant Colonel Murray, Henry William. 4th Australian Machine-Gun Battalion.

During the period 23rd March to 24th April 1918 and 2nd to 7th August 1918 has commanded the 4th Australian machine-gun Battalion with remarkable skill. Under heavy fire from enemy artillery he was successful, by his bravery, in maintaining in the most difficult circumstances a close liaison with French troops.

On Monday 11 November, the diary records that it was a sunny day — no frost. At 11.45 that morning news was received that the Armistice had been signed; hostilities had ceased 45 minutes earlier. The Battalion HQ celebrated.

And so it ended.

9

AFTERMATH

I have returned to these:
The farm, and the kindly Bush, and the young calves lowing;
But all that my mind sees
Is a quaking bog in a mist — stark, snapped trees,
And the dark Somme flowing.

— Vance Palmer, *The Farmer Remembers the Somme*

I t was not until November 1919, twelve months after the Armistice, that Harry Murray embarked for Australia. His length of service could have given him priority for a passage, but perhaps he was in no hurry to return home; he had an opportunity to travel in Great Britain and Europe, and continuing to receive the pay of a lieutenant colonel would have been attractive for a one-time timber cutter. Also, it can be surmised that he had an attachment to Scotland and especially to Clementine Montgomery. He certainly showed no desire to settle in Tasmania, which he had visited only once since leaving in 1908, and when he did return there in 1920, he stayed only a few months. Murray had not availed himself of the chance to return to Australia with the '1914 men' in mid-1918, when Prime Minister Hughes had been prevailed upon to send these 6000 veterans home; as he was told, 'There won't be any left if you don't.'

Further military honours were awarded to Murray in 1919. In June he was made a Companion of the Order of St Michael and St George (CMG). The citation for this honour was written by his divisional commander, Sinclair-Maclagan:

> *This Officer has commanded the machine-gun Battalion of the Division since its inception on the 15th March 1918. His work has been marked by conspicuous gallantry, ability, technical knowledge and devotion to duty. During the period 18th September to 11th November, he commanded the machine-guns of the Division with marked success in the operations which resulted in the capture of the Hindenburg Outpost Line. He also, as Liaison machine-gun Officer with the American Corps, largely contributed to the successful work of the machine-guns of the Corps in the operations resulting in the breaking of the main Hindenburg Line near Bellenglise. He is recommended for high distinction.*

Murray was also Mentioned in Despatches for the fourth time on 11 July.

During 1919, Murray spent little of his time with his unit, and then his military duties were not arduous. A letter from a sixteen-year-old French girl, Edith de St Hilaire, to Dot Cocker, Murray's sister, written in 1919, is held by Murray's daughter. Addressed from Haugest/Somme, it notes that Murray kept a photo of Dot's baby on his mantelpiece and that he was teaching Edith and her sister to play golf. The letter also says: 'If you could see how the boys are found [*sic*] of him it would be a great comfort to you all. We go sometimes driving with him but he is such a tease. He does all what he can to frighten us. I wonder how he was when he was with you. I suppose a mischievous boy.'

From June to September 1919, Murray was granted special leave to study stock raising. With another Australian VC, Donovan Joynt, he led a touring party throughout Great Britain and Denmark for this purpose and also revisited France and Belgium. This activity was part of the AIF Education Scheme that was successful in occupying over 160,000 restless Australian soldiers desperate to return home and waiting for berths in a limited number of transports.

In a letter written to Dot from London on 21 August 1919, he wrote with bitterness of the sights he had seen and made a prescient statement concerning the future of Germany:

I have just returned to London from a trip through France and Belgium. It was very interesting to see the old Battlefields again but very sad to see the absolute devastation of all places. It's rotten to think that the Huns have escaped it. I think we have not been half severe enough with them. They will start almost at once to prepare for their revenge and will profit by their mistakes. I may not live to see the war, but when it comes it will be terrible and the Huns if successful will not forget their humiliation.

Very much an individualist and a conservative man opposed to excessive union power, Murray wrote further in the letter:

It's going to be serious for the people here next winter. Coal will be almost unobtainable and there will be much discontent and unrest I'm afraid — sometimes I fear a revolution of sorts, it will be quickly be crushed & it really would clear the air. I think one would hear less of strikes and the like, in fact it would knock these extreme unions on the head. Men are perfectly absurd nowadays. They want all and expect to give nothing in return. It's perfectly rotten the way the coal miners are behaving & everywhere there's the same tendency & of course it's the public that pays every time.

Murray signed the letter: 'With all the best love for yourself Dottie, From your soldier brother. Harry.'

Harry Murray left England on 19 November 1919 in the Orient Line transport, *Ormonde*. The ship also carried Monash, Birdwood and Brigadier General Evan Wisdom, who had led the 7th Brigade in most of the AIF's major battles of 1917 and 1918. There was also a large contingent of British war brides who had married Australian soldiers.

A month later, the *Ormonde* reached Fremantle, where a large crowd greeted the ship at the wharf. It had been five years less three days since Murray and Monash had left Australia with the second convoy in 1914. Birdwood was given a hearty reception as he waved his Digger's hat from the ship and Monash was also cheered, but the largest volume of applause was for Harry Murray. Former members of his original battalion, the 16th, took charge of the motor car in which he rode, shut off its engine, attached ropes and towed it through the streets. Then he was hoisted shoulder high and carried to the Fremantle Town Hall. When he attempted to address the crowd there, 'He was not permitted to speak until the audience had yelled itself hoarse.' He said to the crowd:

> *I am afraid you have taken the wind out of my sails altogether. All I can do is to thank you most heartily for your welcome to us on returning to our own homeland. This is the moment we have all waited for and fought for. The only other thing I wish to say is that anything I have done or gained I owe not to myself, but to the privilege and honour which I enjoyed of commanding the most magnificent fighters in the world, namely the Australians. I thank you very much for your hearty welcome.*[1]

Proceeding to Perth, Murray and the other notables were given another enthusiastic reception in His Majesty's Theatre; Birdwood, addressed the Diggers and 'diggeresses', as he called the wives. Murray left the ship in Melbourne, where he was again lionised. At the Melbourne Town Hall, on 26 December 1919 it was reported that a woman 'rushed forward and, throwing her arms around his neck, kissed him heartily and presented him with a box of chocolates and a rag doll'.[2]

Murray was not mock modest. He genuinely detested the adulation shown to VC winners and was, undoubtedly, the most retiring of all Australia's VCs of World War I. The Fremantle, Perth and Melbourne incidents made him determined to avoid a further noisy and emotional welcome in Launceston. He crossed to Burnie in northern Tasmania in the steamer *Grace Darling* and, ostensibly, took a train for Launceston. However, he left the train at Deloraine and proceeded to Launceston by car, going straight to his sister Dot's home, where his mother and other relatives awaited him. The large crowd on Launceston station was disappointed and the *Launceston Examiner* of 8 January 1920 reported on Murray's deception:

'The Daredevil of Anzac' or 'Murray the Marvel,' as he is sometimes called, returned to Launceston last evening and, though his coming was not widely known, a large crowd had assembled at the station to welcome him among a party of other Diggers who, having been detained in Melbourne, had crossed to Burnie on the small steamer Grace Darling *for the arrival of the train which was delayed a little over an hour. He [Murray] did not put in an appearance and most of the crowd were disappointed at not being able to catch a glimpse of the man whose intrepidity has made his name honoured wherever there is an 'Aussie.' His modesty no doubt had something to say in his decision to leave the train at Deloraine and motor to the residence of his brother in law (Mr. D. Cocker) [in] Launceston, where his mother was waiting for him.*

He reached Launceston just after 9 o'clock last night and . was met only by relatives and a few friends — just what he desired. There was no cheering crowd, no 'cobbers' to rush him and chair him, and no speeches to vast audiences to make, such as on the mainland.

Murray's former comrades of the Launceston artillery were determined to welcome their famous comrade, formerly Driver Murray, and he did attend a function at the Launceston Hotel on the evening of 10 January. In his response to the welcoming addresses he made a speech which touched on political problems which had arisen in Australia soon after the war. That speech was reported in the *Weekly Courier*:

He was particularly pleased to have the opportunity of once more meeting so many of his old comrades, and he thanked them most heartily and sincerely for the kind welcome they had extended to him. He remembered the many pleasant and instructive days he had spent in the ranks of the Launceston artillery, and he particularly wanted to acknowledge the great service that training had been to him on active service. He could say nothing but good of the Australian Digger. He had, as all soldiers had, his peculiarities, but once understood and properly handled, he was capable of magnificent work. Since his return to Australia he had heard a great deal of political and industrial unrest and the attitude likely to be taken by the returned soldier in the event of any upheaval. With his knowledge of the men comprising the AIF — and he had served with them in the ranks in the early part of the war — he firmly believed that 90 per cent of the Diggers would at once declare for constituted law and order. He recognised that there were great problems to be worked out in Australia, as the outcome of the War, and the burdens of taxation might be somewhat irksome; but they must remember to what lengths taxation in England had been imposed and that, in comparison, we in Australia were getting off lightly. He wished the Old Comrades' Association every

success in its undertaking, and regarded such an association of
great benefit to any unit of the Australian forces. He again
thanked them one and all for their kind welcome and the
splendid reception they had given him.[3]

Murray's speech was an unusual one for a returning hero, touching carefully on a controversial subject of the day. In the immediate post-war years, there were fears that former soldiers could be recruited into bodies advocating civil unrest when there was found to be insufficient work for the fit, or adequate pensions and medical care for the incapacitated. The Russian Revolution of 1917 aroused fear that other countries might follow Russia's path. Many leaders of the AIF greatly feared Bolshevism, and para-military right-wing organisations were formed in which most of the great leaders of the AIF, with the exception of Monash, took a prominent part. Monash did organise a semi-military body to maintain order when the Victoria Police went on strike in November 1923 but firmly resisted appeals made to him over the years to join and take a leadership role in other bodies.

At Palm Beach, Sydney, on 25 January 1920, Harry Murray's former commanding officer and great friend, Douglas Marks, was drowned when attempting to rescue a young woman, Johanna Mary Rogers, who was caught in an undertow. Although a poor swimmer, Marks, who was sitting on the beach fully clothed, discarded only his coat and shoes and entered the water. Both Marks and Miss Rogers drowned, and Marks's body was never recovered. Marks was only 24 years old and engaged to be married.[4] Later in 1920, at the annual meeting of the Royal Shipwreck Relief and Humane Society of NSW, a silver Medal and Certificate of Merit honouring Douglas Marks was handed to his brother Fred. A memorial service held for him at historic St James's Church, Sydney, was crowded out with members of the 13th. The Battalion history noted that 'none of his comrades in arms felt his loss more than his bosom friend and ardent admirer, Col. H. Murray'.[5] Murray named his only son Douglas, and later wrote: 'I have called my boy Douglas after him and, if the boy can live and die but half such a man as Doug Marks, I will be more than content, for no stouter-hearted gentleman, no manlier man, no truer comrade ever lived.'[6]

On 9 March, in Tasmania, Harry Murray was discharged from the AIF. He had been in uniform for five and a half years — one of the longest periods of service of any member of the First AIF. Always a countryman, he now sought a sheep property in Queensland; Tasmania had no prospects for him, and after enduring three bitter winters in France he may well have sought a warm climate. By the end of 1920, he had bought a grazing property, Blairmach, in south-eastern Queensland outside the hamlet of Muckadilla, in long-established cattle and sheep grazing country. Roma was the nearest large town. How he financed this purchase is not known, but he had accrued a large sum in deferred pay, received a grant from the Soldier Settlement Scheme of the day and, as he was still single and not extravagant, he would have had the opportunity to save a considerable sum from his pay. In a letter to C.E.W. Bean, a part of which has been quoted earlier, he stated: 'As you will see I am up in Queensland and have a small grazing property, 15,000 acres carrying about 10,000 sheep. Am busy training them to march in fours etc.' Two sons of a Melbourne merchant family, Jack and Ivor Manton, were sent to Blairmach in the early 1920s as jackeroos, 'to knock the rough edges off them'.[7] The Mantons and Harry Murray became lifelong friends, with advantage to Murray as described later.

On 13 October 1921 at Bollon, Queensland, south-east of Muckadilla, Harry Murray married Constance Sophia Cameron, an estate agent. The marriage was not happy, the couple proving to be incompatible. Murray was reclusive, hardworking and sought a secluded rural life. Constance Murray was vivacious, enjoyed social life and, according to family lore, had ambitions to be the wife of a prominent public figure. Life on a remote sheep station was not to her liking and being a public figure was a role Murray resisted all his life.

The couple separated in 1925 and Murray went to New Zealand. On 11 November 1927 at Brisbane, with Constance Murray as petitioner, a decree nisi, with costs against Harry Murray, was granted on the grounds of his desertion. Nine days later, at the Auckland Registrar's Office, Murray married Ellen Purdon Cameron, niece of Constance. In an interview conducted by David Chalk in 1989, Ellen (Nell) Murray stated that she had first met Murray in the Gresham Hotel, Brisbane, about two years before her marriage to him.

Although there was a considerable difference in their ages — Murray was nearly 47 when he married for the second time and Nell was about 23 — the marriage was a long and happy one and Nell later described Harry as 'a most wonderful husband'.[8] In Nell, Murray was fortunate to find a woman who shared his love of the country life. His nephew, Joseph Cocker, has said: 'If Murray was a son of the soil, Nell was a daughter.' She delighted in rural pursuits, was very fit, being an excellent runner and tennis player, and she took part in many of the tasks required on a sheep station. A direct ancestor of Nell Murray's was John Macarthur of Camden, founder of the Australian wool industry, who as a lieutenant in the New South Wales Corps had left England in 1790 in the *Neptune*, the transport of the Second Fleet which also carried Ann White, Harry Murray's convict great-grandmother.

LIFE ON GLENLYON

After the wedding, Murray and his bride moved to Queensland and stayed for a time with Nell's father, B.J. Cameron, on his property at St George, about 120 miles south of Muckadilla. In the divorce settlement granted to his first wife, Harry Murray lost ownership of the Muckadilla property. He now wished to settle on another station but finance was difficult for him. However, with generous assistance from Nell's family, particularly a cousin of hers, Archie Cameron, and help from the Manton family, he settled on a property, Glenlyon, outside Richmond in north Queensland. The loan from Archie Cameron was settled with a handshake only and, after a decade of hard work, was paid off by the end of the 1930s.

Harry and Nell Murray moved to Glenlyon on 1 April 1928. Until that date, Murray had not had a long-term home of his own. His early life in Tasmania and Western Australia had not been happy. Then followed the war and his short marriage to Constance Cameron. He lived on Glenlyon, apart from some absences in World War II, until his death in 1966. At last, he found happiness with a wife and soul mate, two children, and a property to which he was so attached that he rarely left it. His visits to Brisbane were infrequent, and he made the trip into Richmond, a town of about 300 residents, only about four times yearly.

Glenlyon was a property of 72,000 acres on a blacksoil plain. There was little timber on the property except for some coolabah trees along the creeks and whitewood trees on the ridges. The climate could be extreme: extremely hot in the summer, with frosts common in winter. The property optimally carried about 15,000 pure merino sheep whose wool was of high quality; to quote Murray's son Douglas, on one occasion Glenlyon held the world record price 'for one day' for greasy wool.[9] Until Douglas Murray joined his father on the property on leaving boarding school in Toowoomba in 1948, Harry Murray generally worked it with one man, Jack O'Keefe, who was with him for 35 years from 1930. A loyal and hardworking bushman of the old school, O'Keefe lived a lonely life, taking comfort in his aviary of birds and his favourite drink, rum and port wine mixed.

Two children were born to Harry and Nell Murray: Douglas in 1930 and a daughter, Clem, in 1934. On Douglas's birth, Murray again showed his tendency to conceal his true age, as 'age of father' on the birth certificate is given as 38. He was in fact nearly 50. Both the Murray children inherited their parents' aptitude for the rural life. Douglas worked on Glenlyon until his retirement to Townsville in 1990 when his two sons, Christopher and Donald, took over the property. Clem, described in interviews for this book as 'as good as a man on a property, could do anything', worked in the bush all her life. Clem was proud of a statement made to her at her father's funeral by one of Harry's wartime comrades: 'Harry Murray will never die while you're still alive.'[10]

Helen Murray, an older sister of Harry's, moved to Glenlyon in 1930 and stayed with the family all her life. A gentle lady, she was a much loved aunt to the Murray children. After World War I, many Australian families had a maiden aunt living with them. There was no prospect of marriage for thousands of women after the slaughter of the Great War.

The yearly round of work on Glenlyon as described by Douglas Murray was:

> *Shearing in November and the wool would be sold. November through the Christmas period — general maintenance, the sheep would pretty well look after themselves. Then, about March, the sheep would be due to have their lambs in the next month so you would have to muster the whole place, get the sheep in and clean them, crutching them and also cleaning round their heads so that they could see properly. Then the lambs would come along, so the next job to do with the stock was the lamb marking at the end of June. Then you would get them all in in September and October and jet them all because of blowfly strike. Then round to shearing again. All the rest of your time you would be checking your fences, bore drains and any other maintenance that needed doing on the place.[11]*

There was, however, a social life and friendship on the remote Queensland property. Nell was a very good tennis player, winner of many championships in the Queensland bush, and one of Harry Murray's first tasks on Glenlyon was to build a tennis court. There were three neighbours within a radius of ten miles and they, and others from properties further out, visited Glenlyon on Sundays to pick up their mail and join in a game. Such days would end with a drink of rum for the men 'and a real good pow wow', according to Nell.[12] Most working days ended with a set of tennis. Nell and Harry were keen opponents and their children and visitors joined in. The Murrays were hospitable; visitors were encouraged to stay overnight, although on one occasion Murray was disconcerted by a visitor, a young Scotsman named Duncan. Mindful of his own Scottish connections, Harry enquired of the young man at dinner: 'Which part of Scotland do you come from, Duncan?' 'Glasgow,' was the answer. 'Oh,' said Murray condescendingly, proud of his supposed Highland heritage, 'You're a Lowlander then?' 'Yes,' was the reply. 'My father said never to trust a Highlander. They're too like the bloody Irish!' When Douglas Murray recounted this tale when being interviewed, he said: 'I can still see Dad's face!'

On rare occasions, old comrades made the long trip to Queensland to stay with the Murrays. George McDowell, who had found Murray to be 'as gentle as a woman' in 1916, made several visits. Murray's adjutant of the 4th Machine-Gun Battalion, A.A. Fowles, visited in 1931 and is reported as saying, 'It's a great life up here and I'm looking forward to having another holiday with the C.O. soon.'[13]

Murray's other relaxations and interests were reading — packages of books came from city lending libraries — and maintaining a large vegetable garden. An early riser, he worked in his garden from dawn until called in for breakfast and then again in the evening after tennis. Every visitor to Glenlyon left with a bag of vegetables. Although he had never played the game, he loved listening to cricket broadcasts; one of Douglas Murray's early memories is of Harry and Nell sitting up very late at night listening to a scratchy short-wave broadcast from England of the 1938 England–Australia Test series. Also, he was a prolific letter writer who kept up a correspondence with friends all around Australia.

In Queensland, Harry Murray was almost universally addressed as 'Colonel' and referred to as 'The Colonel'. Only a few close friends called him Harry. Although modest and apparently shy, he had extraordinary powers of command. It was natural for him to take charge and his directions were usually followed without question. His relations with his workers were good, except for the traditional disputes with shearers concerning 'wet' wool. Murray was generally good-natured and easy-going, but a relative working for him found on one occasion that there was steel beneath his calm exterior. Murray instructed the relative to close a gate in the yards. The young fellow, conscious that he was a member of the family, thought that one of the workers should have been asked to perform the task and, pointedly, dawdled over to the gate. He was amazed to hear a parade ground bellow behind him from Murray: 'At the double!'

In interview, Douglas Murray gave three examples of his father's stoicism. Harry followed a boar into a drain on one occasion and was badly gored close to the femoral artery, but he made light of the incident. He was similarly offhand when he was caught for some time in the machinery of the property windmill, resulting in severe injuries to his left knee; his right knee had been damaged in the war. When an old man, he was burning off and was enveloped in the flames. His legs were badly burnt and he was in great pain when walking. Douglas took him to the local doctor but Harry, by then a slight figure, refused to be carried at any stage by Douglas, a big man.

Harry Murray had other distinctive attributes. He showed no fear of heights. When visiting Sydney with his family, the group went to North Head where there is a sheer drop to the rocks below and no safety railing in many places. Murray went right to the edge of the cliff and looked over for some time. His family were agitated by this. He was extremely quick in his reactions and movements. At tennis he had remarkable reflexes at the net although his knee wound restricted his movement at the back of the court. This quickness of reaction is remarked on by several writers describing his actions in battle. Also, 'He never got a shock if someone crept up on him and tried to scare him,' said Douglas, describing childhood games. Another physical attribute of Murray's was that he was tone deaf; he could not distinguish a tune and had to be nudged by Nell to stand up when the National Anthem was played. This makes a mockery of his lyrical description in a *Reveille* article of a bugler playing Gounod's 'Serenade' on Gallipoli.

Summing up his father's character, Douglas Murray chose his words carefully and spoke movingly when interviewed. He said of his father:

> *He was a very, very, highly principled, moral person but when I say that, he would not condemn someone if they made a mistake. He probably could forgive as well if someone did something he did not approve of, he would not completely blackball them. His temperament — he had a pretty placid sort of temperament, with his family anyway. Very rarely went off the handle with us but such was his power of command he only had to speak to us and we obeyed. And he had a really good sense of humour.*

Murray gave evidence of this 'sense of humour' during the war. At Zonnebeke, during the Passchendaele offensive, the 13th Battalion, with a large number of reinforcements in A Company, was in support. A sudden barrage landed near the men as they sheltered in cellars and shell holes. Fortunately, the barrage landed in advance of the troops. Murray relieved the situation by rising out of a shell hole and, smilingly, calling out 'Oo frew dat brick?' This lightened the tension for the young soldiers. The phrase was a caption of one of Bruce Bairnsfather's cartoons of Cockney soldiers' life in the trenches, the most famous of which was: 'Well, if you know a better 'ole, go to it.' These cartoons were very popular during the war.

Murray enjoyed joking about his medals. He would say that his VC, cast from a Russian canon captured at Sebastopol in the Crimean War, was worth only sixpence whilst his DSO, constructed of porcelain and wrought metal, was worth £50. When he was questioned about his decorations in Sydney in 1956, he told reporters: 'I was lucky. They brought decorations by the bucket to my unit, A Company 13 Bn. I always got first go at the bucket. My men were always very loyal to me. I got most of the kudos they deserved, and that's not sob stuff. I'm very sincere in that statement.' When his daughter Clem, as a small child, first became aware of the significance of her father's VC she asked him how he had won it. Harry replied that he saw a bottle of rum on top of an enemy trench, ran out and acquired it for his CO, and was awarded a VC!

In interview, Clem reaffirmed her brother's estimate of their father, stressing the nobility of his character and recalling his admonition to his children not to judge others unfairly. She wondered how a man so 'soft', as she found him, could have performed such exploits in war and she dissolved into laughter when she attempted to count up the variety of birth dates he had given on his army records, his marriage certificate (claiming to be 37 when he was 47) and the birth registrations of his children. She reached a total of seven!

As noted earlier, Murray did not drink alcohol before World War I and did not smoke. He started to do both in the war, although his son Douglas says that on no occasion did he ever see his father adversely affected by alcohol. It was his custom, however, to take cold tea in an overproof rum bottle when he went around the property. According to a family story, a neighbour was overheard to say one day: 'Oh there's no doubt about that Colonel; he upended this bottle of OP rum, and it was in the morning too. He drank a quarter of a bottle and just put the cork back and he never even blinked!' He smoked heavily, rolling his own until his death.

WRITING FOR *REVEILLE*

Between 1929 and 1939, fifteen articles by Murray appeared in *Reveille*, the magazine of the New South Wales Branch of the RSL.

First published in 1927, *Reveille* reached a high standard in those years and is an essential source for researchers writing on World War I. A series, 'Celebrities of the AIF', mostly written by Arthur Bazley in the 1930s, is frequently cited by military historians. Bazley, who joined the AIF at eighteen and was assigned to Charles Bean as his batman from Gallipoli to France and Flanders, was never far from Bean's side, acting as his clerk. Post-war, he assisted Bean in the compilation of his massive history and eventually became acting director of the Australian War Memorial. It is notable that the first 'celebrity' chosen by Bazley for the series was Harry Murray. Many of his words in that article appear again and again in later writings on Murray.

Harry Murray's articles were all drafted in longhand, as he could not type, and reference is made in a letter to the editor of *Reveille* that he must hurry to finish an article and get it across to a neighbour to type so as to catch the mail. Evidence of his admiration of Percy Black is that his first article, which appeared in December 1929, was devoted to his comrade, whom he described as 'The Bravest Man in the AIF'. His second article, 'The Slippery Slide Gallipoli Thrill', a humorous description of portly Major J.P. McGlinn's mishap at Gallipoli, appeared in 1930. In his third article, 'Nation's Best in Gallipoli Graves', he wrote feelingly of the first Gallipoli casualties, saying: 'I think we lost better men in those first few weeks than we ever had afterwards and I give this opinion with a knowledge of those whom we lost and of those who fought on to the end.' He did not expand on this enigmatic statement. His fourth article, on Bert Jacka, 'One of the Best One of the Bravest', was one of many eulogies of Jacka which appeared in *Reveille* in January 1932. Jacka had died of chronic nephritis in Caulfield Military Hospital, Melbourne, on 17 January.

Another eulogy of Jacka in *Reveille*, written by Captain Ken Millar, MC (2nd Bn), contained a curious line: 'He [Jacka] wasn't a "one fight, one V.C. artist" but a V.C. every time he went into action.'[14]

It is a curious line as it raises the proposition that there is some kind of pecking order amongst Victoria Cross winners. But if Jacka was not a 'one fight, one V.C. artist', to repeat the fascinating phrase, then the same could also be said of Harry Murray.

'Training Juniors Field Ranks' appeared in *Reveille* in June 1933. Murray praised officers such as Durrant, Edmund Alfred Drake-Brockman, CO of the 16th, Terence Patrick McSharry, CO of the 15th Battalion when he was fatally wounded at Corbie in August 1918, and 'that dear, kindly, capable gentleman soldier, Lt.-Col. Tilney'. He also paid tribute to Major General William Glasgow, of whom he wrote: 'Such success as I achieved in command of a machine-gun battalion I owe largely to Sir William who was always ready to listen and to counsel, although he was a very busy man.' One wonders how this connection with Glasgow occurred, as Murray's 4th Machine-Gun Battalion was attached to the 4th Division commanded by Major General Ewen Sinclair-Maclagan.

Murray's article, 'Experimental Stage Tanks at Bullecourt', appeared on 1 April 1933. Lengthy articles included 'His Hardest Battle When Discipline Mastered Fear' (December 1935), which was on Pozières, 'Memories of First Bullecourt' (December 1936), 'Capture of Stormy Trench' (December 1937) and 'The First Three Weeks on Gallipoli' (April 1939). In *Reveille* on 1 March 1937, Murray wrote warmly of one of his commanding officers in his 'Col. Tilney Passes: A Lovable Character'. In 'Get Through at Any Cost', which appeared a year later, Murray praised the battalion runners and also wrote favourably of the signallers and cooks.

Of all the Australian Victoria Cross winners of World War I, Murray and Donovan Joynt were the only ones to leave any body of writing. Joynt wrote two books, *Breaking the Road for the Rest* and *Saving the Channel Ports*. Joseph Maxwell's *Hells Bells and Mademoiselles* was, as previously stated, ghostwritten. Murray probably had the ability to write a book on his experiences, but might not have had the time or the inclination to do so.

WORLD WAR II

By the Munich crisis of October 1938, Australia knew that war with Nazi Germany was inevitable, and belated efforts were made to expand the Militia (CMF) and put it in a state of readiness. On 1 November, the government decided to raise the strength of the militia to 70,000 men by voluntary enlistment.[15] In this climate, Murray volunteered once more for military duty, and on 21 July 1939 was appointed lieutenant colonel and given command of the 26th (Militia) Battalion, part of the 11th Brigade, which was the most northerly army unit in Queensland and covered the area between Townsville and Charters Towers. The 26th was usually located at Sellheim. Again, Murray concealed his correct age, stating that he was born in 1885. He was, in fact, 59 years old. His reasons for deception in both wars may well have been that he feared he might have been deemed to be too old. When Murray was appointed to command the 26th Battalion he had not had any connection with the army for nineteen years. That the authorities showed such trust in his retention of his military knowledge is evidence of the high regard in which Murray was held.

In September 1939, when Murray wrote his customary letter to the committee of the 13th Battalion declining, as usual, to attend their annual reunion in Sydney, he sent a donation and wished his old comrades well:

> *Once again my pen and paper must convey greetings and good wishes to you all.*
>
> *How are you all 'A' Company? Just now straining a bit at the leash, like your old Company commander.*
>
> *How I would like a few hours with you — can we not set 'Anno Domini' back twenty years? Still I must not complain. I am still very fit and not so old.*
>
> *I am again in khaki, only A.M.F. but ready for the AIF if the need arises.*

In the men I command I can see the reincarnation of the best Company of the many splendid companies of the old AIF

...

I am in command of the 26th Battalion, A.M.F. — a splendid body of men, all athletes, 60 per cent of them over six feet tall, as keen as men could be and easily controlled.

Of course, it is the old story, volunteers, and the cream of the west. I am afraid they want to get their teeth in, and the old man is a bit with them.

To me, it is a happy omen that the battalion number is a double of the 13th and our colours are the same old Two Blues, only inverted, in diamond shape.

You might wonder what I will do if the need for an overseas force arises! Well, if they will have me, I am going. We licked Fritz once, but this time we will give him Heil. We must end war for all time.[16]

Murray was mobilised for full-time service on 21 October 1941. His World War II records, under the heading 'Examinations and Promotions', show his rank as 'Lieutenant Colonel — No written examination'. Nowhere in his records is there any mention of Murray's attendance at a school or training course until 1941. On 16 April 1918, he was to proceed to the Machine-Gun Training Centre in England for a course, but this movement was cancelled when he was urgently needed to command his battalion at Villers-Bretonneux. Murray's military knowledge to fit him to hold officer rank was all learned on active service. Can any other Australian soldier have reached the rank of lieutenant colonel, from the rank of private, without any formal training away from his unit?

As a young soldier during 1941 and 1942, John Patterson Kane of Sydney served in the 26th Australian Infantry Battalion. In an interview given for this book he recalls Murray as being of 'soldierly appearance', well knit, but a little stooped with age and a lifetime of hard manual work. His turnout was immaculate — as a lieutenant colonel it seems he took more trouble with his uniform than he had as a captain in 1917 — and his 'word of command' on the parade ground was impressive. His manner of speaking to soldiers was measured and calm and he exhibited an air of authority. He was held in high regard by the young men under his command who, in Kane's words, 'would have followed him to the ends of the earth. He seemed to know everything about everyone in the unit.' Although strict, he was humane. On one occasion after an early morning game of tennis, wearing a 'giggle hat', shorts, singlet and sandshoes and with a towel around his neck, Murray was walking towards the showers. A newly joined recruit, not knowing who he was, jocularly said to him: 'Hey mate, it must be pretty crook if they have to have old bastards like you in the army!' Murray replied quietly: 'Oh yes, there is a place in the army for old blokes like me.' Next morning there was a battalion parade and the recruit, to his consternation, saw that the 'old bastard' was a lieutenant colonel with two rows of medal ribbons, including the coveted VC.

Another instance of Murray's informality is given in Polly Underwood's book, *The Reflections of an Old Grey Mare*. As an Army nursing sister during World War II, she was stationed at 116 Australian General Hospital outside Charters Towers. It was her custom on her days off to hitch a ride into town on a garbage truck in order to shop. On one occasion, a private, older than most, thumbed down the truck and shared the trip with her. They talked amiably and on leaving the truck, the elderly private snapped her a smart salute. Some days later, she was told that Australia's most decorated soldier, Colonel Harry Murray, was a patient in her ward. She was amazed to find that the famous colonel and the private with whom she had shared a lift were one and the same person, although she could not understand why he had chosen to pass as a private and hitch-hike when he could have used a staff car.[17]

Patterson Kane was impressed by Murray's physical toughness

during an exercise in which the 26th was opposed to the 31st Battalion. The war game was intended to be as realistic as possible. During the exercise, Murray, accompanied by a lieutenant, noted two men approaching his battalion headquarters. Murray said to the lieutenant, 'What do you see?' The lieutenant replied, 'Sir, I see a couple of swagmen coming towards us,' to which Murray responded: 'I don't believe they are swagmen. I believe they are the "enemy" from the 31st Battalion. When I give you the nod, you tackle the little bloke and I'll take the big bloke.' When the strangers drew closer, Murray winked at the lieutenant and, in Kane's words, 'proceeded to bowl one bloke over in a beautiful rugby tackle and take him captive'. The swagmen were then identified as senior sergeants in the 31st Battalion. Murray was then over 60 years of age.

There is a tradition, often adhered to but for which there is no regulation, that wearers of the Victoria Cross are entitled to a salute regardless of the rank of the person giving the salute. Patterson Kane saw an example of this when the 26th Battalion was inspected on one occasion during the war by the governor of Queensland, Sir Leslie Orme Wilson, who was wearing uniform. As the governor approached Murray, who was standing in front of his battalion, an old soldier, at attention next to Kane in the ranks, whispered to him, 'Watch this!' The governor then proceeded to salute Murray first. 'See,' said the old soldier, 'he's saluting the VC.'

In Australia, in World War II, there was friction at times between Australian and American troops. On 26 and 27 November 1942, in what became known as 'The Battle of Brisbane', violent clashes occurred in which an Australian soldier was shot dead by an American MP and soldiers from both countries were injured, some seriously. In 1942, when Murray was senior officer of the Townsville area, where many Americans were posted, he was notified that the Australian 7th Division, en route to New Guinea, was to be given shore leave in Townsville. Fearing disturbances, Murray acted promptly and with determination, closing all hotels in the city and placing picquets (armed guards of soldiers) outside hotel premises until the 7th had moved on. When news of Murray's edict reached Headquarters in Brisbane, Murray was told by a senior officer, 'You can't do that, Harry.' Murray replied, 'Well it has been done. I'm sure there will be no trouble.' As a result of Murray's actions, the Australians re-embarked without incident.[18]

Murray had hopes of leading his battalion overseas. The 26th was made an AIF unit in 1942 and eventually served in Dutch New Guinea and Bougainville. Murray was seconded to the AIF on 6 August that year but then placed on the Supernumerary List on the 11th, relieving him of his command. In Townsville, he was informed by General Sir Thomas Blamey, Commander in Chief of the Australian Military Forces, that he would no longer lead the battalion. Murray was furious at the decision and was extremely annoyed with Blamey, with whom he had previously been on good terms.[19] Blamey had been a staff officer at Gallipoli and in many of the engagements in which Murray had served in World War I. They met at conferences in 1918 when Blamey, a brigadier, was chief of staff of the Australian Corps and Murray represented the Machine-Gun Battalion of the 4th Division. Blamey was, of course, well aware of Murray's tremendous reputation, and his decision to move Murray from the 26th was a pragmatic one. Murray was 61 years old in August 1942, although according to his records he was 57. In the Middle East in 1940 and 1941, Blamey had to remove a number of older battalion commanders, all with fine records in World War I, who could not perform adequately in modern warfare. He was not going to take a risk with the elderly Murray.

With the termination of his AIF command, Murray was appointed CO of the 23rd Queensland Regiment, Volunteer Defence Corps, a mounted unit which he raised and which came to be known as 'Murray's Marauders'. The unit's role was to train groups of rural workers in guerilla tactics to be adopted if the Japanese landed; to carry out a scorched earth policy if necessary; and to evacuate civilians in the event of invasion. Murray was responsible for an enormous area of land extending from the Northern Territory/Queensland Gulf of Carpentaria junction along the shores of the gulf to Cape York and south to Cooktown. There were few roads in this remote area and the volunteers rode their own horses, carried their own supplies and, at times, lived off the land. It was arduous duty for Harry Murray, who once again gained the respect and affection of his men. Through his connections with the sheep grazing industry and his wartime activities, Murray became a well-known personality in northern Queensland and, far from his native Tasmania, is recalled as an archetypal Queensland bushman.

There were reports on several occasions, never substantiated, that landing parties from Japanese submarines had been sighted on the shores of the Gulf of Carpentaria looking for water. Murray generally had only four men with him on his trips. When his son asked him, in later life, what he would have done with such a small group if he had sighted a submarine, Murray replied: 'Oh, I would have thought of something. We would have dropped a grenade down the conning tower, I suppose!' All said in jest, but Murray, fearless and resourceful, would undoubtedly 'have thought of something'.

On 8 February 1944, Murray's appointment was terminated. He had, at that time, spent several periods in hospital suffering from cellulitis in a leg. In his three periods of service in army uniform — Launceston Artillery, 1902–08; World War I, 1914–19; World War II, 1939–44 — he served full and part-time for a total of sixteen years. It is curious that a man so independent, who chose to be self-employed and self-sufficient for most of his life, who liked isolation, should have so willingly chosen the army life with its discipline, restrictions and mixing with large bodies of men. Yet as far as is known, he enjoyed his service.

10

THE LAST YEARS

Eventually, after years of hard work and surviving the long drought of the 1930s and early 1940s, Murray prospered. During the Korean War, wool prices rocketed, reaching the unprecedented figure of 'a pound for a pound'. Murray made a large income from his wool, invested wisely in stocks and shares, and became comfortably off. He was a generous man and assisted several members of his family with gifts and loans. In some cases, he cancelled the debt after the relative had shown that an effort was being made to repay loan instalments regularly. Douglas Murray has said of his father: 'He was not a mean man.'

With Douglas and his grand-nephew Neil Richards, grandson of his sister Hannah, working with him on Glenlyon, Murray found more time for travel and in the 1940s and 1950s he made several visits to Tasmania to see his sisters. But he still, according to Joseph Cocker, retained his hatred of publicity. When reporters with cameras met him at Launceston Airport on one occasion he warned them that if they took his photograph he would sue them.[1] In 1953 and 1954, he made trips to Brisbane and to Adelaide. In Brisbane, in 1954, Murray was introduced to Queen Elizabeth II. When the Queen asked him what his occupation was, Murray replied: 'In between wars, Your Majesty, I grow wool.' His trip to Adelaide, in 1953, was to attend the wedding of his daughter, Clem. The Murray family drove overland in two cars; Murray accompanied by Neil Richards in one of them. Dressed casually in work pants and shirts, they had trouble with their car when it was bogged, and when they arrived at the prominent hotel where they were booked, reception staff ignored the two rough-looking bushman until a manager approached them. Colonel Murray's proposed visit had received publicity in the local papers and the manager treated him with deference: he was conducted to his room and when he arrived at the dining room for dinner, dressed in a suit and wearing miniatures, as he was to attend a function with South Australian members of the 16th Battalion later, the band played 'God Save the Queen' and the head waiter saluted Murray and his party as they were escorted to their table.

THE VICTORIA CROSS CENTENARY CELEBRATION — 1956

Nell Murray could recall Harry attending only two Anzac Day services during their married life, one of which was a Dawn Service. He did not vary his routine of work on 25 April and he avoided functions to which VC winners were invited. In 1929, Victoria Cross winners were invited, as guests of honour, to dinners hosted by their state governors. In Queensland only one of four VCs, Henry Dalziel (15th Bn), attended. Murray, Edgar Towner (2nd Machine-Gun Coy) and Bernard Gordon (41st Bn) were absent.[2] When the Australian War Memorial was completed in 1941, all VC winners were invited to be present at the opening ceremony. Murray did not attend.

In 1956, VC winners from the British Commonwealth were invited to London to take part in celebrations to commemorate the centenary of the Victoria Cross. All expenses were met by government or ex-service bodies. Murray at first declined to go but changed his mind, stating that he realised that the invitation to attend came from the Queen herself and that he owed Nell a trip after all the years of hard work and isolation she had endured. It is believed that Murray met his own expenses and gave the money that was offered to him to charity.[3]

The Australian World War I VCs who went to London were Thomas Axford, Arthur Blackburn, Albert Borella, John Carroll, George Cartwright, Henry Dalziel, William Dunstan, John Dwyer, Bernard Gordon, Arthur Hall, John Hamilton, George Howell, George Ingram, Reginald Inwood, William Jackson, Donovan Joynt, Lawrence McCarthy, Stanley McDougall, Frank McNamara, Joseph Maxwell, Rupert Moon, Harry Murray, Walter Peeler, William Ruthven, Clifford Sadlier, Percy Statton, Percy Valentine Storkey, Edgar Towner and James Woods. At 75, Murray was the oldest member of the party. The youngest was Bill Jackson, aged 59, who had won his Cross at eighteen in 1916 when serving with the 17th Battalion.

The only VC winner in the Australian contingent with whom Murray appears to have kept in touch was Edgar Towner, who won his VC in 1918 as a member of the 2nd Machine-Gun Company serving with the 24th Battalion in the attack on Mont St Quentin. Towner served in the 26th Battalion under Murray in World War II as his second in command. The two men had much in common. They were both Queensland graziers — Towner's property was at Blackall in central Queensland, south of Murray's — and they were both reclusive. Towner, a bachelor and reputedly eccentric, was a keen geographer who would disappear into the wilderness for months at a time on explorations.

Murray was pleased to see Laurence McCarthy, who had landed on Gallipoli with him as a private in the 16th Battalion. Stanley McDougall had fond memories of Harry Murray for, when he won his VC at Dernancourt in March 1918, Murray had written to him: 'From what I hear, no one in this war has more deserved the VC than you.'[4] John Dwyer, a fellow Tasmanian, was awarded his VC on Murray's recommendation when serving with the 4th Machine-Gun

Company, 4th Division. Dwyer stated that he owed much to Murray
for the training he had received from him in machine-gun tactics.

The majority of the Australian VCs sailed for London in the
liner *Orcades* in May 1956. Murray was delayed as the wool industry
was facing a nationwide shearers' strike and he and his son were
working desperately to get their flocks shorn. He told the press on
arrival in Sydney in June: 'My boy could shear about 30 sheep a day
before the strike. Now he can do 100 without any trouble.' In Sydney,
he and Nell attended a small and very emotional reunion with
23 members of the 13th Battalion, none of whom he had seen since
1919 or earlier. The reunion was arranged by Len Plasto, who had held
a commission in the 13th, founded the 13th Battalion Association in
1927 and organised its annual reunions for decades. A successful
publican in Sydney, he held the licences of the Ship Inn at Circular
Quay, the Royal Hyde Park Hotel, and the Station Hotel, North
Sydney. During the hard times of the Depression he frequently helped
old comrades 'down on their luck' and paid their expenses to attend
reunions.

An article in *Reveille* in July 1956 describes the reunion, which
was held at Plasto's home at Darling Point.

> *The entry of Harry Murray into the assembly of his old comrades
> was an experience difficult to describe to those who have not
> enjoyed the stimulating experiences founded in the mud and
> blood, the glory and the carnage, the spiritual and the material
> and the general holocaust of war.*
>
> *Harry Murray walked in to meet men he had not seen for
> generations, and the years fell away as though by the wave of
> some magic wand.*
>
> *He walked up to Jack Trim. His greeting was:*
>
> *'Hello, Jack, I haven't seen you for 39 years, but you
> haven't changed much.'*
>
> *And then to Rodger Bradley, 'Still playing in the forwards?'*

(Referring to his AIF football activities in the 13th Bn. team in France after World War I.)

To Jack Mutton, 'Remember the rapid firing loading competition?', and to Harry Magney, ex-Superintendent of Police, now somewhat on the weighty side, shaking his hand as he said it: 'You used to be such a slight fellow.'

Then to Jack Prescott: 'Well fancy meeting you,' and to Bill Hughes who was in the battalion sigs: 'Wasn't it at Hébuterne you clocked that 5.9 shell which took your arm off?'

Yes they were there. The men who made history 40 years ago — and the man who wrote out the citation which won for 'Mad Harry' his VC ... Major-General J.M.A. Durrant, C.M.G., D.S.O., original Adjutant of the 13th Bn., and later its Commanding Officer.[5]

A toast to Murray was proposed by Major Theodore Wells, MC, president of the Battalion Association, who had been wounded at Mouquet Farm and Bullecourt.

And in reply, this is what Harry Murray, V.C., C.M.G., D.S.O. and bar, D.C.M., C. de G. — known the whole length and breadth of the Australian Army of the First World War as 'Mad Harry' — said:

'I have never been one to make speeches and have always found it hard to respond to a toast and to express what I want to say. They called me "Mad Harry", but I wasn't mad. Whatever I did, I did to justify something in me which made me feel humble in the face of the great deeds of my fellow-Australians.

'When I got the DCM I wondered why I had been awarded the decoration, because I had seen so many others so much braver than I.

'And because of this, I felt that from the moment I received this decoration I would have to justify the award in their eyes

because they had been so much braver and deserved it so much more than I did — and that is why, perhaps, I did the things I did.

'I have never sought, nor have I taken part in any affairs in life after the war which would attract attention to me because I felt that a medal, once bestowed, and recognition given, was sufficient and it was not right to refer to it constantly. The act had been done and the award given. One should not seek more.

'Tonight has been a great event in the life of myself and my wife. I am glad to be here with my old mates.[6]

Murray's reply is worth noting as, to use a phrase that was applied to Bert Jacka, 'He said what he meant and meant what he said.'

In England, the first event of the VC Centenary celebrations was a thanksgiving service held in Westminster Abbey on 25 June. The next day, 299 VCs paraded at Wellington Barracks and then went by coach to Hyde Park, where they were reviewed by Queen Elizabeth II. The VCs were under the command of the senior VC, in rank, the New Zealander Lord Freyberg. Many of the VCs had sunk into obscurity and it was thrilling for them to be feted. It was a lengthy and exhausting occasion for the heroes, many of whom were elderly men from World War I and earlier conflicts, but they would all have been stirred by the words spoken by the Queen at the parade. Inter alia, she said:

In the past century, 1344 men have won the Victoria Cross — three of them more than once. They were men of all ranks, and they came from all walks of life. They were of different colours and creeds. They fought in many lands and with many different weapons. But their stories are linked by a golden thread of extraordinary courage. Each man of them all gave the best that a man can give, and all too many gave their lives ... They dared mightily and turned their necessity to glorious gain.

The long day concluded with a garden party at Marlborough House attended by Queen Elizabeth, the Queen Mother. At the time of the centenary celebrations, a Victoria Cross Association, later the Victoria Cross and George Cross Association, was formed. With government support, VC winners have gathered in London biannually for a reunion. Murray did not attend any of these reunions, but many other Australian VC winners have made the trip. By November 2002, only 16 winners of the Victoria Cross were still living. Because of age and falling numbers, the reunions of the VC and GC Association are at risk of termination.

After the ceremonies in London, the Murrays spent five weeks on a motor tour of England and Scotland, finishing with a week at Wimbledon for the tennis championship. They then visited Switzerland and France but, unlike most of his World War I colleagues in the party, Murray did not visit the French battlefields. He stated: 'I bypassed the old battlefields. There was nothing I wanted less than to go over the battlefields. That would have been an unnecessary raking up of very sad memories of comrades who never returned.'[7]

The Suez crisis had occurred when Murray was returning to Australia. Isolated, and largely against world opinion, Britain, France and Israel had taken offensive action against Egypt, led by President Nasser, when it assumed control of the Suez Canal. A typical Australian of his generation, a traditionalist and old-fashioned imperialist, Murray gave his opinion when interviewed by *Reveille*. He noted that Londoners 'felt it was time England showed she would not be humbugged any more. Londoners, from businessmen down to labourers, consider Nasser a person drunk at the sight of power.' The Australian prime minister, Robert Menzies, had been appointed to a diplomatic role, and Murray agreed with the Londoners that he was 'the right man for a job of such importance'.

Sir Roden Cutler, later a much admired governor of New South Wales, was with the Australian VCs in London in 1956. He was at that time Her Majesty's Australian minister in Cairo but, because of the political turmoil which required his presence in Egypt, he could spend only a minimum of time with the VCs. When questioned in 2000, he had no clear memories of Murray at the celebrations; Murray spent most of his time with his fellow World War I VCs. But he did recall an interesting sidelight to the tour. A London tailoring firm offered to provide each member of the party with a suit. Sir Roden said: 'I didn't accept and I'm sure that some of the team heaved a sigh of relief, simply because not everyone had a business suit.'[8] The coveted decoration had not brought affluence to many of the heroes.

Harry Murray lived on Glenlyon until his death. He suffered much in his last years from arthritis, his knee wound continued to trouble him, and he walked with a limp. Pain frequently disturbed his sleep and in the night he would go the kitchen and make a cup of tea for himself; on some mornings, Nell found him asleep with his head on the kitchen table. Despite his suffering, he maintained his interest in the property. Nell stated that, 'Each morning, after I had done the chores, he and I would go around the property in a Land Rover. He knew every stick and stone and blade of grass on Glenlyon.'[9]

On 6 January 1966, Nell was driving the family car with Harry as a passenger; they were going on holidays to the south coast of Queensland. Near Condamine, on the Leichhardt Highway, at 5.30 pm, a tyre blew out and the car rolled. Harry was taken to hospital suffering from broken ribs. He had suffered heart trouble for some time, and it is believed the shock of the accident caused his death, which occurred on 7 January in the Miles District Hospital. He was 85 years old.

Nell Murray wrote on 14 March to Bill Connell, an authority on Australian VCs, thanking him for his condolences. In the letter she stated: 'The family and I are much saddened at his passing. His health over the last few years had been very poor and his heart had been weakened by much pain due to arthritis. It would be wrong to wish him back to more suffering; he is now free of all his pain and at peace.

Wonderful tributes have been paid to him for which we are so grateful.'

Aware of his father's dislike of publicity, Douglas Murray wished to hold a private funeral. But when the news of Harry Murray's death was announced a number of his old comrades, including Len Plasto, Theodore Wells and Alan Lilley of the 13th Battalion, and Brigadier Frank North, who commanded the 11th Brigade in World War II, telephoned Douglas and suggested strongly that his father should have a full military funeral. Noting the desire of his father's comrades for this recognition, Douglas agreed, and Harry Murray was buried from St Andrew's Presbyterian Church, Brisbane, with honours. The funeral was widely attended; many 13th Battalion men came from New South Wales — one, Bert Knight of the Bullecourt fight, hitch-hiked from Tamworth — and a few veterans of the 16th Battalion made the long journey from Western Australia. Dozens of wreaths were sent to the church. Theodore Wells delivered a superb oration, concluding with the words: 'He will be remembered not only for his magnificently outstanding record as a soldier, but for his friendliness, his kindness, his modesty and his worthiness as a man.' The coffin was carried from the church on a gun carriage to the Mount Thompson Crematorium, preceded by an honour guard of 150 men from the 6th Battalion, Royal Australian Regiment. Murray's daughter, Clem Sutherland, recalls with emotion seeing three road workers, old soldiers, who removed their hats, stood rigidly to attention, and saluted as the cortege passed by. Major David Kayler-Thompson, who had been awarded a Military Cross for gallantry when commanding a Company of the 1st Battalion Royal Australian Regiment in Korea, carried Murray's medals. It was all a symbolic linking of the infantry of the First AIF and that of Australia's newly formed Royal Australian Regiment.

In his last years, conscious of the difference in their ages, Harry Murray said to his wife that he dreaded her being lonely after his death and that it was his wish that she would remarry. In 1968, Nell married a widower, John Waugh, a grazier from Quilpie and a childhood friend. The marriage was very happy. After John Waugh's death in 1977, Nell moved to Buderim, near Queensland's Sunshine Coast. Her daughter, Clem, joined her there in 1996 and cared for her lovingly until Nell entered hospital on the day before her death. She spent her last hours giving instructions to Clem for farewells to her loved ones, until she passed away at dawn on 2 September 2000, aged 96 years.[10]

11

CONCLUSION

I n his latter years, a mellow Harry Murray would say jokingly to his wife: 'I was the most decorated footsoldier of World War I.' And, for the British forces, so he was; an extraordinary record, as millions of infantrymen served in the armies of Great Britain and its Empire. A study of the records of World War I soldier winners of the Victoria Cross shows that Murray, with six awards, is only approached in number of decorations by John Vereker, Viscount Gort, and by William Coltman. Gort, a Grenadier Guardsman, was decorated five times, winning a VC, DSO and two Bars and an MC. In World War II, Gort commanded the British Expeditionary Force in France in 1939–40. Coltman, serving with the North Staffordshire Regiment, won a VC, DCM and Bar and an MM and Bar.

From April 1915 to October 1918, Murray was present at the Gallipoli landing, Bloody Angle, Quinn's Post, the attack on Sari Bair, Hill 60, the evacuation of Gallipoli, Pozières, Mouquet Farm, Flers, Gueudecourt, Stormy Trench, Bullecourt, Messines, Passchendaele, Hébuterne, Dernancourt, Villers-Bretonneux, Hamel and the breaking of the Hindenburg Line. C.E.W. Bean's account of the First AIF covers six volumes of the *Official History*, approximately 7000 pages. It was an outstanding honour to be mentioned by name in those volumes, yet to Murray belongs the astonishing record of being listed in the indexes no less than 46 times and appearaing in every one of those six volumes.[1] Unequivocally, Bean described Murray as 'The most famous fighter' in the AIF.[2]

It was said of Murray that he was:

A sensitive man — one who always rose to the occasion; practical and careful, yet at the same time reckless of personal safety wherever the situation required it; possessing an inborn grasp of tactical requirements and a sure sense of a vital or dangerous point. It was always to these he personally attended and he made a constant practice of using any pause in the fighting to make a reconnaissance in company with some trusted soldier on any neighbouring or outlying trenches, so that when the Germans next attacked, he had mastered the geography of the position and knew exactly how to deal with the situation. He was one of those who always got the best out of their men. When he was about they always seemed to be equal to about three times their normal effort.[3]

Major General A.S. (Tubby) Allen, who commanded the 7th Division AIF in World War II, said of Murray in 1933: 'One need not go beyond this great soldier for an inspiration. I have never met a man who did not look up to him with admiration.'[4]

In the Australian War Memorial is a letter Murray wrote to Captain G.D. Mitchell, MC, DCM, in June 1939. It is obviously answering an earlier request for Murray's opinion of some writing Mitchell had done on 'Battle Psychology'. Research has not revealed Mitchell's earlier letter but it can be assumed that he had asked Murray to comment on his own attitudes to being in action. This document is one of the few private statements of Murray's that remain. Across the file are the words 'Not to be used under Murray's name in his lifetime.' Also, apparently in Mitchell's handwriting, are the words: 'Dear Baz

[Arthur Bazley, librarian of the Australian War Memorial in 1940]. Here it is for your confidential file. It really shows how an ordinary man trained himself to be a superman.'

In the letter, Murray reveals something of himself:

Firstly please don't run away with the idea that I was in any way heroic. I was, thanks to my mother, just a fair Australian, with sufficient will-power to go through with what I set out to do, and too much racial pride to give way to an enemy of another race.

Major Percy Black, whom I have described as the bravest man in the AIF, was a close friend, and before we landed he and I in a quiet talk resolved and then gave each other a vow that we would never let the enemy prevent us carrying out what we set out to do. Really that we would never take an order from him, the enemy, and he lived right up to that vow.

I was something of a military history student having studied Bellasarius [sic] and Napoleon, and the old British code of an officer and when put in charge of men I had no misconception of my duty.

To speculate on what it was that made Harry Murray such an extraordinary front line soldier, it is necessary to consider his heredity, his family associations, his formative years, his physical and mental attributes, and the opportunity which war gave him.

Murray came of stock which was, in the main, successful and durable. His convict ancestors, Kennedy Murray and Ann White, survived British prisons, the horrors of life on convict transports (especially in Ann White's case) and Norfolk Island, and lived through it all to succeed, finally, in Tasmania. His mother's family, the Littlers, were conscious of their breeding and there were many military and naval figures in that middle-class family. Murray was proud of being an Australian, of his ancestry, and was especially influenced by his mother.

Also, his relatives interviewed for this book stressed that he was intensely proud of his Scottish Highlander ancestry, as he believed it to be. He was imbued with the traditional Scottish virtues of courage, endurance and loyalty and no doubt modelled his behaviour on them. Not surprisingly, he found a natural affinity with Scotland during World War I.

Murray, born in 1880, was the second youngest of nine children. His two brothers were considerably older than he was; Albert was born in 1868 and Charles in 1870. Before Murray was ten they had migrated to Western Australia. From the age of ten until his father's death in 1904, when he was 24, he was the only male child in the house, living with a mother he loved and a father he disliked. Did his mother instil in him a sense of his own importance and confidence that he would succeed in life, as many mothers of famous men have done? Yet until the war he was not notably successful, without a trade or profession and facing a life of hard manual work without prospects. He had, it seems, no girlfriends as he had little to offer financially and was extremely shy. He played no sports and his only social outlet was in the Launceston Artillery. A photograph taken around 1905, when he was in the Launceston Artillery, shows an unhappy young man.

Western Australia brought further disappointments; 'They were not happy years', he said. After his estrangement from his brother, he had to make his own way, but showed the physical and mental strength to endure lonely, hard jobs. Employing a gang of sleeper cutters brought him a measure of success and showed him that he could lead tough men.

World War I was to change Harry Murray's life completely. His motivation to enlist was the same combination as that which caused thousands of Australians to queue at the recruiting depots in 1914 — patriotism, relief from long hours of work at boring jobs, the prospect of an overseas trip, for the working class a good rate of pay ... and the pursuit of glory.

For Murray, a sensitive young man and a reader of military history, there was a strong motivation to succeed at soldiering. An Australian of his generation was reared on tales of the glories of British arms. Practically the only history taught in Australian schools was British history and stories of Wellington at Waterloo, the Light Brigade at Balaclava, the defence of Rorke's Drift, were emphasised and known to every schoolboy of Murray's era. Murray described British warships at Gallipoli as 'Nelson's Bulldogs'. 'Britain loses every battle except the last', 'The Empire on which the sun never sets' and 'The thin red line' were universally known phrases. Now that they were to fight alongside the British, the Australians had a strong urge to prove themselves. How would the unproven AIF compare in battle with the famous regiments of the British Army?

In the 16th Battalion, Murray mixed and worked for the first time with a large body of men and quickly acquired prominence with the machine-gunners — the elite of the unit. He was immediately successful and his self-esteem must have been enhanced. He met Percy Black, who seems to have rapidly become his mentor and whom he admired greatly.

On Gallipoli Murray excelled. Four months after the landing, he was commissioned and had been decorated in a campaign in which decorations were sparingly awarded. He was ambitious and considered a transfer to the British Army if he was offered a commission. He easily and rapidly assumed the trappings and ethos of the officer class; did his family background give him the confidence to blend into a new environment? Then to France, where he was awarded five more decorations, including a VC, and promoted to lieutenant colonel. No other soldier who enlisted in the AIF as a private had such a glittering career.

Murray was strong and well coordinated. All his life, from his early teens, he had been accustomed to hard physical work and his physique was developed by years as a farm labourer, courier and axeman. His comrades spoke of him as being quick, mentally and physically, and his family stress his agility at tennis, his skill as an axeman and his accuracy with a rifle.[5] He retained his vigour into old age.

Although Murray, in one of his articles in *Reveille*, said of himself that he was 'nervous and highly strung',[6] this is not borne out by his record. His son recalls him as 'pretty easy-going'. He took part in numerous actions — indeed, few members of the AIF can have seen so much bloodshed and was extremely fortunate to survive, yet never in writings on him or in interviews is there been any mention of nervous problems. He did not suffer from 'post-traumatic stress disorder', to use a modern term, and he named 'discipline' as the force that sustained him, yet he must have had a most equable nervous system to have endured so much. However, his wife Nell, who knew him better than anyone, said: 'He hated talking about the war ... I think it had a big effect on him really. He didn't want to go to Anzac marches. I think it was too emotional for him, even after all those years. He just didn't want to and if he didn't want to, he didn't. He was a very strong character.' His refusal to visit the battlefields of France and Belgium in 1956 is significant; 'Too many sad memories,' he said.[7]

Yet he wrote in *Reveille* in April 1937:

Surely there is something about that terrible thing called War which manages to call forth all that is best and most unselfish in men. Is it not a fact, that at the bottom of our hearts, we all love it, and love the men who fought and bled with us, and afterwards even the men we have fought against? It is the greatest and most terrible of all human dramas when men in millions — nations in arms — are pitted against other millions, fighting savagely as ants, yearning to kill or be killed. And why? Will it ever be abolished? I wonder.[8]

There is always the tantalising question, when writing about the pre-war life of Harry Murray, what kind of life he was prepared for by his education and environmental experiences. The question is, of course, unanswerable, but what can be said is that he was well equipped, mentally and physically, to survive in the horrendous holocaust of World War I. However, such was the nature of that war that while soldierly ability was a prerequisite for survival, good fortune was probably just as important. It is interesting that Murray has little to say in his writing about luck, of which he obviously had an abundance.

Of his life after World War I, Murray's characteristics which stood out were his modesty, his diligence, his love of the rural life and his devotion to his family. He moved smoothly from soldiering to a civilian, working life. His industriousness — daylight to dusk work which he enjoyed — would have been therapeutic after the traumas of war. Also, he was not subject to self-doubt. He was sure of his goals, sure of his opinions — 'Dad was a King and Country man,' his daughter said — a natural leader, and his authority was not questioned either in civilian life or in war. The post-war civilian life of Harry Murray until the 1940s was anything but easy, however. His failed first marriage left him ruined financially and he had to start all over again with his young second wife, Nell, with a huge debt borrowed to purchase Glenlyon. The struggle to pay off his debts and raise a family and run the large property through the Depression years of low wool prices and drought must have been a dour one. This was a different fight from winning a VC; it was a long, protracted struggle that might have broken the hearts of some men. It is surely proof of a type of determination — to set a goal and to see something through — which he had displayed so often before.

Much has been written here about Murray's modesty and his avoidance of publicity. It should also be noted that although there are photos and portraits of him wearing medal ribbons, neither Murray's family nor the Australian War Memorial possesses a photograph of Murray wearing his medals. This is extraordinary. It is also reputed that he did not wear wound stripes or overseas service stripes on his sleeves when in uniform; emblems usually so proudly displayed by members of the First AIF.

Above all, Murray was brave. In the 1980s, members of the 13th Battalion recalled him in simple terms. 'Murray was an inspiration that night [at Gueudecourt]. He was a tiger. A wonderful man,' said Vic Groutsch. 'He was on his own that bloke. He had no fear,' according to Clarrie James. 'There was no doubt about that. He didn't give a continental.'[9]

The reader of this biography may feel that it is too uncritical of Murray; that it is a hagiography. In reply, it can only be said that to his World War I comrades he was a great hero; to his wife he was 'the most wonderful husband'; to his children, he was a loved and respected father; to his neighbours in the Queensland bush and the young soldiers of World War II he was 'The Colonel', a much admired figure.

The picture that seems to emerge of Harry Murray is one of an uncomplicated man with a good sense of humour who lived a practical type of life and enjoyed it; a man who had no great desire to change the world he lived in. The physical toughness and extraordinary endurance to strain and stress that he demonstrated so often in World War I stood him in good stead in civilian life. Despite his war wounds — particularly the first one, to his knee, which worried him most in later life — and the strains of war on his nervous system, he lived a hale and hearty life for most of his 85 years.

APPENDIX

HARRY MURRAY'S ARTICLES IN *REVEILLE*

'BRAVEST MAN IN THE AIF': MURRAY'S TRIBUTE

(*Reveille*, 31 December 1929, p. 8)

T hus Lt. Col. H.W. Murray, VC, pays tribute through *Reveille* to the memory of Major Percy Black, of the 16th Bn, who was killed at Bullecourt. Before Murray joined the 13th Bn he was with Black in Australia, Egypt and Gallipoli in the 16th Bn machine-gun section and in a letter to the editor, he refers to the death of Black and to the latter's premonition of it as follows:

'I cannot close without a few words about the bravest man in the AIF — Major Percy Black. He was shot through the head when between the front and support German lines and when a few yards in front of A Company of the 13th. He never spoke after he was hit.

'It may be of interest to your readers to know that Black knew Bullecourt was to be his last fight. Two days before the battle he said to me, "Well, Harry, we have been in a few stunts together but this is my last," and added, "I'll have that Hun front line first." And so he did.

'Percy Black was of Scotch parentage and evidently inherited some of the old Scotch superstition, and while realising danger and with the average human fear of the unknown, he was the most truly brave soldier and gentleman I ever knew.'

Referring to the advent of the tanks at Bullecourt — a subject widely discussed in the 14th and 16th Bn Histories — Col. Murray, in answer to the editor's request for his impressions, says:

'One of the main reasons is to do justice to at least one tank's crew, while so much (and unfortunately true) adverse criticism is being directed at the tanks generally, which participated at Bullecourt.

'My own impression was that the failure of the tanks was largely due to the personnel being chiefly mechanics and not soldiers and probably the mechanical crews had not the confidence in their machines necessary for them to show a bold front. One tank, however, did penetrate the German front line and was stopped by a hit, in a communication trench between the front and support lines. The crew bravely brought their guns out of the tank and manned the trenches with us. One tank was stopped halfway through the first wire by a direct hit, and the crew was shot down by machine-guns whilst trying to escape from the burning machines.

'The crews of these two tanks did all that brave men could do. The balance of the tanks was a dismal failure. At the Battle of Hamel and later, the men of the Tank Corps were splendid — brave, keen, efficient soldiers.'

THE SLIPPERY SLIDE GALLIPOLI THRILL

(*Reveille*, 31 March 1930, p. 9)

After six weeks in the trenches swapping bullets often at five yards range with the Turk, our battalion was taken out to Rest Valley. The track was over a steep hill, the descent of which was both smooth and slippery. We had been out a couple of hours, and the men, having picked their 'possies' for the night, were standing about in groups waiting for tea time.

Then we noticed a small party starting to descend the track to the valley. One of the members, when right near the top, slipped and sat down and slid in that position right to the bottom. On nearing us, we found it was a popular field officer of generous proportions. [Major J.P. McGlinn, then Brigade Major of the 4th Brigade.]

However, his popularity did not save the cheers and encores from the Diggers. But the worst was to come. On rising, the officer found that even the good Australian uniform was not equal to the strain it had been subjected to, and the seat of the pants was entirely gone!

This caused a renewed outburst of cheering which, in spite of angry looks, was maintained till the officer had side-stepped past the troops until he reached cover about 100 yards distant. We were all much better for the laugh but I still think that we got extra fatigue for the next three days. It was certainly worth it. Our able MO soon cured the gravel rash!

NATION'S BEST IN GALLIPOLI GRAVES

(*Reveille*, 31 March 1931, p. 7)

Whenever my thoughts turn to Gallipoli, memories come flooding in of the very fine fellows who fell in the first few weeks. Had they been spared, how far they would have gone in places of leadership among the AIF!

There were so many of these gallant fellows that it would be impossible, owing to space limitations, to mention them all. To mention a few would hardly be fair to the others who were equally brave; also, perhaps, it might mean a pang of pain to their dear ones in seeing such names in print. I think we lost better men in those first few weeks than we ever had afterwards, and I give this opinion with a knowledge of those whom we lost and of those who fought to the end.

Often we went hungry on Gallipoli — not through lack of food, but from the inability to eat the fare which was provided such as 'Fray Bentos' hard biscuits and inferior cheese. Even now I recall with horror the sticky mess of a huge cheese, melting on the hillside, into a long streak, almost to the valley below.

Our 'foraging expeditions' in the early hours — between 2 am and 4 am — for a ham or a tin of soft biscuits, or anything else that offered a change from monotonous and unappetising food, often enabled 'high living' for a day or two afterwards for the machine-gunners of the 16th Battalion — a unit with which I was then associated. Several times, to get past sentries on the beach, one of us would impersonate an officer, another his batman, and we would then have a free rein on the inner forage dumps which were comparatively unguarded. Two of us, from below, would tie our booty to a rope which would then be hauled up by our own mates at the top of the cliff. My only hope is that no person — wounded, sick or more deserving than ourselves — went hungry or thirsty as a result.

It was at Durrant's Post that I heard of a grisly but funny incident during the period that the 4th Brigade was resting at Lemnos. The story related to some past war, when a Colonel received a letter from a scientist friend requesting that he send him a skeleton of an enemy's head. The CO instructed his batman — an ex-naval man and a good forager and a hard case — to secure him a head; undamaged, if possible.

Two days later the batman reported to his chief that he had secured a head and mentioned, in casual voice, that as it had not long left its owner and offended the sense of smell, he had taken the liberty to boil it down so that it would not excite the postal authorities in transmission. He duly handed over the skeleton, which safely reached its destination.

GRAVE AND GAY VC'S REFLECTIONS

(*Reveille*, 1 August 1932, p. 13)

One of the most vivid recollections I have of the evening of August 5, 1915, was hearing a bandsman playing on his cornet Gounod's 'Serenade' — this and other selections — as we machine-gunners of the 16th Battalion were coming out of the line to join our unit in Rest Valley.

It was a beautiful afternoon — very peaceful and calm — and the notes of the cornet came floating up the hill with a wonderful sweetness and clarity. Every member of the 4th Brigade who was present will, I am sure, remember this diversion and the wonderful tranquillity which then prevailed — soon to be rudely broken by the attack on enemy territory which we launched that night.

Of that attack, during the darkness, I saw very little. As the advance went on, the machine-guns were close to the fighting but did not actually participate in it. At daybreak, we found ourselves at the foot of a small hill on the top of which was a sunken road held by about 60 Turks. Our units had become somewhat mixed during the night and in the charge to root the Turks out I first saw the Gurkha in action.

Five or six of them joined in the assault on the hill. The Turks stood their ground well and bayonets were used. The bayonet of an Australian [Murray himself] became entangled in a Turk and, while he was trying to free it, another Turk charged him. For a moment it looked as if our fellow would be certainly 'skewered' when suddenly I saw the charging Turk's head fly off. A Gurkha, from behind our man, had thrown his Kukri with deadly aim. By this time the few remaining Turks had bolted. The Australian thanked the Gurkha for saving his life. The Gurkha, however, merely smiled, picked up his weapon, wiped it on the dead Turk's uniform, and strolled off.

The incredulity of a 13th Battalion officer led to his being discomforted, much to the amusement of his mates, the following day. The position of a Turkish sniper was pointed out to this officer, who declared that it was impossible that any enemy soldier would dare to venture so close. Walking off, the officer exposed himself and promptly received a bullet in the foot, causing a flesh wound. He was greatly vexed, probably more so at having his notions about snipers upset than at the pain caused by the wound.

Another thing which I 'feelingly' remember was the plague of fleas in the Turkish dugouts. We were in shorts, and our bare legs were smothered in a few seconds. The Turkish dugouts were not popular with us.

Prior to the August advance we were all more or less sick with dysentery, but the change from the trenches to the comparatively open fighting of the first few days in our new positions seemed to benefit us, and it was certainly interesting. Our guns occasionally found good targets but we too, I'm afraid, gave the Turkish gunners opportunities of which they were quick to avail themselves.

About this time one of our chaps got the shock of his life. It was a hot afternoon and some skirmishing was going on. Suddenly he let out a yell as he received a bang in the side from a rifle bullet and felt a hot stream running down his leg. He turned and rushed down the hill to the dressing station. Dropping on to a stretcher there, he called to the doctor, 'I'm done! I'm bleeding to death! I can feel the blood pouring from my side.' The doctor made a hurried examination and then said, 'My dear fellow, you've been shot through the hot water bottle! The stream you feel is nothing but water escaping from the bottle.' Much relieved, the soldier jumped to his feet and went back to his job.

Also in amusing circumstances was a bullet wound suffered by a machine-gunner near the top of his third finger. He was about the maddest man on Gallipoli and hunted up and down all day in the hope of getting a shot at a Turk in revenge. He did not get much sympathy from his mates, though they were highly amused at his antics, dancing about and cursing.

It was well that we could laugh. One thing I noticed right through the war was how closely comedy and tragedy stalked each other.

EXPERIMENTAL STAGE TANKS AT BULLECOURT

(*Reveille*, 1 April 1933, p. 10)

Looking back over nearly 16 years, my impressions have changed but little in regard to the Battle of Bullecourt.

My attitude as a soldier was always 'ours not to reason why'. If our Higher Command issued an order it was our duty to carry it out as faithfully, completely and efficiently as we could. Had we succeeded in establishing ourselves beyond Riencourt during the first battle of Bullecourt it would have caused the German Higher Command much concern. My sole criticism is that too much was expected of the tanks; too much reliance placed on their effectiveness while they were still in (or little past) their experimental stage.

The ground over which we had to advance at Bullecourt was the easiest I had trodden on, but unfortunately, as we were attacking a re-entrant, the German machine-gunners and riflemen all opened enfilade fire on us, particularly from the right, where the enemy was comparatively unmolested. So severe was this fire at one period that I had to order A Company to lie down for a few minutes until the fire ceased.

Before reaching the German wire I could see that the 16th Bn was getting a heavy time, so I closed up on them to assist. Our casualties were so heavy that by the time we had taken both front and support line it was impossible to go further forward. Our job had originally been to leapfrog the 16th and take Riencourt and dig a trench line in front of it. Major Percy Black, D.S.O., D.C.M., C. de G., was killed between the two lines of trenches, his death being in the nature of a calamity to us there, and the AIF in general. He was the bravest man I ever knew, and I knew hundreds of them.

We held both the German lines — trenches of tremendous strength — but unfortunately for us we were overlooked from the higher ground on our right flank, right in front and rear, and direct front, from Riencourt. The upper stories of the houses in Riencourt were full of enemy troops. This made communication with our headquarters almost impossible, besides rather worrying to our position. So mixed had companies and battalions of the 4th Bde become and so critical was our position that it was decided to try and hold on as long as we could, without moving men to their own units.

We could have held these trenches if headquarters had believed the report that Captain Aarons (16th Bn) and myself made on our position and had given us the artillery support we asked for. This would have allowed our carrying parties to get supplies of bombs and enabled us to harass the German preparation for its counterattack.

Yet our Higher Command could not have come to any other decision for, from two different sources, it had received reports of our being beyond Riencourt. Our request was for heavy artillery fire on positions which — so headquarters was informed from the air, and by our artillery F.O.O. [forward observation officer] — were in our possession. They had also, on the other hand, received a report from the air almost exactly confirming Aaron's and mine, but to shell their own troops was altogether too terrible to contemplate.

So we eventually exhausted our bombs and grenades and had to face the prospect of capture or run the gauntlet of enfilade machine-gun and rifle fire as we made for the openings in the German wire. I never considered it possible to dig in behind the German wire. No body of men could have lasted there one minute, so exposed.

Amid all the tragedy and loss there that morning, one episode gave us complete satisfaction at the time. Most of the wounded having made a dash for the Australian lines, ten of us decided (as Germans were in the next bay of the trench) that it was time for us to go too. So, with seventy to a hundred of the enemy chasing us, we jumped into shell holes on his side of the wire to finish the argument — we would have been sitting shots for them if we had tried to cross the entanglement.

There was some dust and smoke at the time, and the Germans' machine-gunners, unable to distinguish their own men from us, almost completely wiped out our would-be captors. It has always been rather a mystery to me how we managed to cross that wire, it being too high to straddle and too thick to get one's leg through often. I ruined a perfectly good pair of breeches that morning.

I still do not let my mind dwell on the tragedy which cost the lives of so many wonderful comrades that day. Of the ten of us that left the German trench together, only four got back and one of these (Lieut. Tom Morgan) was killed by a shell as soon as he reached our front line. He was one of the best.

A little episode occurred to my runner, L./Cpl. C.W. Stewart, now of Pelaw Main (N.S.W.), that is of interest. He was wounded in the leg (which has been amputated since his return to Australia) and taken prisoner. He had been awarded the MM for bravery (he deserved the VC, as also did his mate, Rollings.) A German soldier tried to take the MM ribbon from Stewart's tunic. Stewart resisted, although passively allowing himself to be 'ratted' of all his valuables. A German officer, hearing the disturbance, asked the reason for it, and on being informed, severely reprimanded the soldier and sent him about his business. Stewart told me about it in London after the Armistice.

TRAINING JUNIORS FIELD RANKS

(*Reveille*, 1 June 1933, p. 2)

I have long felt that some of the soundest and most unselfish of the good work done in the AIF has received very little public attention. I refer to the splendid training given to junior officers by their COs who were in Australia's permanent forces.

Men like Colonels Durrant, Peck and Christie, for instance. How they selected from their junior officers those whom, in their opinion, showed the most fitness for senior command and quietly guided and trained them; passing on their gifts and knowledge; recommending the most suitable works to study; directing their charges in the handling of men, both collectively and individually; and, in short, doing their utmost to pass on all their well-acquired knowledge in order that, when the occasion arose, they would have officers to assume command and maintain the wonderfully high standard of efficiency and discipline that these COs had ingrained in their own battalions.

Of all senior officers, I naturally knew Durrant best, and could tell of many times he set us right. No one ever knew from him that he had done it. He gave us every opportunity of visualising the situations that would arise, and of seeing their solving, guiding us by example and precept, always demanding the best, but always the first to say 'well done' — and it was worth a lot to hear him say that; tempering the strictest discipline with a wonderful comradeship; strafing us in a powerful way all of his own for our misdeeds, but never letting anyone outside the battalion do it; and, above all, teaching us to regard our men as a most sacred charge, to personally see to their wellbeing, and lead them both physically and by example.

Durrant's own standards were high, and so lucidly sound were his own actions and commands that each one felt that he, too, must do his very utmost for the battalion and the AIF.

Durrant started early with me. I had been in the 13th Bn, a newly fledged officer, only for a few weeks when he 'matted' me. It was the first and only time, for when I left the orderly room I knew exactly, as an officer, what was my job. The fault of mine was not very grave — leaving our trenches at Durrant's Post one quiet afternoon for half an hour to see our brigade M.G. officer without having asked permission. Durrant strafed me most thoroughly, and then gave me kind and valuable advice, which I never forgot, and which later steered me safely through much troubled water.

From that time on, my promotions and successes (if any) I owe mainly to his training, and I know if my friend, Douglas Marks, was alive, he would concur in all this. He too had often remarked to me how much we owed to the 'Old Man', as we affectionately called Durrie to each other.

I have no doubt that many others had similar experience with other COs and I trust that an abler pen than mine will take this up and pay tribute to those gallant and unselfish soldier-comrade-mentors of ours whose best was freely given to maintain for Australia the glorious prestige of her troops.

Also, from many of the CMF militia officers, too, we received valuable training. For fear of overlooking some, I hardly like naming any; but since I hope others will do justice to those they knew, I would like to mention Brig.-General Drake-Brockman, the late Lt. Col. T. McSharry, and that dear, kind, capable gentleman soldier, Lt. Col. Tilney.

I cannot close without paying tribute to my guide and adviser after I became a CO — Major General Sir William Glasgow. As new battalions, the M.G. companies were not easy to weld together, and such success as I achieved in command of a machine-gun battalion, I owe largely to Sir William, who was always ready to listen and to counsel, although he was a busy man. He was quick to detect any weakness and always had a sure, firm and clear road to show out of the worst trouble.

HIS HARDEST BATTLE: WHEN DISCIPLINE MASTERED FEAR

(*Reveille*, 1 December 1935, pp. 33, 48)

Throughout history, great generals have always recognised the supreme value of discipline. It has been alleged that, although Australian troops made good soldiers, they lacked discipline. This I could never agree with, because I maintain that it was the discipline, traditions, and the code of the AIF that enabled Australia to play a creditable part in the Great War. Without discipline one can never have an army — nothing but a rabble.

I think it was Thackeray who wrote that he supposed it was because all men were such cowards at heart that deeds of bravery were so universally acclaimed, and doubtless that great writer, with his keen knowledge of human nature, was right. As far as I am personally concerned, I know he was right.

I fully recognise the value of preliminary training and discipline, as without either I could not have done my job. Cowardice — or self-preservation, which is practically the same thing — is the first law of nature, and while some men may be so constituted that they require no artificial stimuli, I cannot make any such claim. I fought many a hard battle (to put it bluntly) between duty and funk, but the hardest of all, in which the decision had to be made in a split second, and while fleeing from the enemy, shall form a part of the following story.

We were attacking in front of Pozières, and A Company of the 13th Battalion had better luck than the troops on either flank, having achieved its objectives. This, however, left both flanks in the air, and soon it became evident that the enemy was trying to cut us off; and at the same time were delivering strong frontal bombing attacks along his C.T. [communication trench]. Immediate retreat was essential, and to effect this under such hostile pressure it was necessary to hold the enemy in check, while retreating along the captured trench, falling back successively on to a number of hastily thrown up strong points.

Unfortunately, we had run very short of hand grenades, and the cool, heady, courageous men who pressed us were well aware of our disabilities and pushed their advantage relentlessly. Cleverly, they mixed their attacks, twice trying an 'over-the-top' enveloping movement, but each time a fierce and deadly response from our riflemen and Lewis gunners taught them the futile and dangerous nature of such tactics.

From thence onwards, they relied upon bombing entirely. Altogether we retired on to seven successive points, we kept the enemy well in check all the time and got all our wounded away. Our men were cool, confident, and grimly determined despite the continuous pressure. After each successive minor retirement, Freddy Doust would send a message to me that he was OK and that was the signal to send most of the front line post back, giving them a couple of minutes start, while we made all the show we could. Then we sent the few remaining riflemen back, following a minute later with the two last Diggers and the officer [Murray himself].

All this was done in orderly manner, with light casualties, and heavier losses amongst the bolder Germans, till we had reached the fifth post. Bad news awaited us there. I was informed that our supply of bombs was almost exhausted and we could only throw an occasional one. Naturally this soon became clear to the enemy who, in consequence, attacked more strongly and confidently. As Company commander, my job was to be the last man away from each successive post; and by that time the Germans were in the next bay of the trench and coming on at a run, to judge by the sound of their exploding bombs.

We reciprocated with our few remaining Mills' bombs, then off we went again. I could hear excited, guttural voices, together with the rattle of enemy accoutrements, and I experienced the usual fierce struggle between the natural promptings and duty, but the discipline of the AIF enabled me to see it out. Even in those hectic moments, I had experienced many a cold shiver as I thought of the bayonets of the counterattacking force, because it seemed to me, as I ran, that I was almost within reach of those lethal, shining blades.

Just before reaching the fifth post, and it looked as if we were clear, a bomb dropped one of the two men in front of me. The survivor, half dazed by the explosion, wounded superficially by metal fragments and not really comprehending what had happened, continued his flight. I jumped over the body of the prostrate man who appeared to be dead, but just as I did so his eyes opened and it was plain that he was alive, but how badly wounded it was impossible to say. His leg was doubled and twisted and, although he did not speak, his eyes were eloquent.

It was then that I fought the hardest battle of my life between an insane desire to continue running and save my own life, or to comply with the sacred traditions of the AIF and stop to help a wounded comrade.

Surely I must be bayoneted if I stopped for an instant. The enemy was coming up at the double, having no opposition. I often dread to think of what I might have done. I was safe enough at the time and all I had to do was to keep going; there was only a straight run 50 yards to my mates, and despite that poor, twisted leg, those mute lips, and pathetic eyes, it was really only the mechanical habit engendered by strict discipline that forced me to do what I did. I dropped onto my shaking knees and pulled him on to my back. He helped like a hero with his one sound leg and off we staggered with Fritz just coming into our bay.

We outpaced him, however, largely because the impetuosity of his advance had more than once been checked. Already he had been pulled up with a jerk four times, and such things test the mettle of the bravest and most seasoned troops. At last I reached a haven of temporary safety and now had others to support us. I was once more among my mates and the wounded Digger was safe, for a little while, at all events.

We were almost at our wit's end, though, as there was a long way to go and still the wily foe maintained his cruel onslaught. It looked as if we were to be reduced to our last resort — the bayonet — but then I heard dear old Bob Henderson's voice calling for me. He was our bombing officer and I called out promptly, 'Here I am, Bob — have you any bombs?' and back came his reply, like a returning wave, and couched in strong Australianese, 'ANY BLOODY AMOUNT! THROWERS TO THE FRONT!'

No need for any more, and now the fierce music of bursting

[German] bombs was mingled with that of our own — sweetest of all sounds. Australia was taking strong command of the situation once again. Bob and his men exchanged deadly compliments with the enemy, beating them backwards for over 100 yards of the trench; the breathless crisis was over at last, and we retired in our own time, strolling over to the jumping-off position which was to be permanently held.

All this happened at night. However bold a man may be by day, much of his courage evaporates by night, but the whole incident impressed upon me, as never before, the supreme value of strict discipline coupled with the force of accepted traditions. I am not ashamed to confess that it was these things that enabled me to do what, after all, was merely my job, and being done all along the front line on both sides day after day. The ability to do such things depends largely upon discipline.

Many men could undoubtedly relate similar experiences and it is with the idea of encouraging their confessions that I have set the ball rolling. For my own part, I can only repeat what I have already written, that without discipline, and rigid training, I could never have done my day's work, and it is to the system of discipline enforced by the AIF that I lift my hat, because it transformed thousands of men — nervy and highly strung like myself — enabling them to do work which without discipline they would have been quite incapable of performing.

MEMORIES OF FIRST BULLECOURT

(*Reveille*, 1 December 1936, pp. 4, 56–9, 63–5)

Captain Mitchell suggested the *Reveille* readers would like to have some of my impressions of First Bullecourt (April 11, 1917), and while his own dramatic and forceful descriptions of our campaigning, with its many episodes and incidents, leave little more to be written, I will nevertheless jot down my recollections of that battle. I must, however, impress upon those who read this article that it is just a Company commander's narrative. Every man in each Company did his job to the utmost, and the danger of the narrative from one man who took part in the attacks is that it may give the impression that his unit was the only one there.

I am able, of course, to write only of what I actually saw, and must condense even that, leaving out many acts and passing over many men who thoroughly deserve to be mentioned — for to record everything one observed or experienced in that great fight would be a task from which even a Homer might well shrink. Again, since I am writing entirely from memory, it is possible that some errors may creep into the narrative, and for these, if there are any, I must apologise beforehand.

My own view of the decision to attack Bullecourt is that the conception generally was sound but that faulty tactics were employed. As the High Command relied chiefly on surprise there could be no preliminary bombardment, but that meant risking a great deal. Too much reliance was placed on the tanks, which at that time were almost untried, certainly unproved; and their personnel did not seem to be well chosen. They were manned by mechanics instead of soldiers. War is admittedly an affair for specialists, but all partaking in front-line operations must be soldiers as well.

In fairness, however, to the drivers of the tanks, who generally did their best, it should be noted that they were acutely conscious of the deficiencies of their machines. We, never having seen tanks in action, did not place any extravagant value on them. All we hoped for was that they would succeed in reaching and breaking through the wire entanglements, thus enabling us to get into the open where rifles and machine-guns would count more than anything else, and enable us to even the scores. I have often wondered whether those responsible merely sent the tanks as an encouraging gesture, relying upon the fighting qualities of the AIF to do the rest; if so, they were wrong. In war one has to deal with stark realities, and men have their limits; for an attack to be successful machinery must play its full part. Had there been a preliminary bombardment followed by a 'creeping barrage', an entirely different story would have been told.

At Bullecourt, the 13th Battalion was at its zenith as a fighting force. Colonel Durrant had thoroughly trained us, both physically and technically. We had been well fed all the time and, in consequence, were as fit as it was possible to be. Owing to a confusion of orders and counter orders, we had been marching for the best part of 48 hours prior to hopping over and, although this was unfortunate, only one man in A Company dropped out. Our job was to support the 16th and then to leapfrog past Riencourt, dig in to the rear of the village and mop it up (as would also the 15th Battalion supporting the 14th) and shoot the Germans at our leisure.

'Great was the risk and glorious the prize!'

Unfortunately, as events turned out, it was the Germans who shot most of the few remaining Australians, of whom — in the running, at all events — I was one until I became too weary to run further.

Early on the morning of April 11, 1917, we were all in the sunken road at Noreuil, still uncertain as to whether we were to attack. I was hoping that the plan would be abandoned because it seemed to be a most desperate gamble. By means of a frontal attack, unsupported by artillery fire, the 4th Division was to assay the task of beating a force of splendidly disciplined, efficient and brave men holding a strongly fortified position.

Hopeless. Hopeless.

All doubts were finally resolved when Captain Parkes, adjutant of the 16th Battalion, came along at the double and gave orders for that battalion to move at once to the jumping-off position, about two miles ahead. Almost immediately afterwards the 13th received similar orders. We realised then it was to be a case of 'box-on'. A few shells were flying about; to minimise casualties and get better walking, we moved in single file with ten yards' distance between platoons. One shell fell right on the narrow track we were following, directly between Nos. 2 and 3 platoons, but, fortunately, hit no one.

At the sunken railway we rested for a bit and had a smoke, and ten minutes before zero climbed the steep bank and lay in open country, Company in line. Our reason for abandoning shelter was to make sure of advancing all together and to accustom the men to being in the open in No-Man's Land. Day was just breaking, visibility being limited to fifty yards. Watches ticked on remorselessly. Zero!!! and off we went.

At first we could see and hear the tanks, which were not going well. Soon a terrific rifle and machine-gun fire broke out, and I wondered how the 16th were faring. We swung along a bit faster, the men keeping a wonderful line. The whole front was now an illuminated panorama of swift stabbing lights, with the blended roar of rifles and machine-guns sounding like the crackle of a bushfire fanned by the wind and racing through a field of ripe wheat — and, like wheat stalks, our men were collapsing before it. Punctuating this sustained and furious roar were the thunderous crashes of exploding shells, hardly needed, however, in face of the more imminent danger.

I could see the rear Company of the 16th getting unshirted Hell. So far, we had practically escaped, but suddenly the ground around, in front, under our feet, leaped to feverish life; spattered, whipped and churned by swathes of machine-gun bullets. I had kept a few yards ahead of our Company in order to watch the flanks and see how they were faring, and I realised at once, from the shifting arc of fire, that the Germans were searching for us; it was plain that they could not see us. I roared out: 'Get down, men, till it passes'; setting the example myself.

It was just then that Lieut. John Brown fell — I saw him topple and felt quite sick. Severely wounded as he was, he walked back to the RAP [Regimental Aid Post] and had his wound dressed, and then started to return to us, but fainted on the way from loss of blood; no lack of morale there. Jack (who belonged to Albury) was an ideal infantryman, brave, capable, cheerful, full of fun and just as full of fight when necessary, strong as two ordinary men, and one of the pick where all were good enough; as good and stout a mate as ever I knew. His exploits, faithfully chronicled, would furnish an epic sufficient almost to fill an issue of *Reveille*. The great game ended for him at Neuve Eglise almost twelve months later.

The intense fire eased off us, swept away like a capricious storm of rain. There was now more light and I could see that the 16th had reached the wire and were being cut to pieces. We couldn't stand that. They had no thought of quitting as they should have done. It was necessary to support them; no use stopping here. A Company responded at once to the call and soon were up to the terrible wire, which of course should have been previously demolished by our artillery. Ahead, halfway through the wire, and ringed by fire, was a lone tank, showers of sparks flying off her as rifle and machine-gun bullets lashed her piteously. Still, the crew, heavily beleaguered, fought gallantly on, serving their guns till they were put out of action.

Bullets whined and spat like burning raindrops about that fatal wire; surely an ant would not emerge alive from such an inferno? What chance had we of getting clear? Still taking all, we were returning nothing. We poured impetuously along the narrow gap made by the tank, scourged by continuous fire up to where it had stopped.

I first tried to get through to the left, but the cursed wire was intact there, and after going a few feet, I saw a machine-gun on the right-hand side of the tank firing at our rear. We rushed around, and sure enough there it was, blazing away furiously. Those German gunners were brave men, since they must have known they would be killed almost immediately — but why mention that when all were brave? They were put out of action speedily.

How we got through the remaining wire, I don't know. A rifle bullet grazed the back of my neck, dropping me for a second. I was done! No, only a false alarm. Up again. The entanglement was just too high to straddle and so crossed and intertwisted that it formed an 8 ft mesh netting of barbed wire on which the enemy fire, converging from all points, sang a ceaseless death song. It was Gallipoli all over again; the marvel was that anybody escaped.

At last, a pitiable remnant, we were over the wire. While rushing forward to join the 16th, we encountered another narrow belt of wire which checked us, but only for a few seconds; and now, at last, our Company — decimated but still unbeaten, the survivors thirsting for revenge — reached the mighty Hindenburg Line. This was what we wanted. There was a fierce, bitter fight for a few seconds with bayonet and bomb and the trench was ours.

Now for the next step; at least there was no wire to stop us this time. The thought of our mates in that wire behind; the sight of Germans ahead firing upon them! No time to waste. Just then Percy Black — the bravest man in the AIF — who had been gallantly leading the remnants of the 16th, threw up his hands and dropped. It was an inspiration to watch the fight that gallant fellow had put up; he was so cool. Another of our best men gone.

Forward again, another fierce, breathless struggle, and the next trench was ours. This was all hand-to-hand stuff, and we were getting a good bit of our own back. But how many good Australian lives would have been saved with proper artillery preparation; it would have been easier for us to have taken the front line if the wire obstructions had been blown away. Losses in the attacking companies at this stage were fully 60 per cent — and we were only starting! We had come prepared for a good deal of open going, and so carried additional SAA [small arms ammunition]. We hadn't sufficient hand-grenades for trench fighting but our losses were too heavy to permit of our advancing, against such opposition, into the open country beyond the second Hindenburg Line. I feel sure that, if we had an adequate supply of grenades, the Germans would never have recaptured that portion of their line taken by the 4th Brigade — we always came out well in a grenade fight which suited our boys to a T.

At this stage the battalions were hopelessly mixed but it was in just one of those situations that Australians were in their element. Our system of discipline permitted the rank and file to give full expression to their individuality in times of intense crisis; every man was a potential officer. German discipline, on the other hand, tended to make machines of men. I am not in any way reflecting upon the military organisation of that mighty race — the war definitely vindicated their qualities as fighters — but their system of discipline, if it had been applied to our boys, would have destroyed one of the Australian's most valuable qualities — 'initiative'.

Hastily organising our defences, we began to draw each unit together, but heavy and persistent counterattacks soon stopped this. These attacks, while keeping us busy, were repulsed easily enough, and wherever possible we organised minor counterattacks ourselves, getting excellent targets in that rapidly changing kaleidoscope, but we had to husband our resources. Roy Wilson boldly took his Vickers gun and crew into a dangerously advanced position, and, so deadly was his fire that he soon made amends for the losses of the 4th M.G. Coy., of which he was an NCO. By taking risks he secured a splendid field of fire, all Germans within range falling like grass before the sweep of giant mower. Yes, Roy did good work that day.

The action now resembled a bushfire which has been partly beaten out, the main blaze being broken up into smaller detached fires, all heavily attacked by groups of fire fighters. German bombing parties counterattacked in force from the right, sustaining a swift and bloody repulse from the 16th. With sufficient numbers, and grenades, I feel sure we could have driven them out of all the trenches.

In that swiftly moving human drama, one episode among many etched itself upon my mind. Before the attack, the 16th had detailed a small party whose job was to fill in the captured trench, after we cleaned up Riencourt, in order to let the cavalry cross. Only one member of this party reached the trenches and, about 9 o'clock, some men reported to me that a man of the 16th was filling in the trench, preventing them from getting along. I went to the place, and sure enough, there he was ON TOP! Quite oblivious of the danger, a splendid target for enemy fire, picking and shovelling industriously and filling the trench.

'What are you doing, lad?' I demanded.

He stopped, and straightening up, told me he had orders from his colonel to fill the trench.

'Get down at once,' I said. 'Don't fill that trench; we want it and you'll be killed if you stay there.'

He grinned uncertainly, hesitated for a moment, and finally prepared to obey, when the sickening familiar thud of a rifle bullet told me he had been squarely hit. He sounded a long shuddering 'Ah-h-h' and toppled over, never speaking again.

For word painting and command of language generally, it is said that Homer has never been excelled, but he had the strangest lack of judgment. In his magnificent epic, Ajax is depicted as defying the lightning. Very wonderful perhaps, and also not a little melodramatic. Would Ajax have faced that steel and leaden death, as did that Digger, armed with a shovel only as Death in a million shapes, 'horsed on the sightless couriers of the air', screamed, whined and sobbed about him? I wonder. Elemental stupidity, magnificent disregard of possibilities, epic obedience. He was, in short, an Australian Digger doing his job.

At another stage of the battle I saw a party of Germans advancing (as they thought) under cover. One of our Lewis gunners, smiling thoughtfully, waited until they had reached a point devoid of cover — then his gun spoke and a spray of deadly missiles did the rest.

Our Lewis gun sections had suffered heavily along with the rest of the attacking force, but the survivors had only one thought; to struggle on with their guns and ammunition, each man carrying three men's loads. One could always rely on such things. The same with the 4th Machine-Gun Company's men; staggering along, they got up to the German trenches with their Vickers and ammunition and served their guns with deadly effect, like the men they were. I haven't the descriptive power to do sufficient justice to their work. All I can say is that they did splendidly.

But, to get back to my narrative. The position now was most critical as, owing to our being in a re-entrant of the Hindenburg Line, the Germans were able to enfilade our rear, particularly from the

Quéant or south side. This made it extremely dangerous for any runners going back with messages. Since both of my runners were casualties, I called for volunteers. Serg. Charlie Trick of A Company offered at once, and with him a mate from the 16th. Captain D.S. Aarons, the senior remaining officer of the 16th, and I, sent messages to our respective COs and, in spite of the difficult and dangerous passage, Trick and his mate got through with them and back again to us with the replies.

As we could see the Germans massing at Riencourt and pouring along a communication trench on our right, we had made an urgent appeal for a barrage on the German positions. We had also stressed the necessity for fresh supplies of grenades and SAA to be sent up under cover of heavy shelling. The guns were there, serried rows of steel monsters, waiting to be used. The shells were there also and, although Colonels Durrant and Drake-Brockman did all that men could do to get us that barrage — and no carrying party of any kind could hope to get through to us without protection — an artillery observing officer, and also an airman, had reported that we were beyond Riencourt, and these reports made our senior officers pause, and finally decide not to shell! General Brand also did what he could to get us artillery support, recognising the extreme gravity of our position, but it was withheld! Mistakes of course, but what tragic ones!

Our gunners were standing by, lanyards in hand, praying for orders to send over a protective curtain of shrapnel and high explosives, more potent far than the fabled shield of Pallas — but orders were orders. And so the guns retained their silent immobility while we fought out the last stages of our hopeless battle in the Hindenburg Line without their assistance. When I think of the lives that could have been saved, even at that stage, I feel like saying hard things, but all men and sections did their best. Mistakes were often made by all of us and it is best to pass over such incidents without further comment.

So the bitterly unequal fight went on, the Germans heavily

reinforced and with endless munitions continuing their ceaseless counterattacks. Our boys fought their losing battle, not with the blind courage of the charging bull, but with smiling lips, and light mocking jests; albeit with keenly observant eyes, ready to give back something just a bit better than they received, despite the mounting odds against them. In dozens we watched them drop. Oh for that barrage! How sweet it would have been to listen to the sudden opening of the full-throated iron chorus — the coughing grunts of the howitzers, mingled with the sharper explosions of the high velocity guns and the deep roar of the long-rangers followed by the crash of descending thunderbolts on the German line.

It was maddening. We could do little more, unaided. Most serious feature of all now was that while the German pressure from both left and right was increasing, our own resources were ebbing fast. We had certainly got the best of the earlier grenade fighting, inflicting heavy losses, but our supplies — supplemented by German bombs that we had found in the captured trenches — were now getting dangerously low. We could have held the front easily by rifle fire but, owing to the heavy demands, our SAA was also diminishing fast. We had to economise and we shortened our line by placing special firing parties in shell holes and short trenches. The beginning of the end!

It was just then that Sergt. Trick brought the reply back. THERE WAS TO BE NO BARRAGE! Unsatisfied longing changed to sickening certainty! It amounted to a sentence of death. Why were we not supported? It had been odds of 20 to 1 against the gallant Trick even going through that fire-swept zone, but he took the odds coolly and won out; as many another did at critical moments. But there was to be no barrage.

We were now being very hard-pressed and fought back bitterly enough; but if enemy losses were heavier than ours, theirs could immediately be made good, whereas ours could not. If only it would snow and give the lads a chance of cover going back. Men who had all along been buoyed up by the expectation of support looked serious and asked, 'What now? We must get back or go as prisoners of war to Germany.' None of us fancied that. It was to be back with a tempest of fire commanding the only line of retreat, and this would intensify immediately we entered it. There was also that uncut wire to cross! Nevertheless, all decided to give it a flutter in small parties, at short intervals, in the hope of attracting less attention. Shortly afterwards, gritting their teeth, our boys plunged into the blood bath, some only getting a few feet before being shot down.

Just here, let me say, I had mentioned that any man who wished to surrender was fully entitled to do so, for the chances of escaping were almost nil. It was like expecting to run for hundreds of yards through a violent thunderstorm without being struck by any of the raindrops. Still they chanced it and soon all entered the fiery lane of blood and death — that is, except ten who tried to cover the retreat. The Germans, by this time, were closing to within ten yards of us on both flanks.

Little Sergeant Gildea, game as a pebble, shouted at last, 'I'm looking for Captain Murray,' and, head downwards, he dashed unscathed through that deadly circle of bullets, buzzing like a swarm of enraged bees. Sole survivor of his little band, he got to me and we kept together until we cleared that stretch of wire. Lieut. Tom Morgan (of Narromine, NSW), game to the core, was there too.

Before we left, a few breathless seconds were consumed in tearing up copies of our code signals and treading them into the mud. Then off we went. So eager were the Germans to get us, they actually followed us out into the open. Great fighters! — we must raise our hats to them. Now we turned for the last and most hopeless fight of the day; completely surrounded as we were, it looked as if it could only end one way, but, owing to the dust, haze and smoke, some of the German machine-gunners mistook their men for fleeing Australians and opened a murderous fire upon them, completely relieving the pressure on us and thus giving us time to get over the wire. All in the day's work, and we offered no objection; at all events we were not the only ones fated to make mistakes that day. Fortunately, they did not see our small party but, as we were negotiating the wire, I felt a rifle bullet cut me across the back, just breaking the skin.

Now, at last, we were practically clear of the intense danger zone and the long strain, physical and mental, took sudden effect. All at once, I felt completely exhausted and unnerved and could only go a few yards at a time. The terrain, not having been cut up by shell fire, offered little cover. We reached one small crater with no shelter in sight beyond it. After a short rest we emerged, and had gone a few yards, when a shell whined viciously overhead, blowing out a splendid crater 20 yards ahead. Good. Just then a machine-gun got on to us and, running feebly, we tumbled into the crater. Putting out my hand, I felt a strip of hot metal from the exploded shell which, strangely enough, acted as a tonic, bucking me up a little bit.

When a man has reached such a stage of physical and nervous exhaustion after hours of desperate fighting, a little thing will revive him. The mind becomes extraordinarily clear and works at great speed, all feeling of fear being absent. Lying down, I began to think. Would this cursed war never end? We couldn't last forever and were now doing all we could. Courage! Why speak of it here? It is a meaningless word. The task was to conserve physical strength and nerve force in the hope that the task would finish before we did. Anyhow, there were plenty more. It was no time for thinking as to how many had been killed that day, and how many were lying wounded back there. Imagination may be a fine quality, but not back there. No, it was no good to a man there. In England they were working busily. I had seen delicate women, some of whom had never before soiled their hands, turning out shells, driving lorries through the streets, unloading, even handling pick and shovel, blistering their delicate fingers. Others again, abandoning maidenly reserve, were warning young men in plain and unmistakable language of the terrible dangers of the London streets, giving them precise and practical instruction in the way to avoid disease that would unfit them for further service — they must keep bodies healthy for their country's sake. Pure women. Wonderful women.

Well, time to be off again. We got up stiffly at last, stumbling and dragging our feet, not caring much, taking no notice at all of the great shells that still plunged and burst all around us. Finally, we reached our old front line and began to see and realise other things. Poor old Tom Morgan was there, siting on a box, his head between his hands. I had never seen him downhearted before, but he had seen his friend 'Bluey' Shirtley killed just before, blown to pieces, and Tom was taking it hard. Just then a German 4.2 landed near Tom and when we picked him up there was a slight smile on his strong lips. He might have been shaking hands with Bluey over on the other side just then. Tom was always smiling and took the game as he found it. Both he and Bluey were officers that it would be hard to replace; cheerful, bright, and ready for anything under all circumstances.

There is not much more to tell. We were relieved at dusk. Colonel Durrant saw to it personally that every man got a feed, and that all had left the trench before he took me along that same narrow track by which we had come forward — was it yesterday, or last year? No, only this morning. I was still so exhausted that I could only walk a few steps at a time. The Germans were still sending over a lot of big stuff, anticipating that supports would be moving to the front, but Durrie would not leave me (as I wanted him to), and let me come along in my own time. There was a strong likelihood of one of those ripping, tearing 5.9s getting us. What did it matter? What did anything matter? It was surely coming to us some time or other.

I wanted to lie down and sleep; sleep above all things, and let Durrant get away from the shelling, but not he. Someone from the relieving battalion had given him a flask of whisky, and he gave me several nips. As a rule a little spirits affects me, but that night it had no more effect than water. At last Durrant got me out and we received a very welcome surprise before we reached Noreuil. A black shape just ahead proved to be good old Ted Plunkett, our quartermaster, who had pluckily led our horses up through the shellfire. This was better. What a feeling of relief to sit back luxuriously while my neddy stepped smartly forward. I felt I could go to sleep and leave it all to him. Besides being game, I think Ted was the best quartermaster in the AIF — certainly a big claim to make — but he managed to keep the tucker up under any circumstances and when we needed something, even something that we really should not have needed, Ted put up such a tale that even our excellent but hard-headed DADOS [Deputy Assistant Director of Ordinance Services], Joe Tuckett, would swallow.

I have mentioned some names in passing, picking out a few deeds from that grim phantasmagoria of struggling, fighting men, but, of course, hundreds of other fine actions were performed that day. Every man who followed his officer through those shrieking fields of fire was a hero. The whole battle was as hopeless as the charge of the Light Brigade at Balaclava, and the effort was sustained far beyond the limits usually assigned to human endurance. Clinging automatically to the discipline of the AIF, the few survivors had to hang on, when, by all the laws, human resources should have been completely expended, and when even mind and body seem to be divorced by a ceaseless succession of stunning and stupendous events. It is only necessary to mention that, in our Company alone, there were 17 unwounded survivors; this will give an idea of the losses as a whole.

To sum up dispassionately, I must repeat that Bullecourt was a mistake on the part of the High Command, for the attempt to carry that strong, cleverly sited and fortified position by infantry assault alone, assisted by a few unproved tanks, was a military blunder of the first magnitude. It amounted to overestimating our infantry and underestimating the German, and it was fatal to underrate such men. Secondly, the one solitary advantage the High Command had relied upon — 'surprise' — was lacking; the Germans having been fully apprised of the attack.

If General Gough's estimate of what was a sufficient number of tanks — twelve — had been correct, with 500 we could have beaten the Germans back to Berlin. The number supplied was totally inadequate, apart from the fact that tanks have very definite limits as major assaulting weapons. They are valuable as adjuncts to infantry (or were, at all events, then) but they certainly cannot take the place of artillery bombardment. At Hamel in 1918, we had 100 tanks, greatly improved and splendidly manned, and they were most effectively employed. In the main, the strategic conception at Bullecourt was sound, but strategy to be successful must take into consideration and accurately assess all tactical factors, after allotting to each branch its real value and proper place in the general scheme, and even then allow a considerable margin for the unexpected.

Before closing, I would like to pay a special tribute to Durrant, whose work shone out even in that assembly of men. From the outset sceptical of a successful issue, he soon found his worst anticipations realised, and knew only too well from the calibre of the attacking force that the attempt would be pushed through, despite the hideous slaughter. Forced to wait in utter futility, and unable to take a hand in the actual fighting while his men were being cut to pieces, his was one of the hardest roles to fill. Early on April 11th, a shell had killed our doctor, and a number of others, and severely wounded Douglas Marks, our adjutant; Durrant being the only unwounded survivor in the vicinity. He saw the business through to the last, himself doing a dozen men's work. Hard work too, and heady work.

At long last the business was ended, all survivors were in and the wounded cared for. I then witnessed the meeting of the four colonels of the 4th Brigade with General Brand, who was waiting in his advanced HQ to see the last of his men come out. The COs came last and exchanged one long look. Weary to death as I was, I flinched at their expression, laden with bitter condemnation of those responsible for the ghastly blunder. Behind those burning eyes, and stern set lips, one could sense the dammed-back floods of denunciation which might break forth at any moment, but no word issued from these iron men. The High Command had blundered, and men had to pay the price; that was all. Had I been responsible, I would have sooner gone through another Bullecourt than have faced those men, although their lips were sealed. They seemed to epitomise in their stern silence all the tragic terror and heroic futility of Bullecourt — bitter grief and stern indignation at the recollection of their men, torn, dismembered, and blown to shreds on that fatal barrier; then the hand-to-hand fighting, the temporary advantage, and finally the grim hanging-on and waiting for the barrage and munitions that never came. In that lightning-like retrospect, one incident stood out cameo like in its clarity — the figure of that youth desperately making a passage for the cavalry that could not come.

Well, it was a quick death, and though it might weaken a man to see his comrades fall, there are worse things than that; far worse. All at once I felt fresh strength flow into my veins. We were going to win. Bullecourt was only an incident.

COLONEL TILNEY PASSES — A LOVABLE CHARACTER

(*Reveille*, 1 March 1937, p. 27)

All members of the 13th and 16th Battalions will learn with sorrow of the passing of Colonel Tilney, so well known and universally loved by all of us.

I remember him in the first days of the forming of the 16th Bn at Blackboy Hill, WA — a kind, keen soldier with a wonderful understanding of the trials and difficulties of the private; ever ready to praise and encourage, and so very slow to blame. Approachable, and always with kindly words of encouragement and advice, he had a genial smile and a calm, unruffled temperament at all times.

I remember when we attacked Dead Man's Ridge in the early days of Gallipoli and we were getting Hades. He was there with his quiet confidence and inspired us and kept us calm under terrific fire. Later, when CO of the 13th Battalion on Gallipoli, in Egypt and in France, he never changed. All of us felt compelled to do our utmost in return for the splendid fair deal we got from him. He was wonderfully strong yet had a quiet sense of humour, was an excellent raconteur, and loved telling the Mess a yarn in a deliberate and witty manner.

Once in Egypt his horse dumped him. The penalty in the Mess for an officer being 'dumped' was to shout for the Mess with a further penalty for divulging the name of a lady. In owning up to the liability over being dumped, he mentioned the name of the mare he was riding; and so fell to the other penalty, much to the delight of the younger element, and to judge by his eyes and smile, more to his.

He could reprimand one in a telling way when occasion demanded it, but I noticed after the 'telling off' he always made a point of showing special and friendly interest in the person incurring the reproof.

It was such men as Colonel Tilney who so quickly trained the raw material of the original AIF into shape and developed and directed the latent possibilities of the AIF rank and file into the splendid force it so quickly became. At the Front, he was one who guided and led it, setting an example of efficient and unselfish leadership and comradeship that lived to the last of the War and still lives in the memory of all who survive.

The Empire, Australia and the AIF owe Colonel Tilney and those other splendid senior officers a tremendous debt for the wonderful training, guiding and leading so freely and unostentatiously given. We are, again, heavy losers in that another of those who did so much has passed on.

GET THROUGH AT ANY COST

(*Reveille*, 1 April 1937, pp. 6, 52)

War is a vast complex — a fearful and wonderful mosaic. From field-marshal to cook, all branches of the service are indispensable and contribute in varying degrees of usefulness to the final victory. I have the thought that we (readers and writers to *Reveille*) should spare the time to chronicle all individual actions, supplying thumbnail sketches of all, from the highest to the lowest. With the Editor's permission, I shall open the ball by a short article devoted to our Runners.

As all know, in war one of the most important of all its multifarious branches is the means of communication. Victory or defeat nearly always depends on keeping the directive brain accurately informed of the position, progress and development of every unit engaged in the battle, together with the exact time of all happenings.

The lines of communication must be kept open for information to be passed back from the headquarters of each attacking unit to each successive HQ, first to battalion and on to brigade, division, corps, army and finally reaching GHQ. However carefully a battle may have been planned in advance, unforeseen happenings often render essential a swift modification of the original plan, and it is of the highest importance that HQ should receive prompt intelligence in order to issue general directions by return to officers in command of the fighting forces; or to despatch reserves or ammunition to points where they may be urgently needed.

An impetus must come from behind, where reserves are held, undeployed and organised; for once any unit is committed to an attack, it is nearly impossible to make any change until the attack has spent its force, and this, with the AIF, meant 'fight till all objectives were taken'. It is impossible to overestimate the importance of a steady flow of intelligence to the commander in his central position as, without it, once he has lost touch with his force, he can exercise little further influence but must rely wholly upon his subordinates to give full and final effect to his plans.

Most important of all intelligence relates to enemy movements, since these cannot be visualised beforehand. There may be, and generally are, unexpected counterattacks and, for that matter, many unexpected developments. Once in possession of such intelligence, the commander can institute prompt measures to deal with the position.

We had many mechanical means of communication such as telephones, 'laddered' ad infinitum, to provide against breakage by shellfire. Also, we had wireless (unfortunately frequently jammed), flares, aeroplanes, rockets, flash lights and even flags — all part and parcel of the 'pomp, pride and circumstance of glorious war'. And, finally, we had our runners, and they never failed us while life remained in their bodies.

Many times they managed to convey vital intelligence and instruction and intelligence backwards and forwards when all mechanical means had failed through temporary obstruction or destruction. With nerve and muscle strained to snapping point, wearied to death by the treacherous mud, sludge and snow, at times when most of us were just content to grit our teeth and hang on where we were, their job was to make their way as rapidly as may be along shell-swept, tortured duckboard tracks with deadly barrages raining from the skies.

Air would be compressed one moment, then rent violently asunder so that even one's voice could not issue from the lips. Words half articulated would be flung back, forced down throats, the air pressure re-inflating the lungs then in act of discharging. Ground shook, trembled and rocked as if the whole of the earth was disintegrating and rumbles following the crashes of one salvo of 5.9s would be caught up and hurled aside by the tearing, blinding, soul-destroying explosions of a dozen others in quick succession in front, on each side, behind; while these again would be furiously displaced by numberless others, until the tiny atoms cowering beneath would feel that there was no such thing as solid earth anywhere; only slimy, fathomless mud, whipped and tormented as if the forces of Hell were taking part in the insensate strife.

How many times runners had to make their way through such conditions, disregarding all questions of personal safety, when the well-being of armies depended upon their speed, all other means having failed for the time being. As they made their way amongst bursting shells falling rain, with debris and loose wire often entangling their feet and dragging them backwards, those men, often mere boys, kept grimly on with one idea 'GET THERE' and surely those words should be written in words of gold.

Get there they did, if not hurled wounded into the fearful mud to die a hideous death. Many, unfortunately, were killed outright. Others just disappeared, but on the other hand, runners frequently got through and helped victory to be snatched out of the fire, saving valuable lives, allowing reliefs and stores to be brought forward to sorely tried troops whose resources, mechanical and physical, were at the point of exhaustion. That was the runners' job and they did their job well.

As I write, I can picture Tommy Ryan and his little band, eyes eager, faces tense, yet lined with grim determination. Tommy's quiet 'Yes, sir,' when receiving orders — he meant it! Also my special escort, Mullavey, whose gameness was a byword and who always, like Hotspur, 'wanted work' and who would urge me to go into No-Man's Land, if there was nothing else doing, and collect a couple of German patrols, or anything else. I remember W. Chaseling, O. Selig, J. McLennan and many others, and finally my own two runners, game to the backbone, loyal and cheerful.

Surely there is something about that terrible thing called War which manages to call forth all that is best and most unselfish in men. Is it not a fact that at the bottom of our hearts, we all love it, and love the men who fought and bled with us, and afterwards even the men we have fought against? It is the greatest and most terrible of all human dramas when men in millions — nations in arms — are pitted against other millions, fighting savagely as ants, yearning to kill or be killed. And why? Will it ever be abolished? I wonder.

The men of A Company, 13th Battalion, set a high standard, and Rollings and Stewart lived right up to it. At Gueudecourt, where the way to Battalion HQ was scourged by shells, thick as the fiery showers in Dante's Hell, these two boys carried message after message, backwards and forwards, always bringing a sandbag of bombs or SAA on the return trips; and then, when daylight came, carrying wounded to the RAP until — as was inevitable — both were badly wounded themselves.

Only urgent necessity made me despatch them that night into the darkness of that screaming Hell and, time and again, I could only wonder if they would ever be seen again; but my feelings can be imagined when later a dark form would step up out of the night, and pantingly convey the welcome news that my message had been delivered and hand me the answer!

Over and over again, our runners attempted and achieved the seemingly impossible. It is surely up to us to recount such incidents as came under our notice. Some episodes were amusing, others just plain tales of devotion to duty and a living up to our standards, if not actually beyond them. I remember in our first attack near Mouquet Farm; really the last attack of our first series there. I had lost both my runners. A Company had had considerable success and I wanted to get a message back to Captain Pulling to ascertain the position of other attacking units. Looking round, I saw a young man who had just joined up and was having his initial baptism of heavy fire.

He seemed made for the job, being lithe, active and young. I asked him if he thought he could get a message through. He agreed at once to try, and asked for my revolver; the rifle was rather in the way for quick work. I gave it to him with instructions to get the message through with all speed and at any cost. Off he darted, and when some distance from our trench was halted by an officer of another unit who asked him where he was going. Promptly, the newly enfranchised one jabbed his revolver into the other's solar plexus, shouting, 'Out of my way; I am a King's messenger', and flashed past the flabbergasted officer without waiting for a reply. He then met a runner, who although hard-pressed himself, still managed to squeeze a few seconds to let me know the right attack had failed and our flank was 'in the air'.

Tribute is also due to our signallers and to their work. Out in the mud, darkness and shellfire, searching for the broken ends of their wires to connect them and restore vital communications with HQ; feeling blindly through acres of disgusting mud; groping, groping, groping, without the excitement of being able to hit back, taking all and giving nothing in return.

Then our cooks — contending with snow, water and mud and shellfire, and the Bête Noir of all cooks — wet, green wood; yet cooking the lads a hot meal, one of the most essential things in war, for, as the mighty Napoleon said, an army marches on its stomach. I can never forget our A Company cook, in the line at Bois Grenier. He had just prepared a special hot evening meal and had all the dixies full — plenty for all, extra meat and vegetables — just ready to dish up, when a big Minnie [a German trench mortar shell fired from a minewerfer] landed on his trench kitchen, scalding his foot terribly and filling with muck all his dixies, which escaped being overturned.

English is a flexible, a descriptive language, but never before had I realised how colourful. That cook was the maddest man in France, hopping about for ten solid minutes directing a stream of vitriolic remarks to all things German, but more especially to the gunner who had just fired the shell. I gathered, among many other things, that the German nation was composed entirely of bachelors and always had been. That Hindenburg knew less about War than building fowl houses; while as for the man who had fired the shell — even the virgins of Gomorrah would have scorned his acquaintance.

So keen was the cook on his job, though, that not only did he refuse to go to hospital, although both foot and leg were terribly scalded, but he wanted to go out and see if he could get some more food. 'The boys must not go short,' he said.

Another valiant band were our stretcher bearers who worked in the open, attending to and carrying out the wounded. Often their work was done while the battle was at its height, with shellfire sometimes worse than a near peril to its carrying parties. It was heavy work, but those chaps stuck it out, and if a popular vote was taken for bravery and devotion to duty, I think the AIF would give the stretcher bearers a majority.

CAPTURE OF STORMY TRENCH: AUSSIES IN GRIM DUEL AGAINST WORTHY FOES

(*Reveille*, 1 December 1937, pp. 10–11, 62–5)

I have written of Bullecourt with all its sorrows, its heroisms, its hauntingly poignant, bitter-sweet memories; and now it is my pleasure to chronicle the happenings of Stormy Trench — happenings which began and ended in complete victory for us.

This time there was no blundering. The attack was soundly planned, tactics brilliantly and accurately executed, and, from start to finish, through all the stubborn fighting of that bitter night, we felt sure of final victory.

It was a midnight epic of barrage and counter-barrage, 'storm against storm racing across the skies', followed by splendid infantry attacks star studded with many a brilliant deed of matchless daring, fierce counterattacks from our great adversaries, loath to admit defeat, and finally the morning! Stormy Trench, torn, tortured, and battered out of recognition, littered by dead from both sides, was ours. Victory is always sweet.

In the main, although all sections, from the High Command down, did their job splendidly, Stormy Trench was distinguished most in the final phases for the work of the Digger, the man, who, when necessity demanded, could always manage to produce something just a little bit better than the enemy, and who, by his loyalty to his officer and his unit and withal his ready initiative, left nothing at all undone to clinch final victory.

The night was one of austere beauty. A mantle of frozen snow flooded by rich moonlight had removed all the ugly scars of previous battles and everything showed out with startling clarity against that illumined sheeting. The Frenchman, when justifying any deed of heroism or unselfishness, says, 'It is for beautiful France'; and France is indeed beautiful. On this occasion, unfortunately, the stillness of the night was rudely broken by bellowing guns, bursting shells and the sight of men struggling like wild animals.

In the account that follows, many acts of individual bravery can only be briefly mentioned, and others left out entirely. It would require too lengthy a catalogue to enshrine all. I am mainly concerned with presenting a bird's eye view of the main engagement. All I can say is that every man was engaged to the limit and, while many were fresh reinforcements, and for the first time face to face with death in all its ugly forms, I saw no blanching in face of those fierce counter-attacks when, time after time, Germany hurled her choicest Die-Hards like thundering waves against us, only to recoil like waves, broken and shattered after the impact. One and all fought coolly, headily, bravely, and the fact that we won, and won against such men, speaks volumes for the men engaged.

The capture of Stormy Trench could quite easily have entailed heavy — nay, disastrous — losses, but due to the clever planning of the staff and the subsequent perfect coordination of all manoeuvres, it fell into our hands with practically no casualties. Holding the position afterwards was a different matter. It called for the most stubborn fighting I have ever witnessed, and it was here that the Digger showed what he was made of.

Even now, after the lapse of twenty years, my heart beats more quickly when I recall the behaviour of our boys — and many of them were mere boys — during those hot and strenuous moments when men were falling all around them. Heavy, accurate shellfire, bitter bombing attacks, and hand-to-hand fighting only made the Digger hang on more grimly and tenaciously. There was no quitting; no thought of it. After repulsing each fresh attack, the survivors would grin feelingly at each other, then prepare for the next, and so it went on till finally the Germans had to confess themselves beaten. Retaking the trench was beyond them, for that night at least. Now I shall proceed to give some details.

We relieved the 15th Battalion at night on February 2, 1917 and were ordered to attack at 10 pm on the 4th. Fortunately the ground was frozen to the consistency of rock, and that was a great relief from the mud and slush we had to wade through a little while back.

It had been the job for our artillerymen to blast gaps in the barbed wire protecting the German trenches. They succeeded on the left but German retaliatory fire had severed our telephone wires and, although these had been repaired and 'laddered', they were cut again.

The consequence was that wire was still intact along the greater portion of A Company's objective, and once our barrage lifted, any delay in crossing that wire would cost heavy losses. Two forward observing officers reported that evening at 4 pm to A Company's HQ that they had been unable to cut the wire. It was finally decided to pass around to the left of the wire and bomb down the trench until all objectives were achieved.

Owing to the uncut wire and a limited 'hopping-off' trench, we could not place the whole Company in front of the gap, so one platoon was placed on the front trenches on our right. They had the difficult task of advancing obliquely under our barrage across No-Man's Land to the gap on our left. Between the right in our front line trench and the next battalion's left there was a considerable gap across the valley. The frost had transformed this quagmire and there was a shallow trench about 18 inches deep connecting. Our boys had to crawl for several hundred yards along this. Moonlight on snow makes men very conspicuous, and we naturally did not want the enemy to spot any unusual movement.

Lieutenant Guy Pulling and his platoon had the nasty job of moving to the right, to the next battalion's trench, and from there advancing obliquely across No-Man's Land when the barrage opened, and they did their work well. Unfortunately, he fell, very severely wounded, just as he led the platoon through the German wire.

The other three platoons crept in single file to the jumping-off trench and along to the right and left, then lay in the frozen snow awaiting zero. The cold was intense, lying in that trench, but it gave us enough cover.

A whisper passed along for permission to smoke — there were nearly twenty minutes to go; minutes of acute tension and suspense, the fear of every moment being seen and wondering what the next half hour had in store for us. Numbers, of course, would never see tomorrow's sunrise, but a cigarette would be a wonderful comfort. A hurried glance from right to left showed men well down, so permission was given. One cigarette had to be lighted from another as any sudden illumination would have betrayed our whereabouts.

Seconds dragged by. Now and again the boom of a heavy gun would sound, a shell whine overhead, then a scarcely noticeable increase came from our own field as gunners warmed them up, preparatory to the barrage, and watches showed now but three minutes to go! The order 'Smokes out' was whispered along; our pulses began to beat faster; the crucial moment was approaching. A last glance at rifles and revolvers, an unbuttoning of pockets holding grenades, and 15 — 10 — 5 seconds!

We were now breathlessly watching, not the front, but our own artillery, when the horizon leapt into quick stabbing flashes and the sweep of steel overhead, like the wings of a million eagles rushing towards their prey, made us jump. About 200 yards ahead we could see the reddish twinkle and pop of our bursting shrapnel and 'Hurrah, we're off', under the swiftly moving changing steel roof of our barrage. And what a barrage! Not a short burst.

Almost it seemed as if the shells were striking an invisible straight edge and bursting, so true and exactly were the fuses set. No fear of rifle or of machine-guns. No one could show out on that parapet and hope to live. We had two minutes to get where that Niagara of steel was falling, all eager and cool, in perfect lines showing in the clear moonlight. Time even to wonder how the other companies were faring and how Guy was getting along with his ticklish job. Now we had almost reached those ruddy smoke smudge pops.

It was hardly safe to stand upright — so close overhead sounded the river of sweeping steel. Better crawling — we must get as close as possible. A glance at my luminous watch dial showed 20 seconds to go before the barrage lifted. Now we were lying prone just ahead of the straight edge, shrapnel shrieking overhead, shells bursting just behind. The air was full of whining nose caps, while empty shell cases hummed as they bounced off the frozen parapet ahead.

Another glance showed about two seconds to go and, as we looked, the barrage, perfectly timed, lifted. Then with a steady, silent, irresistible rush the men poured round the wire and into the trench. This was how it should be done. The trench was deep and wide and the garrison crouching at the bottom had no option but to surrender. No time to waste now. Seconds were most valuable. The selected bombing sections swung along the trench to the right; that splendid dare-devil, Roy Withers, to the fore. No resistance yet; then a bomb or two started to burst around. Traverse after traverse was rushed by those quick, determined men. One dugout was passed whose occupant surrounded, and then we were across the valley and commencing to ascend the hill. Still some hundred yards or more to go, but we were doing well.

Big Roy Withers, noting the entrance to a dugout hidden by a hanging ground sheet, peered in and called on the occupants to surrender. The answer was a shot and Roy was dancing madly with a bullet hole in his ear. 'Split that, and that, you ———!!' he roared savagely as, tearing the pins from two Mills bombs, he hurled both into the dugout. It was a straight shaft with a chamber at the bottom. A yell greeted the double explosion, then dead silence. Of the eight men in the dugout, seven were killed outright, and the only remaining one, an officer, staggered out.

Little was left of the original man who stood upright facing us save the undaunted spirit that still animated his shattered body; nothing more terrible have I ever heard than the indistinguishable growl that issued from that spouting and fearful wound that had been his mouth. We interpreted it as surrender and he was given such attention as was possible, but it would have been a kindness to have shot him. He died that night, having given everything for his country, and surely he met a brave gathering of the very best on the other side. No time for sentiment, though. Holding the trench where we were would have given the Germans downhill throwing in a grenade fight. It was too far to go to the top, for there we would have exceeded our objective and would come under our own barrage, and barrages are no respecter of persons. So we decided to hold on at the bottom of the hill, leaving about 60 yards of flat ground between.

The captured trench was at least six feet deep and four wide, quite undamaged, and it was a treat to see our boys organise it for defence. A bomb stop was speedily built on our right; picks were useless in that frozen earth but in a few minutes the lads had improvised fire-steps. No one was cold now and our casualties had been light. Scotty Thompson moved along quickly, siting his Lewis guns. Corporal Robertson started to enfilade the German trench with rifle grenades.

Our bombing section was stationed at the bomb block with Pte. Bushell, his Lewis gun and crew. Riflemen saw to it that every spare rifle was loaded, including any German ones, and those on the right had a splendid field of fire to sweep, frontally or obliquely. The 4th Machine-Gun Company posted their Vickers about our centre and we were all set and ready for the inevitable counterattack 20 minutes after the taking of the trench.

Sure enough, we were attacked. First there opened on us the most severe high explosive and trench mortar fire we had ever experienced — Tom's Cut and OG 2 given in — and it was frightfully accurate. It was concentrated particularly on our right. Suddenly it ceased and movement was noticed on our right rear. This was thought to be a patrol of Australians, but movement on our right front and a hail of bombs enlightened us. The Lewis gun opened with a rush and a shower of enemy grenades killed or wounded every man except Pte. Bushell, who, after firing one drum, rushed with his gun out of the trench to the top of the mound and, from that position, poured drum after drum into the enemy.

The 2nd bombing section, led by their gallant NCO, raced up to the block and a bomb fight of the first magnitude developed. The heavy losses sustained by No. 1 bombing section enabled the Germans to approach our block and a deadly hail of grenades from front, flank and rear took heavy toll. Our SOS (red over green over red) flared overhead and next instant our artillery opened with a crash, making the earth tremble, as a torrent of lethal steel raced overhead, falling between us and the enemy — no chance of reinforcements reaching them now; even the mighty son of Thetis would have hesitated before entering that wall of screaming, plunging, bursting steel.

The attacking Germans, however, did not want any reinforcements but came on like infuriated tigers, determined to drive us from the position. Owing to their familiarity with the ground, their bombers were giving us merry hell. Only one thing for it; over the top [and] find them. Big Roy scrambled out, injuring his knee rather badly, but he tore down the parados, a grim and shadowy Titan hurling his thunderbolts into the trench.

I saw one group of five he collected, close to our bomb block. Others rushed to the right rear and brought the bayonet into play. The fight was now being carried to the Germans with a vengeance. Still others surged to the right front, where a German bombing section was crouching so close that our grenades were going over their heads. Three were taken prisoner; the others weren't!

The attack began to waver and break before that fierce reception. Many Germans fled; others were bayoneted or shot, but a few escaped. Men were very conspicuous racing over that white blanket and made splendid targets. In the heart of the fighting, Corporal Robertson maintained a heavy enfilade fire with rifle grenades along the German trench. Partially buried twice, and severely shaken, his face lacerated with steel splinters, he kept pumping those grenades over as if he were demonstrating for the benefit of the Germans how it should be done.

I really believe he went through the orthodox movements with each grenade. He made a formidable figure, sitting with his rifle between his knees and the stock on the ground, giving critical glances at his angle and direction at every shot — he had climbed out of those frozen earthen boulders. H.B. Brown [Herbert Basil 'Hard Boiled' Brown, MC, DCM, MM] was also out on the parapet, moving about above his section, directing his fire as coolly as at the range, and after the attack had died down, he helped wounded to the safest spots, and in short, did all that a man might, or could, do.

'Scotty' Thompson (sergeant I should say, but I know Scotty won't mind) was up to his neck in it too, keeping Lewis guns in action. The extreme cold had caused a lot of trouble, but with matches sometimes, and at other times merely by the sense of touch, he went on repairing gun after gun, giving no heed to bomb, bullet or shell. The guns were all important and must be kept going. And so the fight went on all along the trench; nearly all our officers and NCOs were down. Sergeant Scotty McCabe, fairly dancing about his platoon, was telling them in broadest Scotch how to deal with the enemy, and while directing, never missed a chance to get in with rifle or grenade.

Our casualties were now very heavy, as one might expect, but so also were those of the enemy. We were making him pay heavily for every man he killed or wounded. The night was still young, and when the Germans realised that their counterattack had failed, they poured in a smashing shellfire, which again was diabolically accurate. The trench sides were torn off in huge frozen boulders of black earth; it was hard to save men from being squashed to death under them; harder still to find temporary havens for our wounded, getting more numerous every minute. Yet all around, the Digger was cool, cheerful and determined. Men were terribly thirsty. We had plenty of water, but it was all frozen and there was neither time nor opportunity to melt it with Tommy cookers. It used to hurt to see some of the lads trying to get a bit of ice out of their bottles with a pocket knife to quench their thirst.

Throughout all the shellfire, Pte. McQueen was in charge of a carrying party, and he continued to bring grenades and ammunition up. At the outset his party was five strong but casualties reduced these to one, but each one, until wounded, kept going, carrying backwards and forwards through the shell-swept, treacherous area in our rear.

The shelling that followed the repulse of the counterattack continued relentlessly, and the trench was rent and battered beyond description, while casualties were mounting steadily to danger point; but the men were marvellous, despite being blown about and hurled time and time again against the frozen sides of the trench. Not one man was shell-shocked, and although, as I have said before, many of the boys were raw reinforcements, they behaved one and all like veterans.

The fire increased, then chopped off suddenly. It was coming; sure! Suddenly German bombs rained in upon us as another fierce counterattack commenced. Up went our SOS. The watching gunners got busy and the prompt and savage response of our artillery isolated the attack. After a few seconds of savage grenade throwing, our boys rushed, led by such men as Roy Withers, whose joy it was to be where the battle was thickest. This time the repulse was quicker than the last, but hardly had our boys regained the trench when the Germans, very bravely, attempted to rush us, persisting in spite of heavy losses. Those children of Odin certainly fought well.

Three times they renewed their efforts, though bloodily repulsed each time. German infantry has no superior in such cases. Finally, they gave it up and reverted to the machine war. Bitterly accurate shelling took toll of our diminishing numbers. Men were often enough hit squarely, passing at once out of the story; at other times hurled off their feet, often buried, but the lads took what was coming and kept a close watch for any movement over the top, while others kept rebuilding and improving the fire-steps, heaving boulders of frozen earth out of the trench.

Every man did his job. Scotty kept overhauling his guns. All rifles were fully charged — there were plenty of spare ones now, unfortunately, and about 2.30 am the enemy opened a special 'hate' on A Company. It seemed as if no one could survive that deluge of bursting shells which swept the ground like a watering pot, hurling men to and fro like ninepins, but the boys had no thought of anything save holding their ground, and just waited grimly for the counter-attack that must follow, and once again it came.

When the guns ceased their savage orchestration, German bombers made the most determined attempt of the night to capture our block, but they were facing men as determined as themselves. Robertson, in spite of a severely wounded face and a frightful shaking from very near shell bursts, as coolly and accurately as ever, raked the enemy with his rifle grenades, cheering on his bomb throwers at the same time. Roy also, despite his wounded knee, repeated his run along the German trench, hurling grenades as fast as he could pull the pins. Like Coeur-de-Lion, he seemed to rush to the fight as if summoned to a banquet.

Others moved out to meet the onpouring enemy on our right, while riflemen on our left opened such a continuous and heavy fire that it seemed as if we had a machine-gun in every bay. Our gunners did their part well and faithfully. Shrapnel was bursting beautifully overhead, giving enemy reinforcements no chance at all of moving up in support. No troops, however, could daunt that stubborn Company of Diggers. They might all be killed, but they would never admit defeat. And at last even our great foes had to admit that the task was too great, the losses too heavy.

That was the last effort of the night, although their guns roared death and defiance throughout the night. A count of fit men revealed 40 available at this stage — enough to repulse one more counter-attack. After that we would ask Captain Hansen of the 14th for a platoon to reinforce, but no further counterattack came. The enemy had learned his lesson and all had to admit that he had fought well. Stormy Trench, thanks to clever planning and the subsequent efforts of our Diggers, was ours for keeps, and keep it we did.

The long night over, daylight came, and what a shambles it revealed! Gone was the admirable trench we had captured and in its place there remained a boulder-strewn depression — boulders of frozen earth. Wounded and dead were lying along it; men with grey drawn faces but determined jaws — no sign of wavering, even among them. Throughout the night, the Germans had been trying to turn our right flank, and against it they had turned their main efforts.

In a distance of not more than 70 yards I counted 61 dead Germans and 20 Australians, apart from many wounded on both sides. All now were tortured with a raging thirst — all who were alive, I mean; and in spite of the cold were trying to dig a few particles of ice from their water bottles or tins. Gone was the beautiful white mantle of snow for hundreds of yards, both front and rear, blown away by shells, not a vestige remaining.

All was quiet on our front when General Brand decided to relieve A Company and the whole of the 16th Battalion volunteered for the job, although they knew there was hot work ahead. Captain Ahearn and his Company relieved us that night, A Company going on to the 16th for rations and duty. We were treated as only those big-hearted West Australians could treat tired, shell-shaken men. The 16th at the time were in close support, and were doing very heavy night fatigues. We were supposed to take our share, but Colonel Drake-Brockman gave us two hours' work only on any night and we had a big safe dugout to sleep in.

On the morning after being relieved, A Company had no cigarettes and funds were low, so we had a tarpaulin muster [each man throwing coins into a tarpaulin] with fair results. Two of our lads went to the 4th Brigade canteen which General Brand, always thoughtful for the comfort of his men, had as close to the front as possible. They brought back a fair supply.

I have until now purposely refrained from referring to the work of C Company of the 14th Battalion and their gallant commander, Captain Stewart Hansen, who, as our close support, had perhaps the hardest job and the worst time. So splendid was their performance, I felt that by telling something of it separately I might be able to convey a better idea of their courage and superlative performance. They took over the trenches we left, and the Germans knew exactly where those trenches were, and on them fell the tempest of his heavy artillery and protective barrages when attacking us. Their casualties were as heavy as ours.

One of their jobs was to carry SAA bombs and supplies generally to us. I had seen, and afterwards saw, a lot of carrying done, but nothing to equal the work of the 14th's carrying parties, often without officer or NCO, with men staggering under impossible loads and continually scourged by heavy shell fire. Those men not only got their supplies to us, when not killed, but carried them until they found the officer in charge of the captured position, asked him where the supplies were wanted in the trench, delivering them there, and hurrying back for more, and continuing until supplies in the trench were greater than our needs.

They furnished a striking example of teamwork and, as they did not have any chance of participating in the actual hand-to-hand fighting, it was very hard and the most exacting discipline that men could be put to. Too much credit cannot be allotted to those brave, steadfast men of the old 14th and their gallant captain who, sadly enough, paid the big price that night for his country's sake.

THE N.Z. AND A. DIVISION: A HAPPY FAMILY

(*Reveille*, 1 April 1938, p. 18)

The 4th Australian Brigade, of which I was a member, was closely associated with the New Zealanders during the command by General A. Godley of the NZ and Aust. Division. The New Zealanders were a body of men with whom anyone would be proud to be associated. We shared the Egyptian training with its strenuous work and good times, and, in those early days, we accepted each other with some reserve; this, however, being only healthy pride in the respective merits of our own countries and men. We might have had heated differences among ourselves, but woe betide the outsiders who dared the displeasure of either, for they soon found that they had intruded in a family circle incurring the fate generally reserved for such intruders … The conviction of the rank and file of the 16th Bn [Australian] was that the New Zealanders were better men than the Aussies. Often I had been told by New Zealanders that they thought us better than themselves. There could be no doubt, however, of the mutual sentiment towards each other. As time went on this increased. We know that what the New Zealanders could not do as soldiers, could not be done by any other troops in the world.

Who among the 4th Brigade could ever forget the week of farewells at the end of which we Australians of the 4th Brigade were separated from the New Zealanders to be merged into the 4th Australian Division? Although we knew we were going to comrades just as good, it was a wrench to leave these splendid men with whom we had shared our baptism in blood; shared, too, savage dangers, privations and pleasures. In a succession of farewell evenings, each battalion of both NZ and Australian brigades entertained. There were some pranks played too. Our brigade major's sign in front of his tent was placed in front of a latrine, and the latter's sign put in front of his battalion headquarters. Other signs were interchanged, and caused considerable worry to despatch riders. Dr Peter Buck and Lieut. Walker, of the Maoris, were well to the fore with Haka, anecdote and fun. But behind it all was a feeling of sadness; we were leaving our comrades, tried and proved — comrades whom we never found wanting.

THE FIRST THREE WEEKS ON GALLIPOLI

(*Reveille*, 1 April 1939, pp. 10–11, 60–2)

Gallipoli, one of the Empire's most glorious failures. Days of intense, ferocious fighting, followed by nights of fitful, broken slumber, short dozes, sudden violent awakenings, then the morning when from the shallow trenches we faced the Turkish infantry — the most wonderful long-distance marksmen in the world — alert for the least movement. In place of the mercilessly accurate artillery preparation of the Germans in France, we here confronted the machine-gun and rifle fire of the Turks, and in the years that followed I saw nothing so deadly.

The almost complete absence of adequate artillery on both sides made defence infinitely stronger than attack and, when it is remembered [that] the Turks had all the advantages conferred by carefully selected and prepared positions, the wonder is not that we failed, but that we managed to secure a footing at all and hold on as long as we did. It was unquestionably one of the greatest feats of the War.

After a wonderfully pleasant voyage across the Mediterranean, we joined the fleet in Mudros Harbour and were able to glimpse something of the mighty strength of England. Warships of all kinds were there. It was written of Helen that hers was the face 'that launched a thousand ships'. Quite so, but not ships like these. From the Queen Elizabeth, with her batteries of 15-inch guns, down to the destroyers racing and wheeling like seahawks, everything bespoke controlled, efficient and terrible force. Then there were the transports, loaded with troops, horses, munitions; what an inspiring picture it all presented. The Empire was at war and we were all seething with excitement.

We waited at Mudros a few days but there wasn't a dull minute. We yearned for action and, being keyed up, had to do something — so we put in the time cleaning up and oiling our machine-guns and rifles. Knapsacks and haversacks were filled to bursting point and we were ready for whatever the Gods had in store. We had no idea what it might be like, and wasted no time in speculation. We had youth, health and strength; high adventure awaited us. What more could heart of man desire?

In the Anzac Corps, the 3rd Brigade was to lead, whilst we of the 4th Brigade were to land later in the day. We rejoiced in the good luck of our comrades and they certainly justified the confidence reposed in them. At last the great moment had arrived. Troopships began to move off! We could restrain ourselves no longer. Thunderous cheers followed. Ahead of the troopships we could see line after line of warships moving abreast. And now our turn had come. It had seemed to some impatient spirits in the 4th Brigade that we might miss all the fun, but there was plenty to come, if we had only known.

Morning dawned on that smooth sheet of water, the Aegean, famed in history and legend; but a burst of thunder overhead drove all such thoughts from our heads. The British Fleet was engaged and had opened fire on the Turkish defences. Excitement grew almost unbearable; the battle had started, and how was it going? We all looked and listened with painful eagerness as our transport steamed slowly along. Equipment had been donned in readiness, yet still we were a long way back, though now the battleships were coming into view. Who would have missed this crowded hour of glorious life? Looking farther ahead as we drew closer, we could see geysers of stones, earth and dust where the great shells burrowed and burst. The men of the 3rd Brigade were being strongly supported that day.

As we drew closer, our own transport began to quiver and shake from the force of those naval broadsides. We could see the *Triumph*, *Bacchante*, *Queen*, *London*, *Canopus* (to mention but a few) steaming coolly backwards and forwards and, while all of them maintained the traditional regularity of the British Fleet, streams of flame shot outwards from their sides. Stoutly built though they were, one could note the incessant quivering of their steel-clad hulls from the repeated shocks of those discharges. Other effects were noticeable also, as the heavy naval guns gave tongue. Fish turned up, stunned, on the surface of the water.

The battleships, steaming and turning, fired and fired again. It looked as if the Turks must be blotted out; but, on second thoughts, it did not look so well to see those shells bursting so near the beach. Surely our boys must have got further inland by this? Evidently there were some Turks left for us to deal with. By now we had got fairly close and could hear rifle and machine-gun fire, and note the bursting shrapnel of the enemy, who were clearly putting up a good fight.

We were given our dinner. I believe it was ham but none of us took much interest, not then. The drama we were seeing drove all other thoughts from our minds. The cook cut each man a slice and I received the impression that water was scarce. We had not yet become used to mass feeding, but I learnt a useful lesson — not to leave too much to a subordinate where men's rations were concerned.

Colonel Pope was keen to get ashore with his battalion. At 2 pm one of our men was hit by a rifle bullet. Soon we were in a destroyer and, disembarking from it into rowing boats, crowded to the gunwales, began pulling strongly for the shore, soldiers on the oars. Turkish shrapnel was bursting high overhead, but quite harmlessly; my old training in the Launceston artillery told me that. And now other sights and sounds claimed our attention. I had been wondering what species of bird was emitting a low, sweet continuous whistle. Sudden enlightenment came when splinters flew from the bow of our boat and a man just behind me threw up his hands and called out 'Oh!' The whistle was not the song of any bird but proceeded from rifle and machine-gun bullets. The air was full of those leaden songsters now. The shore could not arrive fast enough.

The boat grounded and over I jumped, not waiting for the others as I should have done. We had grounded temporarily on a rock and I submerged over my head; but we all got ashore at last and rushed up to the beach, where we halted. Percy Black mounted his machine-gun in readiness and dug a trench — which, according to our training, we had to do whenever we halted during an advance. The soil was sandy and soon we had a good trench, but were only there for a few minutes before moving off. This didn't matter; at all events we were now definitely at war and would soon see what our opponents were like.

Up till now, our experience of war had been limited to the naval bombardment. Now we were to witness actual consequences in the shape of men wounded, dying, and dead; and other feelings took possession of us. War meant the wounding, mutilation and killing of men — and they were our own men who lay there before us. Doubtless many Turks paid the penalty too — that reflection comforted us a little — and more would follow; we could certainly promise that.

The rattle of machine-gun and rifle fire ahead invited us to rush forward to where the game was being played out, but we were forced to wait. The roar of our shells overhead was sweetest music — we still had the powerful support of Nelson's bulldogs. The naval bombardment swept the enemy terrain, tearing away shrubs and trees, while continual upheavals registered its destructive striking power.

The din of battle seemed to wax louder as we waited, nerves all on edge from the forced inaction. The blended racket of shells, shrapnel, rifle fire and gun fire combined in irregular harmony, and one that continually beckoned us to get in closer; to come to grips. How the great shells hissed, roared and exploded, to the accompaniment of crackling shrapnel from the Turks. Life was being blotted out every minute, hot blood spilt, and still none of us could even guess how the fight was faring. Glancing at the faces of my comrades, their change of expression made me think. The brief experience had transformed them into killers. Lips were tightly compressed, jaws set, eyes alight with blood lust — these were not the boys with whom I had been playing 'banker' a few short hours ago. One could see to what a high nervous pitch they were keyed and it was only their sense of discipline, teamwork, which prevented them from surging forward without orders.

At last the order came to move. It ran through all ranks like an electric impulse. There was an instant movement. Forward! Colonel Pope led the way up Shrapnel Gully (well named indeed) and when we reached Monash Valley we received the welcome order to 'dump packs'. No questioning that order — they weighed 60 to 70 lb apiece. It was now nearly dark. We proceeded up Monash Valley to where it forked and climbed a steep hill (afterwards christened Pope's Hill). The continuous flashing of rifle fire came into sight. No shells now, but those snapping rifles kept up a frightful din; the air simply being saturated with noise.

Near the top we halted. There was some confused shouting and a few shots in front and then a sharp order to man the hilltop and open fire. A rather serious blunder had been made here, the Turks having being mistaken for Indian troops. Colonel Pope, the adjutant (Capt. R. McDonald) and another officer (Lieut. W. Elston) were captured, but the Colonel escaped by knocking his would-be captors down, throwing himself over the steep edge of the hill and rolling back to his men! Good work. We rushed forward, scrambling, slipping, and falling till we reached the top, a plateau, and now at last our long bottled-up impatience found vent as we poured a tremendous fire into the blackness ahead. The enemy response soon died down while our own slackened to a steady, controlled effort.

Percy Black mounted his gun on the extreme left of the hill, the other gun being placed about a hundred yards to the right. It was impossible just then to see what field of fire we had, but we were all 'set' and began to dig in like fury. The long night dragged on, and for me it was a very cold one; owing to my plunge into the sea, I was still (as the immortal Mr. Toots would say, 'very wet') from feet to waist, and I felt absolutely numb.

Dawn showed at last, and all had their rifles ready for a shot. Percy Black grabbed his and, sighting carefully, dropped a Turkish sniper who had been crawling along the side of a cliff about ninety yards away. The poor wretch fell down the steep side, caught his legs in a low fork, and there he hung for days. We all hoped that the shot had killed him and that he did not have to linger in such a position.

Our own casualties began to mount up unpleasantly. One by one men hurtled down the steep hill, often shot through the head. Very little movement could be distinguished in front. The valley on our left was completely unoccupied and was a serious menace; our flank being well and truly 'in the air'. Fortunately, the Turk, being kept too busy, did not take advantage of the fact, but a few determined riflemen planted there could have shot us off the Peninsula.

There was no organised attack on us for some hours, but rifle fire was increasing in both volume and accuracy. Many of our boys were shot, often by invisible marksmen, which is enough to try the stamina of any troops, but the survivors still held their ground. Black never missed a chance with his machine-gun and he was a deadly shot. If any man could claim to have done more than another in stopping the Turkish counterattacks on April 26th and 27th, it was Percy Black. Only for his deadly gunning and determination I am convinced that the Turks would have succeeded in turning our flank and so forced us off Gallipoli.

As the day wore on, the Turks tried to cross some open country and Black caught them in enfilade in lines. They simply sank and died. In one case, when overtaken by the death rain, they hunched together for protection and very few escaped. This drew on Black a concentrated 'hate' from the Turks. A mountain gun shelled him. He got a shrapnel through the ear, and another through his hand, both painful wounds which bled profusely, but still managed to delver his lethal spray whenever opportunity offered. His gun casing was now holed with rifle bullets. Suddenly a party of 70 Turks jumped out of a small depression some 80 yards in front. 'Here they come,' roared Percy, and a steady stream of fire roared from his gun. The nearest of them got to within forty yards of us before collapsing. All were exceptionally brave men who pushed home the attack in the name of Allah, but none was able to get back.

A soldier by intuition, Black pointed out the weakness on our open left flank to an officer and offered to take a few men and line listening posts across the valley, but the officer seemed inclined to disregard the suggestion as unimportant! Some Turkish snipers later got through the unguarded valley, as might be expected, and that officer was one of their first victims.

We were tired enough that night, having had little sleep the night before, but the Turk was keeping us awake and the blaze of rifle fire continued to light up the darkness. Never for one second did it let up during the days and nights that followed. The pressure increased on Tuesday (April 27th) and at times we were 'all out', holding on to our little bit of Gallipoli. We were getting weary from the constant pressure; many of our best and boldest had gone. Harold George (of Claremont, W. Aust.) — one of the gamest boys I ever knew — was shot through the heart. He was acting No. 2 on the gun for Black.

A painful incident occurred just there. At a time when every nerve was strained to hold the enemy at bay, one of our warships dropped four great shells into our midst. They buried deep into the earth and blew out tremendous craters, hurling men high into the air but, fortunately, no one was injured. This made us realise how little damage the spectacular bombardment had wrought among the Turks — howitzers were what were wanted, not naval guns. A distinct note of comedy was supplied by some men as they tried to scramble back to the trench over the loose dirt that was sliding down the steep face of the hill and carrying them like struggling ants with it. Serious as the position was, some of us had to smile. Fortunately, there were no casualties.

Little sleep was to be had on Tuesday night. Wednesday came and water was short. We had to mix kerosene with water for the guns. Though drinking water was precious, whenever the guns ran short and word to that effect was passed along, the boys did not hesitate to part with their precious drops to keep the guns in action.

Wednesday, and still very little sleep. One could see men's heads nodding and drooping — some were sleeping where they stood. But by now the desire seemed to be passing. Recognising how heavy the pressure was, some relief was given. The men of the 16th on the left of Pope's were relieved by a Company from the 13th. They too looked very tired, but I noted among them a particularly game and efficient subaltern in charge of the platoon around our gun. Slight of figure, he was little more than a boy, but was the life of his men. Later I got to know him as Douglas Marks, one of the most brilliant and dashing soldiers on the Peninsula. I also noted a brisk and cheerful captain of the 13th, friendly with everyone, emanating pluck, efficiency, and strength, a fine strong personality. I did not know him but yearned to serve under him; the wish was granted later, for this was Captain (now Brigadier) J.M.A. Durrant, of whom it is unnecessary to say any more just here.

Days and nights pass slowly enough. Such sleep as we could get was sauced with wild dreams. But for the continual rifle fire of the Turks, we might have been living in a dream world. Every hour our men were falling; men whom we had just got to know and like would drop suddenly, limbs all aquiver in death, for the Turk seemed always to aim for a vital part. But the boys kept their spirits up, although it was plain that that the loss of their mates was affecting them. Two would be chatting together when one would pitch forward, and the expression of the survivor would be eloquent of savage, repressed rage. It was a nerve-racking business and there seemed to [be] no ending to it all.

There was a heavy demand on the machine-guns, and Black's weapon was so often hit that it became unworkable. He just put it on his shoulder and walked back to the beach to see if it could be repaired by a ship's armourer, but had the good luck to exchange it for another one instead. The new gun was all brass, and shiny — and what a picture of a returning warrior Percy made as he came up the hill! He might have been Diomed striding back over the plains after interviewing Paris, a splendid physical specimen, afraid of nothing on earth and glorying in his strength and power. Although his arm was in a sling and his head swathed in bandages, his eyes were beaming with joy at the success of his quest; now he could carry on with the good work and we needed him badly.

Just at this moment the *Queen Elizabeth* swung around and fired a salvo from her great rifles. We saw the flashes, then heard what sounded like express trains emerging from tunnels, hurtling over our heads. Somehow we felt more confidant.

We all looked upon the *Triumph* as one of us, and a few weeks later we witnessed a sight that chilled the stoutest-hearted among us, when, about midday, as we were sitting on the lee side of the hill with the great ship almost at our feet, sharply outlined against the blue Aegean, we saw a huge column of smoke and water fly up from her side. Almost immediately she heeled over. A bitter cry arose from our men 'They've torpedoed her!' At once, small craft of all kinds sped to her assistance, and all but 73 of her officers and men were saved. We all had a kind feeling for the Turk who, like the perfect gentleman and brave man that he is, refrained from shelling the rescue parties, although his land guns were within easy range, and by the rules of war he would have been perfectly justified in firing. But the Turk is a gentleman to his fingertips and I really believe he was sorry to see the *Triumph* sink.

And so the game went on, up to the fateful night of May 2nd, when we were scheduled to take the Bloody Angle and other spots ahead of the eastern fork of Monash Valley. Sheer military impossibilities with such troops and munitions as were at our disposal, but one must learn by bitter experience; not that we needed telling, even then. It was a blunder, and, excepting Bullecourt in April 1917, the worst stunt I was ever in. Because of a slight wound, my sergeant would not let me do much. It was a sad and terrible business, and I feel like hurrying over it. The machine-gunners advanced with the infantry, and as we topped the ridge, our men fell like grass before the sweep of an expert mower; but most tragic of all, one of our own machine-guns was firing too low, and added to the massacre until we got the message back and stopped it. Disaster on disaster, following fast and following faster. Our leaders still had something to learn about the Turk and the strength of his defence, particularly in country such as this. Until this disaster overtook us, our casualties, though heavy, were not crushing; but that night the 16th was reduced to the strength of a Company — viz. 240 men!

Sergt. George Demel, leading us over the crest, was killed — the wonder is that anyone survived. He had shown exceptional ability as a soldier, combined with great fitness for command, and would have been an ideal officer for the Western Front. The irony of it was the commission for which he had been so deservedly recommended came next day.

Black carried his gun right forward and remained until all his ammunition was expended and the attack had degenerated into a ghastly failure. Then, almost surrounded, and a target for enemy fire from three sides, he carried it out again. Why he wasn't hit a hundred times I cannot imagine. He was greatly affected by Demel's death when he heard of it.

Bill Lynas, finding he was not required as a signaller just then, gathered several bandoliers and took up a position in front, where he could snipe. When daylight came he could see a lot of Turks lying behind a small rise, shooting at us. They were only 100 yards from him and he picked off nine very neatly, but then had to leave as the men in our trenches mistook him for one of the enemy and commenced blazing at him. Bill always maintained that he would have reached the century but for that. He became a captain afterwards and proved to be one of the best; cool, clever and sufficiently aggressive. [Lynas was awarded a DSO and MC with two Bars.]

The Marine battalions came to our assistance that morning. They were very young-looking, little more than boys to us, and only partially trained, but they lacked neither spirit nor pluck.

As time went on we came down to trench warfare. At Quinn's Post, the opposing trenches were only a few yards apart and Johnny

Turk introduced us to something new — hand grenades. It was here that Doug Marks and his platoon of the 13th fought one of the toughest fights in the history of the AIF. The Turks blew them up and got into the trenches, but Doug and his men were too solid for them and turned them out again, capturing between 20 and 30.

Water and rations now were just as important as ammunition. We did pretty well, foraging in the small hours of the morning. Flies were then so bad that it was impossible to eat or sleep after the sun had risen.

Our medical units did good work from the outset and our own RMO, Captain McGregor, exposed himself without thought of danger, going to the wounded wherever they fell. Finally, on May 1st, he was shot through the forearm. The 4th Field Ambulance had an advanced dressing station quite close to the line, and men of the calibre of Captains H.L. St Vincent Welch, Jeffries, Tom and Rupert Furber, never considered their own safety when life was at stake. The stretcher bearers, too, rose nobly to the occasion. Often they were shot down but, to give the Turk his due, I don't think the shooting was done deliberately. The standard set in those early days became the recognised one for the A.A.M.C., the bravery and efficiency of whose members could hardly have been bettered.

It is impossible to mention everyone in the space of an article, but all will agree that General Birdwood was an outstanding figure. Hardly a day passed that he did not visit different parts of the front line, exchanging cheerful and appreciative words with the Diggers, imbuing every one with fresh determination to succeed. He was placed very high in the estimation of the men, and that regard continues to this day.

Before the Landing we had seen the 29th Division, and all of us were impressed. They looked what they quickly proved themselves to be, a splendid and invincible fighting force. If all Allied troops had been as good as the 29th Division, the war would not have lasted long. One great lesson we learned from the 29th was the inestimable value of adequate training and preparation.

The fight subsided into sniping by day and digging, tunnelling and harassing fire by night, and this kept us busy enough. I was ashore ten days before I found the first 'chats' and I'll never forget the horror and disgust of that. Afterwards we became more used to them, but they were filthy, loathsome beasties just the same.

And now my turn came when a shrapnel bullet pierced my knee. Mates carried me to the beach. I got seasick in the rowing boat that took me to the carrier. At Mudros I was put on the *Franconia*, along with 1850 others, most of them more badly wounded than I was. We had seven doctors on board going night and day, trying to save life, on the operating table. Slight wounds had perforce to go unattended. I lost all count of days on the voyage, but will never forget the 'chats' in their millions on my blanket. All I could do was to turn it every hour and try and keep them on top. Finally Egypt and hospital; all clean at last.

AGAIN READY FOR THE FRAY: HARRY MURRAY'S MESSAGE

(*Reveille*, November 1939, p. 18)

Though Harry Murray, VC, CMG, DSO and Bar, DCM, Richmond, North Queensland, was unable to attend the 13th Battalion Reunion in Sydney on September 30, his cordial remembrances of his association with that unit at Anzac and in France were expressed in the following message:

'Once again my pen and paper must convey greetings and good wishes to you all.

'How are you all, "A" Company? Just now straining at the leash like your old Company commander?

'How I would like a few hours with you — cannot we set old "Anno Domini" back twenty years? Still I must not complain. I am still fit and not so old.

'I am again in khaki, only AMF but ready for the AIF if the need arises.

'In the men I command I can see the reincarnation of the best Company of the many splendid companies of the old AIF.

'Good luck to you all and to all my other grand mates of the Two Blues. Somehow the war has rejuvenated all the old ties of comradeship and as I write I seem to see you all. I got your letter, Cyril Meyer — many thanks. I hope you are all well and enjoy the evening. How are you, Humphrey Browning, Bono, Bernie Rose, Les Cleland, Harry Rollings, Stewart, Arthur Lanigan, Len Plasto, Roger Bradley, Harradine — the names all come crowding in; but I must call a halt. There is a chance of my being in Sydney before long, doing a course of instruction. You must stage an evening, Len, if I do get there. I'll donate my pay to defray expenses.

'I am in command of the 26th Battalion, AMF — a splendid body of men, all athletes, 60 per cent of them over six feet tall, as keen as men could be and easily controlled.

'Of course, it is the old story, volunteers, and the cream of the west. I am afraid they want to get their teeth in, and the old man is a bit with them.

'To me, it is a happy omen that the battalion number is a double of the 13th and our colours are the same old Two Blues, only inverted, in diamond shape.

'You might wonder what I will do if the need for an overseas force arises! Well, if they will have me, I am going. We licked Fritz once, but this time we will give him Heil. We must end the war for all time.

'There is much more I would like to say but you don't want to listen to me for long. Sincerely wishing you all the very best and hoping to see you soon again. Ever yours sincerely,

Harry Murray'

BIBLIOGRAPHY

BOOKS

Bean, C.E.W., *Anzac to Amiens*, Australian War Memorial, Canberra, 1946.

Bean, C.E.W., *The Official History of Australia in the War of 1914–18. Vol. 1: The Story of Anzac From the Outbreak of War to the End of the First Phase of the Gallipoli Campaign, May 4, 1915; Vol. 2: The Story of Anzac from 4 May 1915 to the Evacuation of the Gallipoli Peninsula; Vol. 3: The AIF in France, 1916; Vol. 4: The AIF in France, 1917; Vol. 5: The AIF in France, December 1917 to May 1918; Vol. 6: The AIF in France, May 1918 to the Armistice*. All volumes published by Angus & Robertson, Sydney, 1921–42.

Bean, C.E.W., *Two Men I Knew: William Bridges and Brudenell White, Founders of the AIF*, Angus & Robertson, Sydney, 1957.

Blankfield, A. and Corfield, R.S., *Never Forget Australia: Australia and Villers-Bretonneux, 1918–1993*, Royal Victorian Regiment, Melbourne, 1994.

Charlton, P., *Australians on the Somme: Pozières, 1916*, Methuen Haynes, Sydney, 1986.

Chataway, T.P., *History of the 15th Battalion, Australian Imperial Force*, William Brooks & Co., Brisbane, 1948.

The Congressional Medal of Honor: The Names, the Deeds, Sharp & Dunnigan, Forest Ranch, Calif., 1984.

Coulthard-Clark, C., *Soldiers in Politics*, Allen & Unwin, Sydney, 1996.

Cutlack, F.M. (ed.), *The War Letters of General Monash*, Angus & Robertson, Sydney, 1934.

Dunn J.C., *The War the Infantry Knew, 1914–1919*, Sphere Books, London, 1987.

Facey, A.B., *A Fortunate Life*, Fremantle Arts Centre Press, Fremantle, 1981.

Farrar-Hockley. A.H., *The Somme*, Pan Books, London, 1983.

Gammage, B., *The Broken Years: Australian Soldiers in the Great War*, Australian National University Press, Canberra, 1974.

Gliddon, G., *VCs of the First World War: Arras and Messines, 1917*, Sutton, Stroud, Gloucestershire, 1998.

Grant, I., *A Dictionary of Australian Military History*, Random House, Sydney, 1992.

Grant, I., *Jacka VC: Australia's Finest Fighting Soldier*, Macmillan Australia in association with the Australian War Memorial, South Melbourne, 1989.

Horner, David, *Blamey: The Commander in Chief*, Allen & Unwin, Sydney, 1998.

Joynt, W.D., *Breaking the Road for the Rest*, Hyland House, Melbourne, 1979.

Keegan, J., *The First World War*, Hutchinson, London, 1998.

Kent, D., *From Trench and Troopship*, Hale & Iremonger, Sydney, 1999.

Laffin, J., *Guide to Australian Battlefields on the Western Front, 1916–1918*, Kangaroo Press and Australian War Memorial, Sydney, 1992.

Laffin, J., *The Battle of Hamel*, Kangaroo Press, Sydney, 1999.

Laffin, J., *Damn the Dardanelles*, Sun Books, South Melbourne, 1985.

Liddell Hart, B.H., *History of the First World War*, Pan Books, 1972.

Longmore, C., *The Old Sixteenth*, 16th Battalion Association, Perth, 1929.

Mackaness, G., *Poets of Australia*, Angus & Robertson, Sydney, 1946.

Maitland, G.L., *Tales of Valour From the Royal New South Wales Regiment*, n.p., 1992.

Maxwell, J., *Hells Bells and Mademoiselles*, Angus & Robertson, Sydney, 1932.

Mead, G., *The Doughboys America and the First World War*, Allen Lane, Penguin Press, London, 2000.

Mitchell, G.D., *Backs to the Wall*, Angus & Robertson, Sydney, 1937.

Monash, J., *The Australian Victories in France in 1918*, Angus & Robertson, Sydney, 1936.

Moorhouse, G., *Hell's Foundations: A Town, its Myths and Gallipoli*, Hodder & Stoughton, London, 1992.

Needham, Ann, Riddler, Laurel, Hadley, Merle and Scott, Phyllis, *The Women of the 1790 Neptune*, Ann Needham, Dural, 1992.

Nichols, B., *The Colonial Volunteers: The Defence Forces of the Australian Colonies, 1836–1901*, Allen & Unwin, Sydney, 1988.

Percival, J., *For Valour: The Victoria Cross, Courage in Action*, Methuen, London, 1985.

Pollard, A.O., *Fire-Eater: The Memoirs of a V.C.*, Hutchinson, London, 1932.

Prior, R. and Wilson, T., *Passchendaele: The Unknown Story*, Yale University Press, New Haven, Conn., 1996.

Rule, E.J., *Jacka's Mob*, Angus & Robertson, Sydney, 1933.

Sadlier, P.S., *Paladin: A Life of Major General Sir John Gellibrand*, Oxford University Press, Melbourne, 2000.

Sampson, R. (ed.), *The Burford Sampson Great War Diary*, n.p., 1992.

Schuler, P.F.E., *Australia in Arms*, T. Fisher Unwin, London, 1916.

Serle, G., *John Monash: A Biography*, Melbourne University Press, Melbourne, 1982.

Smyth, J., *Milestones*, Sidgwick & Jackson, London, 1979.

Smyth, J., *The Story of the Victoria Cross, 1856–1963*, Frederick Muller, London, 1963.

Stewart, Alexander Caldwell, *Service on Land and Water, 1939–1946*, J.C. & M. Stewart, Brisbane, 1995.

Thompson, Alastair, *Anzac Memories: Living With the Legend*, Oxford University Press, Melbourne, 1994.

Underwood, Polly, *The Reflections of an Old Grey Mare*, self-published, c. 1985.

Wanliss, N., *The History of the Fourteenth Battalion, AIF*, 14th Battalion Association, 1929.

White, T.A., *Diggers Abroad: Jottings by a Digger Officer*, Angus & Robertson, Sydney, 1920.

White, T.A., *The Fighting Thirteenth: The History of the Thirteenth Battalion, AIF*, Tyrrells Ltd, Sydney, 1924.

Wigmore, L., *They Dared Mightily*, 2nd edition (revised and condensed by Jeff Williams and Anthony Staunton), Australian War Memorial, Canberra, 1986.

Wilson, Patrick (ed.), *So Far From Home: The Remarkable Diaries of Eric Evans, an Australian Soldier During World War I*, Kangaroo Press, Sydney, 2002.

Winter, D., *Haig's Command: A Reassessment*, Penguin Books, Harmondsworth, 1992.

JOURNAL ARTICLES

[Anon.], 'Again Ready for the Fray: Harry Murray's Message', *Reveille*, 1 November 1939, p. 18.

[Anon.], 'AIF Celebrities (1) Lt. Col. H.W. Murray', *Reveille*, 30 August 1929, p. 4.

[Anon.], 'AIF Nearly Lost Murray V.C.: He almost "Walked Out" on Gallipoli', *Reveille*, 1 September 1934, p. 20.

[Anon.], 'A Chip Off the Old Block', *Reveille*, 31 October 1931, p. 11.

[Anon.], 'First Bullecourt Lieut.-Col. Murray's Graphic Narrative Acclaimed', *Reveille*, 1 January 1937, pp. 3, 15–16.

[Anon.], 'Harry Murray, V.C., Home Again: Describes London Centenary Celebrations', *Reveille*, 1 October 1956, p. 4.

[Anon.], '13th Battalion Reunion', *Reveille*, 31 October 1930, p. 20.

[Anon.], '13th Battalion Reunion', *Reveille*, 1 November 1932, p. 26.

[Anon.], 'Two Daredevils: Jacka — Murray', *Reveille*, 29 June 1929, p. 22.

[Anon.], 'V.C. Dinner Big Parade', *Reveille*, 30 November 1929, p. 8.

[Anon.], 'War Hero Guest at Reunion', *Reveille*, 1 July 1956, pp. 6–7.

Allen, A.S., 'The "Daddy" of the 45th Bn.', *Reveille*, 1 July 1933, p. 3.

Blair, D.J., 'An Australian "Officer-Type"? — a Demographic Study of the Composition of Officers in the 1st Battalion, First AIF', *Sabretache*, Vol. 39, March 1998, pp. 21–7.

Brand, C.H., '4th Brigade's Exploits an Epitome', *Reveille*, 31 October 1930, p. 21.

Burness, Elizabeth, 'Collection Note: The Death of Major Percy Black', *Journal of the Australian War Memorial*, No. 15, October 1889, pp. 45–6.

Chalk, David, 'The Great Harry Murray', *Wartime: Official Magazine of the Australian War Memorial*, No. 8, 1999, pp. 28–33.

Crumlin, Joe, 'In the Steps of the 4th Brigade', *Journal of the Australian War Memorial*, No. 16, April 1990, pp. 39–43.

Cusack, Jack, 'Most Decorated Soldier: Australia's Quiet Hero', *Reveille*, 1 February 1966, p. 15.

Ford, H.C., 'With the 13th: August in Gallipoli', *Reveille*, 1 August 1932, pp. 64–5.

Francis, C., 'Australia's Most Decorated Soldier: Lieut.-Colonel Harry Murray, V.C.', *Reveille*, 1 February 1967, p.11.

Herring, Sydney, 'Fighting 13th: Some Memories', *Reveille*, 31 August 1929, p. 21.

Knowles, Bert, 'Bullecourt Tragedy Retrospect', *Reveille*, 30 April 1931, pp. 15, 26.

Lincoln, Merrilyn, 'Henry William Murray', *Australian Dictionary of Biography*, Vol. 10, pp. 641–3.

C. Longmore, 'Celebrities of the AIF No 74: Major Percy Black, D.S.O., D.C.M., 16th Battalion', *Reveille*, 1 October 1936. p. 6.

Loughran, H.G., 'Hill 60 4th Brigade Attacks', *Reveille*, 1 August 1933, pp. 36, 52–3.

McLoughlin, Frank, 'Celebrities of the AIF No 46: Sgt Stan McDougall, V.C., M.M., 47th Bn. AIF', *Reveille*, 1 June 1934. p. 7.

Millar, Ken, 'Boarding System: Jacka a Victim', *Reveille*, 31 January 1933, p. 8.

Miller, M. Geoffrey, 'The Death of Manfred von Richtofen: Who Fired the Fatal Shot?', *Sabretache*, Vol. 39, No. 2, June 1998, pp. 16–28.

Murray, Harry, '"Bravest Man in the AIF": Murray's Tribute', *Reveille*, 31 December 1929, p. 8. [Murray's articles are listed in chronological order.]

Murray, Harry, 'Slippery Slide Gallipoli Thrill', *Reveille*, 31 March 1930, p. 9.

Murray, Harry, 'Nation's Best in Gallipoli Graves', *Reveille*, 31 March 1931, p. 7.

Murray, Harry, 'One of the Best, One of the Bravest', *Reveille*, 31 January 1932, p. 3.

Murray, Harry, 'Grave and Gay V.C.'s Reflections', *Reveille*, 1 August 1932, p. 13.

Murray, Harry, 'Experimental Stage Tanks at Bullecourt', *Reveille*, 1 April 1933, p. 10.

Murray, Harry, 'Training Juniors Field Ranks', *Reveille*, 1 June 1933, p. 2.

Murray, Harry, 'His Hardest Battle: When Discipline Mastered Fear', *Reveille*, 1 December 1935, pp. 33, 48.

Murray, Harry, 'Memories of First Bullecourt', *Reveille*, 1 December 1936, pp. 4, 56–9, 63–5.

Murray, Harry, 'Col. Tilney Passes — A Loveable Character', *Reveille*, 1 March 1937, p. 27.

Murray, Harry, 'Get Through at Any Cost', *Reveille*, 1 April 1937, pp. 6, 52.

Murray, Harry, 'Capture of Stormy Trench: Aussies in Grim Duel Against Worthy Foes', *Reveille*, 1 December 1937, pp. 10–11, 62–5.

Murray, Harry, 'The N.Z. and A. Division: A Happy Family', *Reveille*, 1 April 1938, p. 18.

Murray, Harry, 'First Three Weeks on Gallipoli', *Reveille*, 1 April 1939, pp. 10–11, 60–2.

Oakley, Gary, 'Australian Memorial at Bullecourt', *Journal of the Australian War Memorial*, No. 23, October 1993, p. 48.

Pedersen, Peter, 'The Ghosts of Anzac', *Journal of the Australian War Memorial*, No. 2, April 1983, pp. 34–4.

Russell, Julie, 'Ellis Silas: Artist at Gallipoli', *Journal of the Australian War Memorial*, No. 9, October 1986, pp. 54–5.

Tilney, L.E., 'Night March 4th Bde., Steadiness', *Reveille*, 1 August 1932, p. 47.

Wells, T., 'Celebrities of the AIF No. 75: Lieut.-Col. D.G. Marks, D.S.O., M.C.', *Reveille*, 1 November 1936, pp. 6–7.

White, T.A., 'Lieut. H.B. Brown: An Appreciation', *Reveille*, 1 November 1938, p. 10.

Wilson, Graham, '"Everything on its Belly" — Feeding the First AIF', *Sabretache*, Vol. 41, September 2000, p. 11.

Winn, R.C., 'Stormy Trench', *Reveille*, 1 February 1938, p. 7.

Wray, F.W., 'The Fourth Brigade at Anzac', *Reveille*, 1 August 1933, pp. 6–7, 62.

AUSTRALIAN WAR MEMORIAL — UNIT WAR DIARIES

4th Australian Machine-Gun Battalion. Item No. 24/4/1. Roll no. 432.

13th Australian Infantry Battalion. Item No. 23/30/1–23/30/53. Roll no. 45.

14th Australian Infantry Battalion. Item No. 23/31/1–23/31/53. Roll no. 46.

15th Australian Infantry Battalion. Item No. 23/32/1–23/32/48. Roll no. 47.

16th Australian Infantry Battalion. Item No. 23/33/1–23/33/39. Roll nos 48–9.

4th Australian Infantry Brigade. Item No. 23/4/1–23/4/33. Roll nos 8–9.

4th Australian Division. Item No. 1/48/1–1/48/17; 1/48/33–1/48/32; 1/49/1–1/49/33. Roll nos 831–834.

OTHER

Murray, Harry, *Some Reminiscences*, written at the request of his son, Douglas, unpublished, c. 1950.

[Web site] Lucas, Nathaniel and Gascoyne, Olivia, *First Fleet, 1788.* Subheading: *Harry Murray.*

NOTES

PREFACE

1 C. Longmore, *The Old Sixteenth*, 16th Battalion Association, Perth, 1929, p. 4.

2 T.A. White, *The Fighting Thirteenth: The History of the Thirteenth Battalion, AIF*, Tyrrells Ltd, Sydney, 1924, p. 4.

CHAPTER 1: TRADE OR CALLING — BUSHMAN

1 A. Needham, L. Riddler, M. Hadley and P. Scott, *The Women of the 1790 Neptune*, Ann Needham, Dural, 1992, p. 169.

2 Interview, Douglas Murray, son of Harry Murray, Townsville, 24 October 2000.

3 Interview Joseph Cocker, nephew of Harry Murray, Launceston, 19 July 2000.

4 Interview, Joseph Cocker.

5 Harry Murray, letter to G.D. Mitchell, 1939.

6 Murray to Mitchell, 1939.

7 Interview, Douglas Murray.

8 *Daily Telegraph* (Sydney), January 1920.

9 C.E.W. Bean, *The Official History of Australia in the War of 1914–18*, Vol. 4, Angus & Robertson, Sydney, 1933, p. 293.

10 C. Longmore, 'Major Percy Black, D.S.O., D.C.M., 16th Battalion', *Reveille*, 1 October 1936, p. 6.

11 C.E.W. Bean, *The Official History of Australia in the War of 1914–18*, Vol. 1, Angus & Robertson, Sydney, 1921, p. 499.

12 G. Wilson, '"Everything on its Belly" — Feeding the First AIF', *Sabretache*, Vol. 41, September 2000, p. 11.

13 Ibid., p. 32.

14 H. Murray, Reminiscences, unpublished MS, p. 3.

15 Silas, Diary, 25 February 1915.

16 C. Longmore, *The Old Sixteenth*, 16th Battalion Association, Perth, 1929, p. 36.

17 H. Murray, 'The First Three Weeks on Gallipoli', *Reveille*, April 1939, p. 10.

CHAPTER 2: ON GALLIPOLI

1 P.A. Pedersen, *Monash as a Military Commander*, Melbourne University Press, Melbourne, 1985, p. 62.

2 H. Murray, 'The First Three Weeks on Gallipoli', *Reveille*, April 1939, pp. 10–11, 60–62.

3 Ibid., p. 60.

4 H. Murray, Reminiscences, unpublished MS, p. 3.

5 Murray, 'The First Three Weeks on Gallipoli', p. 60.

6 Ibid., p. 61.

7 Murray, Reminiscences, p. 2.

8 *Australian Dictionary of Biography*, Vol. 9, p. 613.

9 Murray, 'The First Three Weeks on Gallipoli', p. 62.

10 R. Simpson (ed.), *The Burford Sampson Great War Diary*, n.p., 1997, p. 103.

11 A.B. Facey, *A Fortunate Life*, Fremantle Arts Centre Press, Fremantle, 1981, p. 263.

12 Murray, 'The First Three Weeks on Gallipoli', p. 62.

13 C. Longmore, *The Old Sixteenth*, 16th Battalion Association, Perth, 1929, p. 66.

14 Interview, Joseph Cocker.

15 C.E.W. Bean, *Anzac to Amiens*, Australian War Memorial, Canberra, 1946, pp. 156–7.

16 C.E.W. Bean, *The Official History of Australia in the War of 1914–18*, Vol. 2, Angus & Robertson, Sydney, 1924, p. 679.

17 Murray, 'The First Three Weeks on Gallipoli', p. 61.

18 P. Schuler, *Australia in Arms*, Fisher Unwin, Sydney, 1916, p. 246.

19 G. Serle, *John Monash: A Biography*, Melbourne University Press, Melbourne, 1982, p. 234.

20 Bean, *Official History*, Vol. 2, p. 662.

21 Murray, Reminiscences, p. 4.

22 J.R. Crumlin, 'In the steps of the 4th Brigade', *Journal of the Australian War Memorial*, No. 16, April 1990, p. 42.

23 [Anon.], 'AIF Nearly Lost Murray, V.C.', *Reveille*, 1 September 1934, p. 20.

24 Murray, 'The First Three Weeks on Gallipoli', p. 62.

25 D.J. Blair, 'An Australian "officer-type"? — a Demographic Study of the Composition of Officers in the 1st Battalion, First AIF', *Sabretache*, Vol. 39, March 1998, p. 21.

26 H.G. Loughran, 'Hill 60: 4th Brigade Attacks', *Reveille*, 1 August 1933, p. 53.

27 J. Maxwell, *Hells Bells and Mademoiselles*, Angus & Robertson, Sydney, 1932, p. 3.

28 Ibid., p. 13.

29 Loughran, 'Hill 60', p. 53.

30 T.A. White, *The Fighting Thirteenth: The History of the Thirteenth Battalion, AIF*, Tyrrells Ltd, Sydney, 1924, p. 51.

31 *Australian Dictionary of Biography*, Vol. 10, p. 642.

32 P. Pedersen, 'The Ghosts of Anzac', *Journal of the Australian War Memorial*, No. 2, April 1983, p. 42.

CHAPTER 3: PRELUDE TO THE SOMME

1 E.J. Rule, *Jacka's Mob*, Angus & Robertson, Sydney, 1933, p. 28.
2 H. Murray, 'The N.Z. and A. Division: A Happy Family', *Reveille*, 1 April 1938, p. 18.
3 Rule, *Jacka's Mob*, p. 35.
4 *Australian Dictionary of Biography*, Vol. 9, p. 442.
5 G. Moorhouse, *Hell's Foundations: A Town, its Myths and Gallipoli*, Hodder & Stoughton, London, 1992, pp. 231–2.
6 I. Grant, *Jacka VC*, Macmillan Australia in association with the Australian War Memorial, South Melbourne, 1989, p. 59.
7 N. Wanliss, *The History of the Fourteenth Battalion, AIF*, 14th Battalion Association, Melbourne, 1929, p.105.
8 Ibid., p. 123.
9 H. Murray, Reminiscences, unpublished MS, p. 4.
10 Rule, *Jacka's Mob*, p. 58.

CHAPTER 4: THE SOMME OFFENSIVE — POZIÈRES AND MOUQUET FARM

1 C.E.W. Bean, *Anzac to Amiens*, Australian War Memorial, Canberra, 1946, p. 264.
2 C.E.W. Bean, *The Official History of Australia in the War of 1914–18*, Vol. 3, Angus & Robertson, Sydney, 1929, p. 720.
3 E.J. Rule, *Jacka's Mob*, Angus & Robertson, Sydney, 1933, p. 70.
4 Bean, *Official History*, Vol. 3, pp. 729–30.
5 Ibid., pp. 761–3.
6 Ibid., p. 769.
7 H. Murray, 'His Hardest Battle: When Discipline Mastered Fear', *Reveille*, 1 December 1935, pp. 33, 48.
8 T.A. White, *The Fighting Thirteenth: The History of the Thirteenth Battalion, AIF*, Tyrrells Ltd, Sydney, 1924, p. 66.
9 Ibid., p. 72.

10 Ibid., p. 74.
11 H. Murray, Reminiscences, unpublished MS, p. 5.
12 White, *The Fighting Thirteenth*, p. 75.
13 Bean, *Official History*, Vol. 3, pp. 862–977.
14 Ibid., p. 876.
15 Ibid., pp. 994–5.
16 A.H. Farrar-Hockley, *The Somme*, Pan Books, London, 1983, pp. 252–3.
17 J. Keegan, *The First World War*, Hutchinson, London, 1998.
18 Bean, *Official History*, Vol. 3, p. 944.

CHAPTER 5: STORMY TRENCH — WINNING THE VICTORIA CROSS

1 T.A. White, *The Fighting Thirteenth: The History of the Thirteenth Battalion, AIF*, Tyrrells Ltd, Sydney, 1924, p. 80.
2 Ibid.
3 C.E.W. Bean, *The Official History of Australia in the War of 1914–18*, Vol. 3, Angus & Robertson, Sydney, 1929, p. 919.
4 White, *The Fighting Thirteenth*, p. 85.
5 C.E.W. Bean, *The Official History of Australia in the War of 1914–18*, Vol. 4, Angus & Robertson, Sydney, 1933, p. 35.
6 White, *The Fighting Thirteenth*, p. 86.
7 Bean, *Official History*, Vol. 4, p. 37.
8 White, *The Fighting Thirteenth*, p. 90.
9 D. Chalk, 'The Great Harry Murray', *Wartime: Official Magazine of the Australian War Memorial*, No. 8, 1999, p. 33.
10 George Stanley McDowell Collection. AWM. PR 00276.
11 R.C. Winn, 'Stormy Trench', *Reveille*, February 1938, p. 7.
12 Patrick Wilson (ed.), *So Far From Home: The Remarkable Diaries of Eric Evans, an Australian Soldier During World War I*, Kangaroo Press, Sydney, 2002, pp. 38–9.

CHAPTER 6: THE FIRST BATTLE OF BULLECOURT

1 C.E.W. Bean, *The Official History of Australia in the War of 1914–18*, Vol. 4, Angus & Robertson, Sydney, 1933, p. 253.
2 H. Murray, 'Memories of First Bullecourt', *Reveille*, December 1936, p. 56.
3 Bean, *Official History*, Vol. 4, p. 250.
4 Ibid., p. 258.
5 Ibid., p. 260.
6 Ibid., p. 264.
7 Ibid., pp. 270–1.
8 Ibid., p. 277.
9 Ibid.
10 Ibid., p. 295.
11 Murray, 'Memories of First Bullecourt', p. 4.
12 T.A. White, *The Fighting Thirteenth: The History of the Thirteenth Battalion, AIF*, Tyrrells Ltd, Sydney, 1924, p. 96.
13 Bean, *Official History*, Vol. 4, pp. 316–17.
14 White, *The Fighting Thirteenth*, p. 98.
15 Murray, 'Memories of First Bullecourt', p. 64.
16 Ibid., p. 65.
17 C.H. Brand, 'Terrible Price Paid', *Reveille*, January 1937, p. 3.
18 B. Knowles, 'Bullecourt Tragedy: Retrospect', *Reveille*, April 1930, p. 15.
19 Bean, *Official History*, Vol. 4, p. 351.
20 Published in *Aussie*, 16 February 1918.

CHAPTER 7: MESSINES AND PASSCHENDAELE

1 G.D. Mitchell, *Backs to the Wall*, Angus & Robertson, Sydney, 1937, p. 106.
2 T.A. White, *The Fighting Thirteenth: The History of the Thirteenth Battalion, AIF*, Tyrrells Ltd, Sydney, 1924, p. 100.

3 Mitchell, *Backs to the Wall*, p. 106.
4 White, *The Fighting Thirteenth*, p. 127.
5 White, *The Fighting Thirteenth*, pp. 126–7.
6 Ibid., p. 102.
7 Interview, Joseph Cocker.
8 R. Prior and T. Wilson, *Passchendaele: The Unknown Story*, Yale University Press, New Haven, Conn., 1996, p. 61.
9 G. Serle, *John Monash: A Biography*, Melbourne University Press, Melbourne, 1982, p. 290.
10 White, *The Fighting Thirteenth*, p. 103.
11 J.C. Dunn, *The War the Infantry Knew, 1914–1919*, Sphere Books, London, 1987, p. 475.
12 White, *The Fighting Thirteenth*, p. 103.
13 Ibid.
14 Serle, *John Monash*, p. 283.
15 Patrick Wilson (ed.), *So Far From Home: The Remarkable Diaries of Eric Evans, an Australian Soldier During World War I*, Kangaroo Press, Sydney, 2002, p. 86.
16 White, *The Fighting Thirteenth*, p. 107.
17 Prior and Wilson, *Passchendaele*, p. 98.
18 N. Wanliss, *The History of the Fourteenth Battalion, AIF*, 14th Battalion Association, Melbourne, 1929, p. 236.
19 White, *The Fighting Thirteenth*, p. 112.
20 Ibid., p. 112.
21 Wanliss, *The History of the Fourteenth Battalion*, p. 254.
22 Ibid., p. 115.
23 T.A. White, *Diggers Abroad: Jottings by a Digger Officer*, Angus & Robertson, Sydney, 1920, p. 119.
24 C.E.W. Bean, *The Official History of Australia in the War of 1914–18*, Vol. 5, Angus & Robertson, Sydney, 1937, p. 729.
25 White, *The Fighting Thirteenth*, p. 121.
26 Wilson (ed.), *So Far From Home*, p. 168.

27 Interview, Joseph Cocker.

28 White, *The Fighting Thirteenth*, p. 90.

CHAPTER 8: LIEUTENANT COLONEL H.W. MURRAY — 1918

1 C.E.W. Bean, *The Official History of Australia in the War of 1914–18*, Vol. 5, Angus & Robertson, Sydney, 1937, p. 122.

2 Ibid., p. 123–4.

3 Ibid., pp. 358–9, 394–5.

4 G.D. Mitchell, *Backs to the Wall*, Angus & Robertson, Sydney, 1937, p. 265.

5 M. Geoffrey Miller, 'The Death of Manfred von Richtofen: Who Fired the Fatal Shot?', *Sabretache*, Vol. 39, No. 2, June 1998, pp. 16–28.

6 Interview, Douglas Murray.

7 C.E.W. Bean, *The Official History of Australia in the War of 1914–18*, Vol. 6, Angus & Robertson, Sydney, 1942, pp. 266–9.

8 Ibid., p. 327.

9 J. Monash, *The Australian Victories in France in 1918*, Angus & Robertson, Sydney, 1936. pp. xxii–xxiii.

10 Bean, *Official History*, Vol. 6, pp. 488–9.

11 War Diary, 4th Australian Machine-Gun Battalion.

12 Bean, *Official History*, Vol. 6, pp. 604–5.

13 Ibid., p. 684.

14 Ibid., p. 947.

15 A.O. Pollard, *Fire-Eater: The Memoirs of a V.C.*, Hutchinson, London, 1932, pp. 248–9.

16 *Launceston Examiner*, 8 January 1920.

CHAPTER 9: AFTERMATH

1 *West Australian*, 20 December 1919.
2 *Hobart Mercury*, 27 December 1919.
3 *Weekly Courier*, 15 January 1920.
4 *Sydney Morning Herald*, 10 September 1921.
5 T.A. White, *The Fighting Thirteenth: The History of the Thirteenth Battalion, AIF*, Tyrrells Ltd, Sydney, 1924, p. 167.
6 T. Wells, 'Celebrities of the AIF No. 75: Lieut.-Col. D.G. Marks, D.S.O., M.C.', *Reveille*, November 1936, p. 7.
7 Interview, Douglas Murray.
8 Interview, Nell Murray.
9 Interview, Douglas Murray.
10 Interview, Clem Sutherland, daughter of Harry Murray, Buderim, Queensland, 3 February 2001.
11 Interview, Douglas Murray.
12 Interview, Nell Murray.
13 [Anon.], 'Murray V.C.: Praise for *"Reveille"*', April 1931, p. 8.
14 K. Millar, 'Boarding System: Jacka a Victim', *Reveille*, January 1933, p. 8.
15 D. Horner, *Blamey: The Commander in Chief*, Allen & Unwin, Sydney, 1998. p. 121.
16 *Reveille*, November 1939, p. 18.
17 P. Underwood, *The Reflections of an Old Grey Mare*, self-published, c. 1985.
18 A.C. Stewart, *Service on Land and Water: 1939–1946*, J.C. & M. Stewart, Brisbane, 1995, p. 15.
19 Interview, Nell Murray.

CHAPTER 10: THE LAST YEARS

1 Interview, Joseph Cocker.
2 'Where Do V.C.s Go in Peace Time?', *Reveille*, November 1929, p. 8.

3 Interview, Joseph Cocker.
4 F. McLoughlin, 'Celebrities of the AIF No. 46: Sgt Stan McDougall, V.C., M.M.', *Reveille*, June 1934, p. 7.
5 [Anon.], 'War Hero Guest', *Reveille*, July 1956, pp. 6–7.
6 Ibid.
7 [Anon.], 'Harry Murray V.C. Home Again: Describes London Centenary Celebrations', *Reveille*, 1 October 1956, p. 4.
8 Communication from Sir Roden Cutler, 7 December 2000.
9 Interview, Nell Murray.
10 Interview, Clem Sutherland.

CHAPTER 11 CONCLUSION

1 Noted in the address by Lieutenant Colonel A. Lilley to the 41st reunion of the 13th Battalion, 1967.
2 C.E.W. Bean, *The Official History of Australia in the War of 1914–18*, Vol. 5, Angus & Robertson, Sydney, 1937, p. 730
3 [Anon.], 'AIF Celebrities (1) Lt. Col. H.W. Murray', *Reveille*, 30 August 1929, p. 4.
4 A.S. Allen, 'The "Daddy" of the 45th Bn.', *Reveille*, 1 July 1933, p. 3.
5 Interview, Clem Sutherland.
6 H. Murray, 'His Hardest Battle: When Discipline Mastered Fear', *Reveille*, 1 December 1935, p. 48.
7 [Anon.], 'Harry Murray VC Home Again: Describes London Centenary Celebrations', *Reveille*, 1 October 1956, p. 4.
8 H. Murray, 'Get Through at Any Cost', *Reveille*, 1 April 1937, p. 52.
9 David Chalk, 'The Great Harry Murray', *Wartime: Official Magazine of the Australian War Memorial*, No. 8, 1999, p. 32.

INDEX

AAMC = Australian Army Medical Corps, AEF = American Expeditionary Force, AFA = Australian Field Artillery, BEF = British Expeditionary Force, Bn = Battalion, Bty = Battery, Coy = Company, MG = Machine Gun, RA = Royal Artillery, RAMC = Royal Army Medical Corps, Regt = Regiment, RAR = Royal Australian Regiment, VDC = Volunteer Defence Corps

*before name indicates killed in action or died of wounds.